# Let the People Rule?

## Direct Democracy in the Twenty-First Century

Edited by Saskia P. Ruth, Yanina Welp and Laurence Whitehead

ROWMAN & LITTLEFIELD INTERNATIONAL
London • New York

Published by Rowman & Littlefield International, Ltd.
6 Tinworth Street, London SE11 5AL, United Kingdom
www.rowmaninternational.com

In partnership with the European Consortium for Political Research, Harbour House, 6–8 Hythe Quay, Colchester, CO2 8JF, United Kingdom

Rowman & Littlefield International Ltd.is an affiliate of Rowman & Littlefield
4501 Forbes Boulevard, Suite 200, Lanham, Maryland 20706, USA
With additional offices in Boulder, New York, Toronto (Canada), and Plymouth (UK)
www.rowman.com



**British Library Cataloguing in Publication Data**
A catalogue record for this book is available from the British Library

ISBN: HB 978-1-78552-257-4
ISBN: PB 978-1-78661-266-6

**Library of Congress Cataloging-in-Publication Data**

ISBN 978-1-78552-257-4 (cloth : alk. paper)
ISBN 978-1-78661-266-6 (paperback : alk. paper)

∞™ The paper used in this publication meets the minimum requirements of American National Standard for Information Sciences—Permanence of Paper for Printed Library Materials, ANSI/NISO Z39.48-1992.

**More from the ECPR Press Studies in Political Science series:**

**Global Tax Governance**
ISBN: 9781785521263
*Peter Dietsch and Thomas Rixen*
'Tax specialists may think they have little to learn from a book on global tax governance, especially one that concludes that the best solution is to create a new International Tax Organisation (ITO). They would be wrong. Anyone concerned with international taxation will benefit from this excellent collection of essays about the nature and possible resolutions of the conflicts within and between states about fiscal sovereignty, tax competition, and domestic and international equity that underlie the international tax discussion. The authors do not always agree with each other and few readers are likely to agree with all of them. But this book makes clear what is really at issue in this discussion and shows why even the recent prodigious efforts of the OECD-G20 BEPS group are most unlikely to produce any lasting solutions. For nation-states and economic globalisation to coexist, something like an ITO may indeed prove necessary.'
**Richard Bird, University of Toronto**

**Decision-Making under Ambiguity and Time Constraints**
ISBN: 9781785521256
*Reimut Zohlnhöfer and Friedbert W. Rüb*
'Associated with the work of US political scientist John W Kingdon, for more than three decades, the multiple-streams Framework has informed the work of numerous policy scholars from all over the world. Featuring an excellent line-up comprised of well-known and more junior contributors, this edited volume offers a timely overview of key comparative, empirical-methodological, and theoretical issues raised by the Multiple-Streams Framework. This coherent book will interest the many policy scholars who draw on this now classic Framework.'
**Daniel Béland, Johnson-Shoyama Graduate School of Public Policy, University of Saskatchewan**

**New Perspectives on Negative Campaigning**
ISBN: 9781785521287
*Alessandro Nai and Annemarie Walter*
'The study of negative campaigning has mostly been about American elections. Refreshingly, the essays in this book look at what happens in other countries. By so doing, they truly offer new perspectives and thus advance our understanding of attack politics. Recommended to anyone interested in elections and campaigns.' **John G Geer, Vanderbilt University**

# Contents

# List of Figures and Tables

*Figures*



*Tables*

# Abbreviations

| | |
|---|---|
| ANFPP | Asociación Nacional de Fonavistas de los Pueblos del Perú |
| CAFTA | Central American Free Trade Agreement |
| CDU | Christian Democratic Union (German political party) |
| CL | Civil Liberties |
| CCP | Comparative Constitutions Project |
| ECI | European Citizens' Initiative |
| EEA | European Economic Area |
| EP | European Parliament |
| EU | European Union |
| FH | Freedom House |
| FMP | Free Movement of Persons |
| FONAVI | Fondo Nacional de Vivienda (Peru) |
| JNE | Jurado Nacional de Elecciones (National Jury of Elections, Peru) |
| MAS | Movimiento al Socialismo (Socialist Movement, Bolivia) |
| MDDs | Mechanisms of Direct Democracy |
| PiS | Law and Justice (Polish Political Party) |
| PO | Civic Platform (Polish Political Party) |
| PPERA | Political Parties, Elections and Referendums Act 2000 |
| PR | Political Rights |
| RedGob | Red Euro-Latinoamericana de Governabilidad para el Desarrollo |
| SEA | Single European Act |
| SNP | Scottish National Party |
| UN | United Nations |
| USSR | Union of Soviet Socialist Republics (Soviet Union) |

# Contributors

**ROCÍO ANNUNZIATA** holds a PhD in Political Studies (École des Hautes Études en Sciences Sociales de Paris) and in Social Sciences (University of Buenos Aires). She works as Associate Professor of Contemporary Political Theory at the University of Buenos Aires and as Professor of the Master in Political Science and Sociology at the Facultad Latinoamericana de Ciencias Sociales (FLACSO). She is also researcher at the National Council of Scientific and Technical Research (CONICET), and director of the project 'Between administration and negativity: forms of non-electoral citizen participation in contemporary Argentina' at the University of Buenos Aires.

**BRIGITTE GEISSEL** is Professor of Political Science and Political Sociology at Goethe University Frankfurt a.M. and Head of the Research Unit 'Democratic Innovations', and was Speaker of ECPR Standing Group 'Democratic Innovations' (2010–15); she has had fellowships, research or teaching positions at various universities/institutes such as Harvard Kennedy School (USA), Social Science Research Center Berlin, the Universities of Berlin, Darmstadt, Muenster and Illinois (USA). Her research interests include democratic innovations, political actors (new social movements, civil society, political elites, citizens). Her recent work has appeared in many publications including *Comparative Sociology*, *West European Politics* and the *European Journal of Political Research.*

**FERNANDO MENDEZ** is Senior Researcher at the c2d. Apart from his work at c2d he also directs the eDemocracy Centre, which is affiliated to the c2d, and is the coordinator of the Preference Matcher research consortium. He holds a PhD in Political Science from the European University Institute, Florence. He has published across various fields in journals such as the *British Journal of Political Science*, the *Journal of European Public Policy*, *Publius: The Journal of Federalism*, *Party Politics*, *Quality & Quantity* and *Public Law*. His most recent books, *Patterns of Constitution Making* (Ashgate 2013), *Referendums on European Integrations* (Cambridge University Press 2014) and *Voting Advice Applications in Modern Political Campaigns and Elections* (IGI Global forthcoming) reflect his interdisciplinary interests.

**MARIO MENDEZ** is a senior lecturer in the Department of Law at Queen Mary University of London. His research interests are in the field of EU, UK and comparative constitutional law. Recent publications include a co-authored monograph entitled *Referendums and the European Union: A Comparative Inquiry* (Cambridge University Press, 2014) and *The Legal Effects of EU Agreements: Maximalist Treaty Enforcement and Judicial Avoidance Techniques* (Oxford University Press, 2013).

**LEONARDO MORLINO** is Professor of Political Science at LUISS, Rome (Italy). His most recent books include: *La calidad de la democracia en America Latina* (IDEA, 2014), *Changes for Democracy* (Oxford University Press, 2012), *Democracias y Democratizaciones* (CIS, 2008) and *Democratization and the European Union: Comparing Central and Eastern European Post-Communist Countries* (Routledge 2010, with Sadurski). He was also one of the three editors of the *International Encyclopedia of Political Science* (8 volumes, Sage Publications, 2011), awarded with the Honorable Mention of Dartmouth Medal for reference publishing in all domains of knowledge.

**GABRIEL L. NEGRETTO** is an associate professor of Political Studies at the Centro de Investigación y Docencia Económicas (CIDE), Mexico City. He holds a law degree from the University of Buenos Aires, and both a Master of International Affairs and a PhD in Political Science from Columbia University. He has been visiting scholar at the Kellogg Institute for International Studies and visiting professor at Columbia University, Princeton University, the New School for Social Research, Universidad de la República, Universidade de Sao Pablo, and Universidad Torcuato Di Tella. He specialises on constitutional politics, institutional change and design, and Latin American political institutions. He has published numerous articles on these topics in American, European and Latin American academic journals, such as *Comparative Political Studies*, the *Journal of Politics*, the *British Journal of Political Science, Law & Society Review*, the *Texas Law Review*, *Latin American Politics and Society*, the *Journal of Latin American Studies*, *Government and Opposition* and *Desarrollo Economico*, among others. His most recent book is *Making Constitutions. Presidents, Parties, and Institutional Choice in Latin America* (Cambridge University Press, 2013).

**MATT QVORTRUP** is Professor and Chair of Political Science at Coventry University. He studied politics at Oxford University, and earned his doctorate from Brasenose College in 1999 on a study entitled 'Constitutional implications of the use of the referendum'. He subsequently gained a graduate Diploma from the College of Law. Before joining Coventry University, he taught at the London School of Economics and University College London. As a practitioner, he was head of the Gun Crime Section in the British Home Office (2002–3). He was a special envoy for the US State Department in Cyprus (2004–5) and in the Sudan in 2009.

**SASKIA P. RUTH** is a postdoctoral fellow in Political Science at the NCCR Democracy at the University of Zurich and the Centre for Democracy Studies in Aarau, Switzerland. She holds a Diploma in Latin American Studies and a PhD in Political Science from the University of Cologne (Germany). Her research focusses on the quality of democracy, the crisis of representation in Latin America, and the phenomenon of clientelism and populism. Her article 'Clientelism and the utility of the left–right dimension in Latin America' has recently been published in *Latin American Politics and Society*.

**PASCAL SCIARINI** is Professor of Swiss and Comparative politics and currently head of the Department of Political Science and International Relations at the University of Geneva, Switzerland. His main research topics are decision-making processes, direct democracy, Europeanisation and political behaviour. His work on these topics has appeared in several journals, such as *Comparative Political Studies*, *Electoral Studies*, the *European Political Science Review*, the *Journal of Legislative Studies*, the *Journal of European Public Policy*, *Regional and Federal Studies* and *West European Politics*. His most recent book, which he co-authored with Manuel Fischer and Denise Traber, is *Political Decision-making in Switzerland: The Consensus Model under Pressure*, Basingstoke/New York: Palgrave/Macmillan (2015). He is also one of the editors of the *Handbook of Swiss Politics*, Zurich: NZZ Libro (2014).

**UWE SERDÜLT** is Vice-Director of the Centre for Research on Direct Democracy (c2d) and worked as a lecturer at various European universities, but mainly at the University of Zurich and ETH Zurich. Research led him to Poland (PU Cracow), Japan (Waseda and Ritsumeikan University) and the USA (University of Pittsburgh, PA). He studied history, political science and computer science at the Universities of Zurich and Geneva.

**STEPHEN TIERNEY** is Professor of Constitutional Theory in the School of Law, University of Edinburgh and Director of the Edinburgh Centre for Constitutional Law and ESRC Senior Research Fellow with the Centre for Constitutional Change. The Fellowship was awarded to study the referendum process. He served as independent adviser to the Scottish Government on the technical aspects of the referendum for six months in 2012, and in January 2013 was appointed constitutional adviser to the Scottish Parliament's Referendum (Scotland) Bill Committee, which helped frame the process rules for the referendum. He currently serves as Legal Adviser to the House of Lords Constitution Committee.

**YANINA WELP** is Regional Director for Latin America at the Centre for Research on Direct Democracy (Center for Democracy Studies Aarau). Her main areas of study are the mechanisms of direct and participatory democracy in Latin America and digital media and politics. She has published extensively on these topics in several academic journals and books. Her most recent contributions are *Digital Technologies for Democratic Governance in Latin America* (UK: Routledge, 2014, co-edited with Anita Breuer), *Democracias en Movimiento* (Mexico: UNAM, co-edited with Daniel Zovatto and Alicia Lissidini) and *La dosis hace el veneno. Análisis de la revocatoria de mandato en América Latina, Estados Unidos y Suiza* (Quito: CNE, co-edited with Uwe Serdült).

**JONATHAN WHEATLEY** holds a PhD in Social and Political Sciences from the European University Institute in Florence. After gaining his doctorate, he was a Research Fellow at the Osteuropa Institut, Free University Berlin, before becoming Regional Director at the Centre for Democracy in Aarau (Switzerland) with responsibilities for the Commonwealth of Independent States and the Western Balkans region. He is now a lecturer in Comparative Politics at Oxford Brookes University. In addition to publishing a number of scholarly articles, Wheatley has also published a book entitled *Georgia from National Awakening to Rose Revolution: Delayed Transition in the Former Soviet Union* (Ashgate, 2005), an analysis of the political regime in Georgia from 1988 to 2004.

**LAURENCE WHITEHEAD** is a senior research fellow in Politics at Nuffield College, Oxford University. His latest books are *Illiberal Practices* (with Jacqueline Behrend, Johns Hopkins University Press 2016), *Latin America: A New Interpretation* (Palgrave, 2006 second revised updated edition 2010) and *Democratización: Teoría y Experiencia* (Fondo de Cultura Económica 2011). His most recent edited publication is *Caleidoscopio de la Innovación democrática en América Latina* (with Yanina Welp, FLACSO, Mexico, 2011). Among recent articles there is 'The Westminster system: model or muddle?' in the *Taiwan Journal of Democracy*, May 2013; and 'Enlivening the concept of democratisation: the biological metaphor' in *Perspectives on Politics*, July 2011. He is editor of an Oxford University Press series, *Studies in Democratization* and President of the *Conseil Scientifique* of the Institute des Ameriques, Paris, and belongs to the steering committee of the Red Euro-Latinoamericana de Gobernabilidad para el Desarrollo.

# Acknowledgements

This book began with the RedGob Annual Conference on 'New experiments of direct democracy: consequences for governability and development', which took place in Aarau, Switzerland, in December 2014. We are very grateful to the Conference Committee, especially to Leonardo Morlino, Manuel Alcántara Saéz, Detlef Nolte and Bert Hoffman for their organisational support and important intellectual contributions to the conference. We also want to thank the Centre for Democracy Studies in Aarau for their support in hosting this event as well as our colleagues Uwe Serdült, Nicola Aubert, Daniel Bochsler, Micha Germann and Pedro Capra from the Centre for their stimulating comments at the conference. We are grateful for the financial support the Swiss National Science Foundation (SNSF) and the Avina Foundation provided to organise the conference, which led to this volume.

We also want to thank Alejandra Barahona de Brito for her assistance in editing parts of this book. Our gratitude goes as well to the ECPR Press team and the anonymous reviewers of our book proposal. Their useful comments helped us to further improve this project.

# Preface

*Leonardo Morlino*

Looking back at the past decades a curious paradox draws our attention: there has been the diffusion of democratic regimes in different areas of the world as well as growing dissatisfaction about how these regimes actually work, both in recently established and longstanding democracies. How is it possible that the global diffusion of democracy, which implies the legitimation of this institutional arrangement, can coexist with such levels of dissatisfaction, disenchantment and delegitimation? How can such a paradox be explained?

Let us begin by clarifying a few key aspects. First, the experience clearly shows the global diffusion of democracy since the early 1970s. Even where traditional or authoritarian regimes prevail – in some Arab countries, for example – there is a fairly high percentage of people who claim to favour democracy. In Latin America – even in Venezuela, which is among the countries experiencing deep uncertainty about the effectiveness of their democracy – a high percentage of citizens support democracy. So what is happening?

Democracy became the 'only game in town' after the failure of military and non-military authoritarianisms alike, and the later collapse of the communist regimes. This rendered obsolete the dictum usually attributed to Churchill that 'democracy is the worst form of government except for all others'. Democracy became widely accepted. But when its key mechanisms were set in motion, disillusionment and alienation also emerged. So democracy has high levels of legitimation and is not challenged worldwide, but in recently democratised countries, not only do authoritarian legacies take time to fade because they are often a part of ongoing domestic political conflicts, but citizens also had very high expectations regarding the new democratic political institutions. These institutions can alleviate suffering by limiting the violation of civil rights and freedoms, but they cannot deliver a welfare state for everyone, even when social rights are legally enshrined. Hence, the origins of discontent are hidden, but durable, authoritarian legacies together with unfulfilled high expectations.

In the old-established democracies, where social rights have existed for years because of welfare systems supported by high gross domestic product and international economic prominence, the lives of citizens have become poorer, less safe and more economically insecure after years of growth as a result of globalisation and the worldwide economic crisis (2007–14). Deep discontent has therefore become widespread. In fully fledged democratic regimes, the difficulties of solving government and policy problems have not cast doubt on democracy as such, but on the ability of democratic regimes to respond to citizens' needs. The result has been the growth of both right- and left-wing protest parties.

The feelings and consequent behaviour of citizens in new and old democracies have different origins and causes, but irrespective of their origin they have produced widespread dissatisfaction or 'global discontent'. As early twenty-first century Argentina shows, this does not call into question democracy in the countries where such attitudes develop; rather what comes under attack are the insurmountable and unsustainable limits of the mechanism of representation within a democratic regime. In fact, on the one hand, what new and old democracies practise alike is representative democracy; but on the other hand, the aspects of democracy that have been criticised in the past and today are precisely representative mechanisms, including elections and parliaments. The most recurrent criticism refers to a characteristic of representative democracy that 'identifies a decision-procedure for selecting political personnel with one for selecting policies or laws', and 'In choosing the one the people choose the other. But it is assemblies or parliaments which make laws and governments that make decisions and not the people' (Hirst 1988: 202).

This and other limits of democracy have been central to debates in political science and political philosophy in recent decades. Deliberative democracy has been at the heart of recent philosophical debate, involving Rawls, Habermas and others. Rawls advocated a political society that can guarantee equal rights and fair citizen participation in the future, whereas Habermas emphasised how fair procedures and clear communication lead to legitimate consensual decisions by citizens. Equal rights, fair participation, transparent communication, and open debates are at the core of the deliberative democratic processes. Consequently, political decisions must be the product of fair and reasonable debate among citizens. In this way the representative limits of deciding 'who', but not 'what', can be overcome and citizens can effectively become the principals of a democratic deliberative process that has removed the limits of representation and implemented a real direct democracy, which can enjoy much stronger citizen legitimation.

Some scholars argue that deliberative democracy can be compatible with both representative and direct democracy, but others believe that direct citizen participation and involvement is the only way to innovate and legitimise democracy. This is the position of James Fishkin, one of the most influential scholars supporting deliberative democracy (see in particular Fishkin 2011), who argues that deliberative democracy is a subtype of direct democracy, characterised by: information (participants have access to reasonably accurate information that they believe is relevant to the issue); substantive balance (arguments offered by one side or from one perspective are answered by considerations offered by those who hold other perspectives); diversity (the major positions held by the public are represented by participants in the discussion); conscientiousness (participants sincerely weigh the merits of the arguments); and equal consideration (arguments offered by all participants are considered on the merits regardless of which participant puts them forward). Cohen (see in particular Cohen 1989) stresses citizen participation, involvement and consequent democratic legitimation.

Scholars and citizens in new and old democracy alike are even more critical of the limits of representation mechanisms. As Mair (2013: 16) has stated:

> parties are increasingly failing in their capacity to engage ordinary citizens … parties can no longer adequately serve as a base for the activities and status of their own leaders … Parties are failing because the zone of engagement – the traditional world of party democracy where citizens interacted with and felt a sense of attachment to their political leaders – is being evacuated.

That is, in an actual context where there are objective reasons to see the limits of representation (people decide who, not what) and where there are real problems that are difficult to cope with, in an intellectual context where those limits are emphasised and alternatives are envisaged, the crisis of intermediate structures, such as political parties, can be considered as a sort of last step to distance the people even more from representative democracy.

It is hardly surprising then that citizens are attracted by the ever-present possibility of direct democracy and that new and old democracies have adopted institutional solutions to implement it. The European Social Survey (from 2012), which has been analysed by Kriesi, Ferrin and others (Ferrin and Kriesi 2016), confirms that direct democracy is supported among twenty-nine European countries, along with liberal democracy and social democracy. What Europeans want is a final say on key issues via referendums or similar procedural mechanisms. More specifically:

> two-fifths of Europeans (39.6 per cent) responded with a 10 on the direct democracy question, that is, they require democracy to provide citizens with the final say by referendum for major new laws. Thus, a significant portion of European citizens view liberal democracy as we know it as not sufficient in terms of procedures for what they understand as democracy. (Kriesi et al. 2016: 80)

Several scholars have looked at citizen discontent with representation mechanisms and, in some cases, support for direct democracy (see for example Pharr and Putnam 2000, Torcal and Montero 2006, Norris 2010, Dalton and Welzel 2013), which has produced a response by politicians in a number of countries. As shown by Altman (2014) and others, different mechanisms of direct democracy (MDDs) have been adopted in several countries, with Uruguay and Ecuador being the Latin American countries with most MDDs.

It was in this intellectual, political and research context that members of the Red Euro-Latinoamericana de Gobernabilidad para el Desarrollo (RedGob), an association created years ago under the leadership of Laurence Whitehead, met at the Centre for Democracy Studies Aarau in Switzerland in December 2014 to begin a new research project to reflect on the contemporary development of direct democracy. The key question of the project *Let the people rule? Direct democracy in the twenty-first century* is the extent to which direct democracy can help solve the pervasive crisis of representative institutions around the world and whether existing and future direct democratic mechanisms can contribute to relegitimising democracy. This question needs to be explored at various levels since MDDs can be implemented at the local, regional, national or supranational levels. Furthermore, it is important to examine the different MDDs that have been introduced in different places from Europe to Latin America, and the former Soviet Union area to Sub-Saharan Africa. Finally, direct democratic mechanisms should be considered in detail with their own characteristics on different aspects: how have specific mechanisms reshaped constitutional design? To what degree have direct democratic mechanisms changed political processes? And how are they affecting different policy-making domains? The ultimate goal of this kind of analysis would be to promote a fuller understanding of the impact of MDDs to representative democracies and to whether these mechanisms can address global democratic discontent and give democratic processes a new lease of life. Under the guidance of the three editors, the authors of this book have addressed all these questions and provided in-depth, thoughtful replies that are worthwhile to reflect on for all readers.

## References

Altman, D. (2014) *Direct Democracy Worldwide*, Cambridge: Cambridge University Press.

Cohen, J. (1989) 'Deliberative democracy and democratic legitimacy', in A. Hamlin and P. Pettit (eds) *The Good Polity*, Oxford: Blackwell: 17–34.

Dalton, R. J. and Welzel, C. (eds) (2013) *The Civic Culture Revisited: From allegiant to assertive citizens*, Cambridge: Cambridge University Press.

Ferrin, M. and Kriesi, H. (eds) (2016) *How Europeans View and Evaluate Democracy*, Oxford: Oxford University Press.

Fishkin, J. (2011) *When the People Speak*, Oxford: Oxford University Press.

Hirst, P. (1988), 'Representative democracy and its limits', *Political Quarterly*, 59(2): 199–213.

Kriesi, H., Saris, W. and Moncagatta, P. (2016) 'The structure of Europeans' views of democracy: citizens' models of democracy', in M. Ferrin and H. Kriesi (eds) *How Europeans View and Evaluate Democracy*, Oxford: Oxford University Press: 64–89.

Mair, P. (2013) *Ruling the Void: The hollowing out of western democracy*, London and New York: Verso.

Norris, P. (2010) *Democratic Deficit: Critical citizens revisited*, Cambridge: Cambridge University Press.

Pharr, S. J. and Putnam, R. D. (eds) (2000) *Disaffected Democracies: What's troubling the trilateral countries?* Princeton: Princeton University Press.

Torcal, M. and Montero, J. R. (2006) *Political Disaffection in Contemporary Democracies: Social capital, institutions, and politics*, London: Routledge.

*Chapter One*

# Direct Democracy in the Twenty-First Century

*Saskia P. Ruth, Yanina Welp and Laurence Whitehead*

One of the biggest challenges to democratic legitimacy over the last two decades has been the crisis of democratic representation. To tackle this problem, an ever growing number of established as well as new democracies around the world have included mechanisms for direct democracy (MDDs) in their constitutions to complement representative political institutions, thereby enabling citizens to become more directly involved in the decision-making process. For the purpose of this book, we define MDDs as a set of procedures allowing citizens to take political decisions directly through a vote beyond the regular election of representatives (see for example Butler and Ranney 1994, Hug and Tsebelis 2002, Uleri 1996). These procedures are regulated either by the constitution or by law. Some are triggered automatically (i.e. mandatory referendums), some by political actors in power ('top-down' procedures), and some call for the prior collection of citizen signatures ('bottom-up' procedures). The results of the activation of these mechanisms may be binding or merely consultative. In short, there are many different MDDs, and their manifold and varied effects on representative democracy in different contexts remain understudied and deserve far more scholarly attention. This volume rests on the observation that such mechanisms have become increasingly central in worldwide efforts to legitimise political change within democratic systems (across several domains), and on the assumption that this trend is most likely to continue, and indeed may well intensify.

Before the Second World War the use of MDDs was associated either with authoritarian regimes (e.g. the Nazi regime) or with the exceptional case of Switzerland. This picture changed after the end of the war and with the third wave of democracy in Latin America and Eastern Europe (Serdült and Welp 2012). MDDs now exist in law and practice in diverse settings and various world regions. In their seminal work *Referendums around the World* (1978), Butler and Ranney observed only a few countries that had legally instituted MDDs (e.g. Puerto Rico held the first of what would become a sequence of status votes in 1967). Today, some 150 countries allow their citizens a direct say on political issues (Kaufmann and Waters 2004).

The practice of direct democracy has spread not just across countries and regions, but also across levels of government. In recent years, the use of MDDs at the national and supranational levels of government has become increasingly frequent. Examples range from European Union (EU) referendums (Mendez et al. 2014), to referendums held during the transition to democracy in the post-communist countries (Auer and Bützer 2001; Walker 2003) and in many Latin American countries, with the 'participatory turn' initiated in the 1990s (Welp and Serdült 2009). At the same time, the number of subnational-level MDDs has also increased, as shown by the cases of Germany, Japan, Poland and Peru.

MDDs are becoming increasingly relevant, not just because of the growing frequency of their use but also because of the extension of their scope. In Latin America, referendums held to legitimise constitutional replacements were portrayed by political leaders as means to carry out a 'political revolution', as in Venezuela (1999), Ecuador (2007–8) and Bolivia (2006–9) (*see* Negretto, Chapter Three in this volume). Moreover, the use of MDDs has increased in processes of self-determination, not only in post-conflict countries such as Montenegro (2006) but also in wealthy regions with consolidated democracies, such as Quebec (1995) and Scotland (2014). Catalonia has yet to hold an official referendum of self-determination, but it is likely to do so in the near future. The use of MDDs is also on the national agenda of EU member states, most recently and prominently the referendum in the United Kingdom to determine whether to remain or leave the EU in 2017. Such referendums are not just used to resolve constitutional or territorial conflicts. Venezuelan president Nicolás Maduro (2013–) is likely to face a recall referendum that may lead to his removal from office before the end of his term. This would be the second recall referendum against the Venezuelan head of state in less than fifteen years in the only country that has organised a recall referendum against a president.

The increased importance of MDDs is also the result of popular demand, with the growing demand for politicians to become more responsive and accountable to the interests of citizenries. Calls for direct democracy and for the reinvention of democracy are a part of the discourse of new political leaders and parties on the left and right alike. Parties like Podemos in Spain and the Alternative für Deutschland in Germany, among others, champion more direct citizen intervention in the policy-making process.

But effects of MDDs are not always as virtuous as their promoters claim, and they can create new legitimacy problems. For this reason, it is crucial to discuss the precise contours and consequences of current MDDs. To cite one example, the European Citizens' Initiative (ECI) has been celebrated by many as a step towards more responsive democratic governance and greater citizen control over European institutions but has been attacked by many others for being insufficient. The ECI is a petition mechanism intended to introduce topics to the European Commission agenda, but it does not involve a vote and is non-binding. The institutional design of MDDs has become a matter of heated debate in various national contexts, particularly concerning what kind of topic should be submitted to a direct vote. The most recent debates occurred in the Netherlands and Switzerland. An initiative was held in the Netherlands in April 2016 to allow citizens to pronounce themselves on the EU–Ukraine Association Agreement. Although it was a non-binding vote, the rejection of the EU–Ukraine Association Agreement by Dutch citizens complicates the decision-making process at the EU level (*see* Mendez and Mendez, Chapter Twelve in this volume). Similarily, Switzerland has held controversial referendums on the expulsion of foreigners and immigration quotas which led to an endangerment of the bilateral agreements with the EU (*see* Sciarini, Chapter Eleven in this volume).

Given the increase in MDDs and the likelihood of their further proliferation it is of paramount importance to study their consequences for representative democracy. This innovative volume addresses this critical and hitherto neglected issue. It is structured around an overarching research question: to what extent can such mechanisms help to solve the global crisis of representative institutions and reinforce democratic legitimacy? This central question begs many more, such as: How easily can political elites manipulate referendums that authorise the replacement or amendment of democratic constitutions? To what extent do MDDs resolve conflicts in situations of extreme polarisation? Do mechanisms such as recall referendums strengthen or undermine democratic accountability and governability? How consequential are direct democratic decisions for specific policies, who is to implement them, and can political actors reinterpret them afterwards?

The specialist contributors to this volume cover many different aspects of direct democracy. While some chapters focus on individual types of mechanisms – e.g. mandatory referendums or recall referendums – others cover a broader range of MDDs in a comparative setting. In the first stage-setting chapter, Laurence Whitehead juxtaposes the 'fiction' of representation and the 'faction' of direct democracy, to discuss two standard objections to direct democracy: the presupposition of a small compact community and the potential manipulation of the demos (or principal) by organised 'factions'. In contrast, large political units delegate authority to 'representatives' whose responsiveness is assured through the regular and frequent renewal of mandates via competitive elections. But critics of this model counter that this presents a mythical account of how 'representation' really works; in practice, the agents manipulate their inattentive principal, rather than acting at its service. Whitehead finds partial merit in both sets of criticism, questions the starkness of the separation between the two models and suggests that various combinations are possible. But just as there is no one 'right way' for all democracies, each alternative option presents problems as well as advantages. Demands for more legitimate forms of democratic expression will continue to fuel various experiments and diverse combinations of the two models.

The first part of the volume focuses on the use of MDDs to legitimise constitutional reforms and address sovereignty issues. The chapters in this section direct our attention to the broader legal and socio-political background shaping the choice of MDDs, and their political legitimacy. How fully are established political forces consulted? How are the timing and wording of referendums decided? Are such referendums held in contexts with 'strong' or 'weak' constitutional cultures?

Gabriel L. Negretto begins by looking at the highly problematic relationship between citizen participation and constitution making. Although voting in referendums and electing a special constituent body are the most widely accepted mechanisms of citizen participation in framing a new constitution, they present many problems for democratic regimes that lack mechanisms for the replacement of the constitution. Negretto argues that citizen involvement in constitutional rewrites can only be compatible with the preservation of representative institutions if the process is regulated by an institutional or political agreement between the government and the main opposition parties. This agreement, in turn, depends on whether established parties are able to retain popular support and institutional influence when the organisation of the process is decided. The argument is supported with empirical evidence from recent episodes of constitutional replacements in Latin America.

Jonathan Wheatley goes on to explore a specific type of constitutional referendum – the 'power consolidation referendum'. This is used in an instrumental manner to amend a constitution so as to augment the powers of the executive. Wheatley investigates the conditions under which such referendums are likely to be held. He considers a number of factors that may explain power consolidation referendums, including the existing constitutional framework, the process by which the existing constitution came into being and the extent to which a 'culture of constitutionalism' prevails in the territory concerned. He explores the impact of these factors on a number of cases in two very different regions of the world in which power consolidation referendums are frequent: the former Soviet Union and Sub-Saharan Africa.

The following two chapters by Qvortrup and Tierney, informed by the Scottish independence referendum in 2014, illustrate the complexities of MDDs as applied to the question of the independence of a new democracy. Precedents such as Quebec and prospective imitators such as Catalonia show that the Scottish experience is not a one-off case. But who is entitled to deliver a majority verdict? Can expatriate citizens take part, or only those who would constitute the demos if the secession occurred? A resulting breakaway will also be highly consequential (of major constitutional significance) for citizens in the rump democracy that would emerge. Thus, a secessionist majority will not just legitimate a new democracy but also disrupt (arguably even delegitimate) the larger pre-existing one.

Matt Qvortrup presents a comparative historical overview of independence referendums since the mid-nineteenth century. He considers some of the claims made in earlier independence referendums: When and why have these referendums taken place? When and why are they won? Do they exacerbate ethnic conflict? Should there be a special majority for independence referendums, and how does the wording on ballot influence outcomes? Stephen Tierney looks at the Scottish process and the lessons it might offer for self-determination referendums elsewhere. He emphasises the importance of a 'good process' to ensure the credibility of self-determination referendums. Issues of process involve the power of initiation, setting the franchise, question framing, independent oversight, and fair and transparent funding and spending rules. Given the heat the debate generated in the last few weeks of campaigning, it was essential that the process be fair and be seen to be so by both sides: in short, that both winners and losers agree to accept the result.

The volume shifts from constitutional mechanisms and independence referendums to the use of MDDs to resolve day-to-day political questions, and their impact on political processes and policy outcomes. The following chapters address topics such as recall referendums to bridge the divide between the electorate and wayward representatives and the role of MDDs at the local, national and supranational levels of government. Yanina Welp and Saskia Ruth contend that many analyses of MDDs report contradictory effects on political processes and public policy. While some studies associate MDDs with the deepening of democracy, others highlight how they offer opportunities for political manipulation and the concentration of power in the executive. To systematically distinguish between the potentially positive or negative effects of MDDs, the authors propose a classification of the motivations of political actors who call for these mechanisms. They complement their actor-centred approach by examining the institutional design of MDDs, the constellation of relevant actors in referendum processes, and the normative function of such mechanisms. They test the usefulness of their classification by applying it to eighteen Latin American countries between 1900 and 2014.

Rocío Annunziata theorises about the conflictive relationship between recall procedures, democratic representation and citizen participation. Based on the Latin American experience, and on recent contributions to political theory, she contends that recall procedures are in tension with contemporary democratic transformations in the region. She discusses the limitations of recall referendums in strengthening incentives for political representatives to honour their campaign promises in the context of 'post-promissory representation'. Annunziata then examines how far recall referendums institutionalise the possibility for citizens to reject the decisions or actions of political representatives, and recommends enhancing deliberation and communication between representatives and citizens rather than relying on 'instruments of rejection' such as recall procedures.

Uwe Serdült and Yanina Welp undertake a related comparative analysis of recall referendums. They draw a global map of recall referendums, investigating the variety of legal provisions and identifying institutional targets (national and/or local, executive and/or legislative). They provide illustrative case studies to test the extent to which recalls fulfil different functions, depending on the main agent initiating the process and the question that is being decided (removing an elected authority or resolving a policy or institutional conflict).

Brigitte Geissel looks at the Federal Republic of Germany. The German political system has rested on the principles of representative democracy since its founding in 1949, but the concept of representative democracy is under increasing stress and participatory concepts are gaining ground. Since the 1990s, all German federal states have introduced MDDs to their state constitutions (at the state and the local levels). Geissel offers an overview of the regulation and use of these instruments at different levels of government and examines their expected and perceived effects.

Swiss direct democracy is often seen as a model in terms of citizens' participation. However, Pascal Sciarini argues that the Swiss model has been under strain over the last few years due to globalisation and Europeanisation, and because of the extension of direct democracy to new international treaties, with the share of internationalised issues that are submitted to a direct democratic vote increasing substantially between the 1960s and the 2010s. Sciarini shows that although the Swiss government has been fairly successful in using direct democratic means to decide on foreign policy questions, the popular initiative 'against mass immigration' introduced by the Swiss People's Party on 9 February 2014 contradicts the bilateral agreement with the EU on the Free Movement of Persons (FMP). The decision has since put Swiss-EU relations under considerable strain.

In the final chapter of this volume Fernando Mendez and Mario Mendez focus on some of the paradoxes of accommodating direct democracy within a multi-level polity such as the EU. They map the diffusion of direct democratic instruments in the EU over time, and note a critical juncture that roughly coincided with what EU scholars refer to as the 'end of the permissive consensus' and the growing politicisation of the EU.

In the concluding chapter the editors examine the comparative lessons and broader implications of this rich array of studies. Taken together, the chapters of this volume powerfully document both the historical and recent proliferation of direct democratic correctives to conventional structures of representation. But they also make clear that such innovations are not easy to integrate into inherited systems, and that even when they do address some genuine legitimacy deficits, they may also generate new and equally problematic democratic tensions.

## References

Auer, A. and Bützer, M. (2001) *Direct Democracy: The Eastern and Central European Experience*, Aldershot: Ashgate.

Butler, D. and Ranney, A. (1994) *Referendums around the World*, Washington, DC: American Enterprise Institute.

Hug, S. and Tsebelis, G. (2002) 'Veto players and referendums around the world', *Journal of Theoretical Politics*, 14(4): 465–516.

Kaufmann, B. and Waters, D. (2004) *Direct Democracy in Europe*, Durham, NC: Carolina Academic Press.

Mendez, F., Mendez, M. and Triga, V. (2014) *Referendums and the European Union: A Comparative Inquiry*, Cambridge: Cambridge University Press.

Serdült, U. and Welp, Y. (2012) 'Direct democracy upside down', *Taiwan Journal of Democracy*, 8(1): 69–92.

Uleri, P. V. (1996) 'Italy: referendum and initiatives from the origins to the crisis of a democratic regime', in M. Gallagher and P. Uleri (eds) *The Referendum Experience in Europe*, Basingstoke: Macmillan: 106–25.

Walker, M. (2003) *The Strategic Use of Referendums*, New York: Palgrave Macmillan.

Welp, Y. and Serdült, U. (2009) *Armas de Doble Filo*, Buenos Aires: Prometeo.

*Chapter Two*

# Between the 'Fiction' of Representation and the 'Faction' of Direct Democracy

*Laurence Whitehead*

> *Because [the] territory [of modern states] is much larger than that of the ancient republics, the mass of their inhabitants, whatever form of government they adopt, have no active part in it. They are called at most to exercise sovereignty through representation, that is to say in a fictitious manner.*
>
> Benjamin Constant, (1988 [1813])

> *[I]n a democracy the people meet and exercise the government in person; in a republic, they assemble and administer it by their representatives and agents. A democracy, consequently, will be confined to a small spot. A republic may be extended over a large region ... a pure democracy, by which I mean a society consisting of a small number of citizens, who assemble and administer the government in person, can admit no cure for the mischiefs of faction.*
>
> James Madison (1987 [1788])

## The fiction of representation

Although this volume focuses on MDDs in Latin American, Europe, the former Soviet Union area and sub-Saharan Africa, the present chapter refers back to foundational issues in the emergence of the democratic tradition, as indicated by the opening quotations. And although John Keane has persuasively reconstructed the neglected non-canonical history of democracy, thus underscoring a richness and diversity that has been screened out in orthodox Western narrative, this chapter starts out from the conventional reference points of Athens and Philadelphia, since innovations are most clearly displayed by contrast with classical origins.

In the statement quoted above, Madison was, of course, seeking to promote his draft of a federal constitution for the thirteen states of what became the USA, so he needed to simplify the alternatives. The anti-federalists feared that the bottom-up and local-scale participatory politics of the revolutionary period would be swamped by the centralised powers that the proposed constitution would confer on a national government that was responsible for a territory already as large as Poland, and expected to become much larger still. Madison needed to persuade the American people that – as Montesquieu had argued half a century earlier – only very small units could be governed directly; and also that a territorially extensive republic could preserve liberty and respond to the will of the people, through the design of suitably 'representative' political institutions.

Among the design features in this scheme, public office would be open to all adult citizens (even though, in practice, a select stratum including many lawyers and merchants were expected to predominate; and, of course, women, slaves, and native Americans were not included). Various 'checks and balances' (including frequent elections, dual sovereignty and bicameralism) were included and a Bill of Rights was soon added, so that although the result was a large republic, the representatives of the people would not become tyrants.

In due course the formula of 'representative constitutional government' became the template for what we now regard as a modern democracy. Yet as the Madison quote indicates, the advocates of the 1787 constitution regarded it as an alternative to democracy rather than its embodiment. A century later James Bryce reiterated that interpretation of the document as follows:

> Had it been attempted four years earlier or four years later, at both which times the waves of democracy were running high, it must have failed. In 1783 the people, flushed with their victory over England, were full of confidence in themselves and in liberty, persuaded that the world was at their feet, disposed to think all authority tyranny. In 1791 their fervid sympathy with the Revolution in France had not yet been damped by the excesses of the Terror nor alienated by the insolence of the French government and its diplomatic agents in America. But in 1787 the first reaction from the War of Independence had set in. Wise men had come to discern the weak side of popular government; and the people themselves were in a comparatively humble and teachable mind. (Bryce 1891: 639)

Since the triumph of the federalists in 1787–8, Madison's stark and intuitively appealing contrast between compact (but impractical) direct democracy and large-scale representative democracy has become something of an axiom. But this contrast was always quite parochial and too schematic, and has now been further invalidated by the arrival of electronic means of communication, which abolishes the old barriers of time and distance. The parochialism is apparent when one compares it with article VI of the *Déclaration des Droits de l'Homme et du Citoyen* adopted by the French National Assembly in August 1789 (rights reaffirmed in the currently operative 1958 Constitution of the Fifth Republic): 'La Loi est l'expression de la volonté générale. Tous les citoyens ont droit de concourir *personnellement, ou par leurs représentants* à sa formation' (author's emphasis). The multiple inscriptions of direct democracy within the Swiss constitutional system offered a much stronger contrast with Madison's axiom over the course of the subsequent century. No doubt the contemporary Swiss Confederation is an extreme counter-example, but it is also a strikingly successful variant in a close-to-average scale modern democracy. Although influenced by the Federalist Papers the Swiss constitution-makers were not bound by all its doctrines, and they in turn went on to influence others-most notably in Uruguay, and less happily in Bosnia, but also (to a lesser degree) even in California.

So Madison's polemic against direct democracy was context-bound and parochial. It was also always too schematic. In what sense? Here, for example, is what Thomas Jefferson wrote in 1816 (at the time of Madison's presidency):

> Divide the counties into wards of such size as that every citizen can attend, when called on, and act in person. Ascribe to them the government of their wards in all things relating to themselves exclusively. A justice chosen by themselves, in each, a constable, a military company, a patrol, a school, the care of their own poor, their own portion of public roads, the choice of one or more jurors … . by making every citizen an acting member of the government, and in the offices nearest and most interesting to him, will attach him by his strongest feelings to the independence of his country, and its republican Constitution. (Jefferson, 1977, 556–7)

Although this proposal was never adopted in the form stated, its spirit informed a variety of subsequent developments in various states. Moreover, although ratification of constitutional amendments by popular vote has never been allowed under the 1787 text, many of the state constitutions adopted in the following century require direct sanction by a majority of the electorate for any amendment to take effect.[1] In any case, these principles demonstrate the scope that exists for bridging the direct/representative democracy divide.

Just as direct forms of democracy were mixed in with the representative variant from the earliest days of the American Republic, so also in the supposedly pure city state democracies of ancient Greece, representative and direct variants also always coexisted. Aristotle's description of the Constitution of Athens in 325 BC makes the details clear: at periodic 'sovereign' assemblies 'the people must confirm in office those magistrates whom they consider to be performing their duties satisfactorily' (1959, Chapter 43); the King-Archon (responsible for cases of impiety and for first hearings of homicides) and four superintendents of mysteries 'are elected in the assembly by open vote' (Chapter 57); 'all military commands are filled by open vote' (Chapter 61); and most court hearings are decided by the vote of 500 jurors, or up to 1,500 in the most important cases (Chapter 68). Again the distinction between direct democracy and representative government is far too schematic to capture the really existing rules and procedures of this city state, even at its most 'purely' democratic (i.e. when many public duties were assigned by lot).

1. According to Bryce: 'As the republic went on working out both in theory and in practice those conceptions of democracy and popular sovereignty which had been only vaguely apprehended when enunciated at the Revolution, the faith of the average man in himself became stronger, his love of equality greater, his desire, not only to rule, but to rule directly in his own proper person, more constant. These sentiments … found large scope in local government' (1891: 450–1). Bryce also noted that in many state constitutions the method of amendment comes very close to the Swiss referendum, and adds: 'It is not uncommon for proposals submitted by the legislature in the form of constitutional amendments to be rejected by the people. Thus in Indiana, Nebraska, Ohio and Oregon, the legislature submitted amendments extending the suffrage to women, and the people in all four states refused the extension' (1891: 452–3).

More broadly, even when direct participation in 'assembly' style democracy is most strongly encouraged, there are evident practical limitations that impede the proceedings from acting as the unmediated expression of the popular will. Some citizens have flocks to herd; some doctors must be on call for their patients; some seamen must catch the tide. Some may arrive after the assembly has begun, others will have to leave before the end. Not everyone can speak at once, and the order of the agenda is also consequential. So whoever controls the timetable can influence the outcome. Decisions must be transcribed and recorded (not all can or will read, or be equally diligent in checking the minutes). In fact not everyone can speak: some will be shy, some deaf, some inarticulate.

In brief, even in the most compact and participatory polis citizen engagement will always be uneven and selective: and no public assembly can dispense with at least informal reliance on the leadership of a few who may claim to 'represent' the collective opinion, but who in practice also shape – and may well capture – it. Here enters the theme of 'faction'. According to Madison:

> By faction I understand a number of citizens, whether amounting to a majority or a minority of the whole, who are united and actuated by some common impulse of passion, or of interest, adverse to the rights of other citizens, or to the permanent and aggregate interests of the community … the smaller the society, the fewer probably will be the distinct parties and interests composing it; the fewer the distinct parties and interests, the more frequently the majority will be found of the same party; and the smaller the number of individuals composing a majority, and the smaller the compass within which they are placed, the more easily will they concert and exercise their plans of oppression. (Madison et al. 1987 [1788], X)

Although the Federalist Papers have captured the mainstream Western political imagination, and thus entrenched an extremely negative image of the intolerance, instability and irresponsibility of faction-dominated assembly government in the ancient world,[2] that is not the only possible reading of the available evidence. Machiavelli used Livy to underscore the relative absence of factional 'ingratitude' in Rome as compared to Athens: 'the city was never deprived of its liberty by any of its citizens, so that there was no great reason to suspect them, or, consequently, to offend them in a thoughtless way' (1997, Chapter 28). And as Aristotle's account of the restoration of Athenian democracy in 403 BC reads:

> The Athenians appear, in fact, both publicly and privately, to have behaved with unsurpassed moderation and fairness to those who shared the guilt of earlier misfortunes. They not only abstained from any form of victimisation, but actually drew on state funds to repay Sparta … (1959, Chapter XIV)

2. According to Madison, 'such democracies have ever been spectacles of turbulence and contention,' and 'have ever been found incompatible with personal security or the rights of property; and have in general been as short in their lives as they have been violent in their deaths' (Madison et al. 1788 [1987], X).

Morreover, in 403 BC the Athenians swore 'the first general amnesty in recorded history – a publicly enacted, ritualistic declaration of forgetfulness of the "bad" – that is, anti-democratic – deeds of the years prior to 403, an oath sworn by all Athenians on the restoration of democracy' (Cartledge 2009: 85). In similar vein, Jon Elster's review of recent scholarship on Athenian democracy between 403 BC and 322 BC, sums the issue up as follows: 'Athenian democracy ... must be considered a great success, largely because of its elaborate system of checks and balances, which prevented rash decisions by the citizens and abuse of power by military and political leaders' (1999: 253). Aristotle added that: 'the constitution then established has continued until today [approximately 80 years] accompanied by a steady growth of the power of the masses' (1958, Chapter XV). Most persuasively, Paul Cartledge has just published his thorough and authoritative assessment of the various forms and stages of *demokratia* in Greek antiquity, which basically confirms Aristotle's account, and underlines *inter alia* the significance of such fourth-century BC features as the writ alleging unconstitutional proposals, and the separation between decrees and laws (Cartledge 2016: 221–5).

So Madison was promoting a selectively hostile account of the evidence available to him about the ancient world, and was also caricaturing early American experiences of town hall meetings that were dear to his anti-federalist opponents. It is worth recalling that in New England even a city as large and expansionary as Boston was still governed by a primary assembly of all those who qualified as citizens, until 1822. As we have seen, Jefferson still promoted this model of 'ward republics' thirty years after Madison's philippic. By then, the evils that he had associated with pure democracy ['a rage for paper money, for an abolition of debts, for an equal division of property, or for any other improper or wicked project'] had indeed materialised – but in Paris, not in Boston; and as a consequence not of the passions of a direct citizen assembly, but through the unrestrained dictates of the National Assembly, the first sovereign body composed of 'representatives' of the French people. From a contemporary Swiss perspective it is hard to accept an equation between cantonal democracy and unstable tyranny, or to share the assumption that a large modern society can only be governed by remotely elected congressmen (let alone by party machines controlled by professional politicians that only pretend to represent local constituents). Comparative historical experiences are much more varied and nuanced than that.

In Madison's defence, it has long seemed a self-evident reality that no large modern state or society can routinely be governed directly by the entire body of its citizenry. But according to the 'fiction' of representative democracy they do 'rule', at least in the sense of approving the overall process of decision-making; selecting representatives who are delegated under specified conditions (constituencies and term limits, among others) to make laws and decide particular policy questions on their behalf. To be more precise, the voters as a collective body may 'rule' in these senses, even though each individual voter can only exercise such a minute fraction of the overall electoral authority as to be inconsequential (and in that sense 'fictitious'). For any of this to be meaningful a large body of citizens must 'participate' directly and personally in certain defined spheres of political life – as voters, party activists, jury members, local councillors, and perhaps even (as in certain Swiss cantons) voters in public assemblies, even though on an individual cost–benefit analysis it is irrational to make so much effort for what is in effect zero personal influence.

Is this why Constant regarded popular sovereignty as 'fictitious' (see opening quotation)? Jeremy Bentham also wrestled with similar issues at about the same time,[3] but it has proved a particularly continuous theme in French scholarship on representation and democracy. Pierre Rosanvallon, for example, has argued that representation is founded on a 'necessary fiction', but not because of its futility for the individual. Rather, he stresses the contrast between two conceptions of 'representation' in the French republican tradition: the juridical conception concerns the indivisible unity of the republic as the expression of an abstractly conceived 'people', and the sociological counterpart reflects the reality of social diversity. In his view, the inherent conflict between these two ideas generates a chronic 'crisis of representation' in the French political system. The 'necessary fiction' of representation arises from the need to integrate social diversity into the unity of the political body (1998: 41).

This is a very 'top-down' understanding, which no doubt reflects the exceptionally centralised origin of the French Republic. As Rosanvallon also notes, the National Assembly was initially conceived not as a gathering of representatives each with their own constituencies and mandates, but as the foundational expression of a general will – the source of citizenship and representative government, not its consequence (1998: 38). The concentration of French politics in Paris and the repeated cycles of personalist leadership (Bonapartism to Gaullism) among other elements, might suggest that the 'fictional' nature of representative government is an oddity of France, and not a matter of general significance.

Bruno Latour's (2012) more general analysis of the 'crisis of political representation' provides more universal arguments. It is not just in France that political discourse involves the improbable claim that the wishes of millions of citizens can somehow be mimetically translated into the decisions of a political regime (or indeed a personal leader) without deception or betrayal.[4] To do justice to this line of thought we need to differentiate 'fiction' from outright 'falsehood'. The fictional nature of political representation refers to the hopes and expectations required to make it work – claims that must have some basis in reality, and can be defended from challenge by the presentation of verifiable evidence, even though wishful thinking and self-deception are also built in.

3. As insightfully discussed in David Runciman (2008, 137–40).

4. In Chapter 12 ('Invoquer les fântomes du politique'), the author presents a very ambitious general interpretation of the paradoxes of political discourse, which he contrasts with other ways of operating such as through law, religion and, above all, science. He sees complaints about a 'crisis of representation' as a recurrent phenomenon that he attributes to a rationalist misunderstanding about what political discourse necessarily involves, namely endless cycles of rhetorical promises that are doomed to be challenged and replaced by more of the same.

This general approach needs to be grounded in comparative study and empirical evidence. In his last book, Peter Mair (2013) presented a carefully documented account of what he termed the 'hollowing' of Western democracy. His study, and most of the associated literature, is strongly 'presentist' in its diagnosis. This refers to the multiple indications that by the early twenty-first century membership of parties, confidence in parliaments, satisfaction with electoral processes and outcomes, and identification with democratic institutions were all in serious decline in most of the Western world. A huge scholarly literature has grown up for the measurement, tracking and explaining of such tendencies. The financial crisis of 2008 and subsequent disappointments make it hard to distinguish between underlying secular trends and possibly more conjunctural factors. Although Mair was focused on contemporary Western Europe it is clear that similar tendencies can also be identified in the western hemisphere, and elsewhere.

## Beyond fictions and factions

For the purposes of this volume what matters is the widespread perception (whether or not it proves justified) that inherited constitutional models of representative government are in trouble in most parts of the democratic world, and require adjustment. How such troubles compare with the earlier history of democracy is worth considering, but not here.

When evaluating the various innovations currently being proposed and introduced it is important to recall the foundational debates and prior experiences of both direct and representative democracy, and to resist the notion that only one of these two forms is truly legitimate. The burden of this chapter is that mixed and combined variants have been more common and constructive than the purists of either camp tend to recognise. The spaces in between classical direct and representative forms of democracy have been filled out in many competing ways – by the intermediation of disciplined parties; by federal and local forms of experimentation; by the interposition of bureaucracies, regulatory and monitoring agencies; and by diverse variants of deliberation, participation, petition and sortition at both national and local levels. But all this mixture and experimentation comes at a price – it works better in some settings than others – and the many variants suggested by theory and experience should be regarded as provisional, subject to review. Each solution is likely to throw up unintended consequences and, thus, to generate further challenges in its turn.

Evidently we are surveying a wide range of cases, and the alternatives under consideration rest on contextual conditions that vary substantially, both from time to time and spatially. For example, the core responsibilities of contemporary citizenship presume literacy, a certain degree of numeracy, some sense of community or shared identity, and conditions of human development that allow citizens to make autonomous political judgements. Small cohesive communities may have more scope for direct forms of self-government than large impersonal cities. Traditions and collective beliefs about who should participate, how much, and when, are not uniform across the globe. So there is not a 'one size fits all' correct balance between direct and representative forms of democracy. But constitutional forms of national government with plausible claims to the status of democracy are widely prevalent in the twenty-first century, and have been normatively in the ascendant for the past generation. That has meant the privileging of electoral processes to select and rotate national public officeholders and parliamentarians. 'Representative government' in this sense, has come to be seen by many (including a large sector of the political science community) as the essence of modern constitutional democracy.

In reality, however, the 'direct' components of a democratic system remain present, even when of reduced visibility. Constitutional government involves a set of rules and restraints that are binding on leaders as well as citizens. However, it is also possible to construct localised arrangements for some aspects of direct decision-making by open assembly within larger systems that are predominantly indirect. For example, the Bolivian and Mexican constitutions now allow for traditional practices known as *usos y costumbres* to settle various policy matters in communities designated as 'Indian' and are therefore entitled to activate what are supposed to be time-honoured methods of local government. Indeed, even in one-party Communist China the 1998 law on Village Council elections:

> allows village assemblies – comprised of all adult village residents – to discuss and decide on matters such as village expenditures and revenues, applications, plot allocations, family planning actions, and collective contracts. On paper, these rights amount to a form of direct (as opposed to representative) democracy. In this respect, the legal rights of Chinese villagers exceed those given to citizens in most liberal democracies … . In addition, all adult villagers were given the express right to run for election, to directly nominate candidates, and to recall [Village Council] members before their term of office is complete. (Wright 2015, 62)

Even in more traditional representative systems there are some direct as well as indirect procedures to consider. Parliamentarians may be empowered to represent their constituents, but they are also expected to consult with them: receiving letters and petitions from voters, perhaps making themselves available for periodic face-to-face meetings with those they represent, or explaining themselves to their activist supporters. But there is no uniformity between legislatures over such matters: not even such a fundamental representative procedure as the receiving of petitions is necessarily accepted.[5] Then there is peaceful direct action. Citizens with strong opinions about a particular policy choice (a military adventure or the siting of an

5. The right of petition was taken up by the USA following the British practice, so in the pre-Civil War period John Quincy Adams led the campaign for the abolition of slavery by promoting petitions to Congress in that sense. But southerners, led by Henry Clay, vehemently resisted on the grounds that the federal Congress had no jurisdiction on this matter. This was the 'gag rule' controversy that raged between 1836 and 1844. The eventual compromise was that such petitions would be received and archived, but not read.

airport, for instance) have the right to express their views collectively and publicly in open demonstrations. Again there is no 'one size fits all' formula, but the general position is that all forms of representative democratic government also involve a variety of avenues of citizen participation that constrain the discretional powers of professional politicians, and that allow for direct involvement in political life from unelected members of the public at large.

Viewed from this broad perspective direct forms of democracy encompass a very diverse array of possibilities. Citizen participation may be information generating, advisory or mandatory. Those involved may be everyone who is affected, all voters, large collectivities within the encompassing society, single-issue minorities, or much smaller and more fragmented participants. Individuals may write to representatives; municipalities may organise to defend local objectives; interest groups may lobby or protest; party conferences may overrule nationally elected leaders; constitutional amendments may be ratified or rejected; or citizens may even vote to secede. Some recent variants include the spread of recall procedures; the proliferation of citizen accountability agencies (ombudsmen or *defensores del pueblo*); participatory budgeting; procedures requiring legislators to deliberate on laws proposed by the public; and the direct election of police commissioners. What all these many and varied forms of direct democracy have in common is the intention to lubricate the relationship between the political class and the citizens on whose behalf it purports to act. In this sense representative and direct forms of democracy can be mutually supportive, bridge legitimacy gaps and assist in the democratic steering of public policy choices.

But although direct and representative forms of constitutional government can flow together to improve the workings of democratic politics, they are also inherently prone to clash. Such conflicts should be of particular concern where old-established practices of representative government are under stress or challenge. David van Reybrouck (2014, Chapter 1) provides a striking inventory of what he calls the 'democratic fatigue' of contemporary Europe. They are also likely to raise more difficulties in contexts where untried forms of democratic experimentation are being attempted as emergency responses to what is perceived as citizen disenchantment with 'really existing' constitutional regimes. A recent review of such experiments in Latin America suggests that while most were intended as genuine improvements aimed at addressing real and strongly felt deficiencies in the existing frame of governance, they typically introduced new complexities and anomalies that might often prove more unsatisfactory than the problems they were expected to tackle (Welp and Whitehead 2011).

From time to time constitutional reforms may be needed, and when this arises it is common to seek direct approval through a referendum. Unless the citizenry as a whole are allowed some direct means to authorise or reject proposals that alter the fundamental principles of a democratic regime, there will be no assurance that the rulers still acknowledge their condition as agents, rather than owners, of the collective enterprise. But this raises a further foundational question (who is to be included in the 'citizenry as a whole'?), the denominator without which no numerical majority can be defined. Any referendum or plebiscite whether mandatory or only consultative,[6] can only be held once the territorial boundaries and electoral qualifications applicable to a given political jurisdiction have been determined. Let us now turn to some brief conceptual observations about the logic of different forms of direct democracy are in order. Since the business of modern government is complex, ordinary citizens will need help in order to intervene successfully and to avoid unintended consequences. Some of this assistance can be provided by experts, but their advice will need to be sifted, their credentials assessed, and their professional biases corrected. It is hard enough for professional politicians to exercise such oversight, and much more problematic for the inexperienced and occasional citizen-legislator. Moreover, modern policy making is largely sequential. Each decision needs to be taken with a view to its second- and third-round effects, and to the anticipated reactions of the interests affected.

Choices made through direct citizen participation have to be simple and stark. Representatives can take the necessary time to deliberate and to assess the full consequences of a policy move, and to monitor successive phases of implementation, whereas their principals can only make immediate broad-brush judgements. But this way of presenting the alternatives can seem technocratic and elitist. The exponents of direct democracy are liable to decry the mystification of policy making behind the backs of ordinary people. Perhaps more direct interventions may be broad-brush and immediate, but even so they may introduce correctives that respond to the felt needs of the bulk of the population, and that reflect popular feeling, including well-founded distrust of *partidocracias* and insiders whose privileged lifestyles insulate them from everyday realities

The Brazilian constituent assembly of 1987–8 and the eventual ratification of the presidential form of government in 1994 provide a useful demonstration of how representative and directly consultative forms of decision-making may be pursued in tandem. After two decades of military rule, millions of Brazilian citizens came onto the streets to demand immediate direct presidential elections *(direitas já)*. Although they were unable to obtain that ambitious objective they did secure transition to an elected and civilian administration, and eventually, in 1987, the Congress was reconstituted as a constituent assembly with a mandate to write a democratic constitution.

In view of its imperfect legitimacy, this assembly was keen to secure popular consent for its efforts. It therefore invited direct participation from the wider society. Specifically, it agreed to receive suggestions from any association, local assembly or neighbourhood committee. It also established a programme of public hearings in Brasilia at which such bodies would have the right to present themselves and give their opinions. Moreover it provided for the consideration of amendments to its draft, provided they received the backing of at least 30,000 voters and three associations. In the event it received 122 popular amendments promoted by 12.25 million signatures. Of these amendments, eighty-three were

6. The terminology is variable here. For many the two words are synonyms, but in Australia, for example, a referendum is a direct vote to modify the constitution, whereas a plebiscite is a direct vote on any other matter.

found to be valid, and ten days in August 1987 were dedicated to public hearings at which each proposal was presented to the plenary by three sponsors, with ensuing debates between assembly members and members of the public.

At the end of a complex negotiation process the document was not ratified by a plebiscite, but just approved by the assembly. However, one crucial matter that could not be resolved there was the form of government that was to be adopted. Consequently, in 1993, the electorate at large was offered a threefold choice between presidential, parliamentary and monarchical forms of government. Although elite opinion strongly favoured the middle option, the citizenry proved firm in their preference for presidentialism, and it was the wisdom of the masses that prevailed (to no obvious detrimental consequences).

Thus constitution making in Brazil sidestepped the 'representative' versus 'direct' dichotomy, and demonstrated that intermediate solutions need not generate ungovernability. This is particularly striking considering the vast continental scale of the federation, and its acute social inequalities and severely uneven regional levels of development. In the end, Brazil's 1988 constitution has proved more durable and authoritative than its six predecessors, and some of its success can be attributed to the popular participation it invited.

As noted, it was a legislative assembly that crafted the rules of the game in Brazil, taking almost two years to elaborate an all-encompassing constitutional text. Although the form of government was decided by plebiscite, it was the legislators who wrote the overall package who adopted it. The same was true of the constitutions that emerged from the American and French Revolutions. It was not until Napoleon overturned the Republic and was made First Consul for Life that the Roman procedure of direct authorisation of the ruler by plebiscite was reintroduced.[7] A classic observation in the literature about this matter is that whereas representative governments can craft complex and modulated responses to difficult challenges, in a plebiscite or consultation voters can only say 'yes' or 'no' to a prefabricated package.[8] So who sets the question? How is the timing determined? And once the result is known, how is the aftermath to be managed? As the history of recent referendums in democracies around the world makes plain, the intervention of professional politicians cannot be eliminated by resort to this particular instrument of direct democracy. To the contrary, most referendums are generated, manipulated and reinterpreted by a stratum of political experts who use the political capital derived from a plebiscitary verdict to pursue an agenda of their own (often directed against their equally professional political rivals).

Thus far the spaces of contention considered here are at the national and constitutional levels. Yet as most of the case material in this volume shows, similar challenges over the interaction between direct and representative forms

7. Three previous plebiscites in revolutionary France had authorised constitutions, not personal rulers. Napoleon was 'elected' by 3.5 million votes to about 8,000 – the kind of result that continues to discredit some forms of plebiscitary consultation to this day.

8. At most it may be possible to ask two linked questions, more than that generates unmanageable confusion over the outcome.

of democratic legitimation also arise at the level of provinces, municipalities and cantons; and also supranationally (concerning ratification of the Maastricht and Nice Treaties of the European Union, for example). These procedural issues can affect not just the foundational rules of entire political systems, but also more down-to-earth sectorial questions (such as participatory budgets or the redrawing of district boundaries).

One example out of many will have to suffice here. In 2003 the Westminster Parliament enacted a Regional Assemblies law for England, to complement the devolution it had provided to Scotland, Wales and Northern Ireland. The idea was to establish three regional assemblies for the North East, the North West, and Yorkshire and Humberside. In November 2004 the North East proposal was put to a regional referendum – and rejected by 77.9 per cent of those who voted, on a 49 per cent turnout. In sharp contrast to the strong sense of local identity expressed in the three devolved regions, this direct testing of public opinion demonstrated to their political representatives in London that the English did not favour a fragmented *demos*. The remaining two proposed regions were not even consulted, and the whole initiative was simply dropped.

The topic of referendums clearly provides a rich and diverse array of possible linkages between direct and indirect forms of democratic government. But it is far from exhausting the range of possibilities. One important rival variant of direct democracy is 'participation by lot' as commended in 1970 by Robert Dahl (1970: 149–50). This option is currently being promoted by Van Reybrouck, under the label of 'sortition', whereby political responsibilities are distributed throughout the citizenry by lot. Two good illustrations of what he has in mind concern the Belgian upper chamber following the abolition of the Senate in 2014, and the House of Lords, if hereditary peerages are eventually abolished in the UK. In both cases, it is possible to argue that law making would be more legitimate, and no less effective, if the backstop chamber was composed not of another cohort of party political operatives, but of a directly representative cross section of the population at large. Van Reybrouck acknowledges some of the difficulties, and makes proposals to circumvent them. Thus, sortition could be combined with other selection procedures, intended to screen out those least equipped for, or interested in, the task.

The list of direct democratic forms could be extended further with the same result. Direct popular assemblies can provide elected representatives with information and support, but they can also generate a conflict of powers. Legislative initiative by petition can enrich the work of a parliament, but it can also undermine the cohesion and legitimacy of regular legislative processes. Surveying the entire field of possibilities, any direct democracy arrangement of consequence will have the potential to curb the discretion, and perhaps weaken the authority, of elected political representatives. The risk is greatest when the direct democracy channel is binding, national and open ended. Reconciliation between the two democratic forms is more likely when the direct component is advisory, local and focused. But there is no single formula applicable in all contexts for maximising the legitimacy gains and minimising the risks to policy cohesion. Direct democracy initiatives that may initially serve as salutary correctives to the failings of sclerotic systems of representation may subsequently develop dysfunctions of their own that are equally in need of correction from the other side.

As argued in a recent volume on the future of representative democracy (Alonso et al. 2011), the historical and sociological conditions that generate effective and legitimate forms of parliamentary representation in one setting or era may no longer provide the same underpinnings in a different place or at a later point. In late eighteenth-century North America, congressmen (property-owning white gentlemen) might travel by horseback for a month in order to take up the seats in Washington, DC. Today, constituents are 'represented' in a very different way by multi-millionaires funded by super Political Action Committees and communicating via digital social media. In the future, technology is likely to produce many new forms of political organisation, including some that are more instantaneous and direct than ever before. Horizontal communication may be displacing vertical channels of accountability.

Moreover, this brief discussion of other problems of reconciling direct and representative forms of democracy has left out some crucial informal channels of intermediation. The commercial media, the security services and the money power of corporate interests need to be taken into account. Innovative and more direct forms of democracy may disrupt traditional models of democratic representation, but they are not alone. If parliaments no longer protect citizens from intrusive security surveillance, direct democracy may offer the best (or only) means of re-establishing the right to privacy. If media moguls can capture or intimidate elected representatives, direct expressions of citizen sovereignty may be required to curb the excesses of the Fourth Estate.

In conclusion, the shifting balance between direct and representative forms of democracy is likely to remain a core and contentious issue of dispute, generating many new experiments and not a few false trails, over coming decades. This volume provides an early *tour de horizon* and demonstrates both the richness and variety, and also the incompleteness, of the innovations that are in prospect.

## References

Alonso, S., J. Keane and W. Merkel (eds) (2011) *The Future of Representative Democracy*, Cambridge: Cambridge University Press.

Aristotle (1959) *The Athenian Constitution*, London: Everyman's Library.

Bryce, J. (1891) *The American Commonwealth*, New York: Macmillan.

Cartledge, P. (2009) *Ancient Greek Political Thought in Practice*, Cambridge: Cambridge University Press.

—— (2016) *Democracy: A Life*, Oxford: Oxford University Press.

Constant, B. (1988 [1813]) *Political Writings*, Cambridge: Cambridge University Press.

Dahl, R. (1970) *After the Revolution? Authority in a good society*, New Haven: Yale University Press.

Elster, J. (1999) 'Accountability in Athenian Politics', in B. Manin, A. Przeworski and S. Stokes (eds), *Democracy, Accountability and Representation*, Cambridge: Cambridge University Press.

Fung, A. and E. O. Wright (eds) (2003) *Deepening Democracy: Institutional innovation in empowered participatory governance*, London: Verso.

Gastil, J. and P. Levine (eds) (2005) *The Deliberative Democracy Handbook: Strategies for effective civic engagement in the twenty-first century*, San Francisco: Jossey-Bass.

Jefferson, T. (1977) *The Portable Thomas Jefferson*, London: Penguin.

Keane, J. (2010) *The Life and Death of Democracy*, London: Pocket Books.

Latour, B. (2012) *Enquêtes sur les modes d'éxistence*, Paris: La Decouverte.

Machiavelli, N. (1997) *Discourses on Livy*, Oxford: Oxford University Press.

Madison, J., A. Hamilton and J. Jay (1987 [1788]) *The Federalist, or, The New Constitution* by Alexander Hamilton, James Madison, and John Jay, Everyman's Library, London: J. M. Dent & Sons.

Mair, P. (2013) *Ruling the Void: The hollowing of western democracy*, London: Verso.

Manin, B. (1997) *The Principles of Representative Government*, Cambridge: Cambridge University Press.

Rosanvallon, P. (1998) *Le peuple introuvable: Histoire de la représentation démocratique en France*, Paris: Gallimard.

Runciman, D. (2008) *Political Hypocrisy: The mask of power, from Hobbes to Orwell and beyond*, Princeton: Princeton University Press.

Van Reybrouck, D. (2014) *Contre les élections*, Arles: Babel.

Welp Y. and U. Serdült (eds) (2014) *La dosis hace el veneno: Análisis de la revocatoria del mandato en América Latina, Estados Unidos y Francia*, Quito: Consejo Nacional Electoral.

Welp, Y. and L. Whitehead (eds) (2011) *Caleidoscopio de la innovación democrática en América Latina*, Mexico City: FLACSO.

Wright, T. (2015) *Party and State in Post-Mao China*, Cambridge: Polity.

*Chapter Three*

# Constitution Making in Democratic Constitutional Orders: The Challenge of Citizen Participation

*Gabriel L. Negretto*

## Introduction

There are several possible institutional channels of citizen involvement in constitution making. In Western constitutional law, the two standard mechanisms are the referendum and the election of a constituent body independent of the ordinary legislature. These procedures are well established in the historical practice of constitution making following the foundation of a new state or during the inauguration of a new democratic regime. However, they are highly problematic in the context of an existing democratic constitutional order in which there is no regulation for the replacement of the constitution.

Organising an ad hoc referendum and deciding on the election, composition, and powers of an independent constitution-making body may lead to severe conflicts between the different branches of state power as well as between government and opposition. More ominously, in a weakly institutionalised environment a popular leader and his party can take advantage of the legal vacuum and use channels of citizen participation to hijack the process and redistribute power in their favour. In a separation of powers system, a referendum on whether the constitution should be replaced can be used to delegate the power to organise the process to the incumbent president. The election of a constituent assembly under the rules decided by the executive may provide members of his party with unilateral control over this body and the ability to claim sovereign power to replace or intervene in the legislature and other state powers. The end result of such a process is likely to be the erosion of representative democracy.

I argue that voting in referendums and electing special constituent bodies in constitutional rewrites can only be compatible with the preservation of representative institutions if the process is regulated in advance by means of an institutional or political agreement between the government and the main opposition parties. Reaching such agreement, in turn, depends on the distribution of political power between the forces supporting the old constitutional order and those favouring its replacement. Specifically, participatory but executive-led constitution making tends to occur in a presidential regime when at the time of deciding the organisation of the process new parties advocating radical reform win executive office without achieving majority control of the legislature. I support this argument with a comparative analysis of recent processes of constitutional replacement in Latin America.

This chapter starts with a discussion of the mechanisms of popular participation available in different forms of constitutional change. This is followed by a discussion on the problem of how to channel popular participation in the replacement of democratic constitutions and on the alternative routes of institutional regulation of this process. A final section analyses the conditions under which irregular replacement of the constitution may enhance citizen participation while eroding representative institutions. A brief conclusion follows.

## *Citizen participation in constitutional change*

The two main mechanisms of formal constitutional change are amendment and replacement of a constitution. In the first case the legal continuity of the constitution is preserved through partial textual revisions; in the second, the constitution in force is abrogated and a new constitution created (for this distinction, see Negretto 2012, 2013). Citizen involvement in constitutional change is considered to be essential for the adoption of important amendments and invariably for the creation of new constitutions. This participation may be required as a matter of principle or on consequentialist grounds. The classic distinction between constituent and constituted power postulates that only the people, not existing state authorities, should be the authors of the constitution (Paine 1995 [1791]). Some authors argue that the right of citizens to participate in the conduct of public affairs in general and in constitution building in particular is a contemporary international norm (see Banks 2008). Citizen involvement in constitutional change may also be demanded because of its expected beneficial effects on constitutional design and democracy (see Widner 2008; Ginsburg et al. 2008, 2009; Eisenstadt et al. 2015).

However, the involvement of citizens in constitutional change has widely diverse meanings and can be channelled in many different possible ways. I discuss here only procedures that provide citizens with the ability to make proposals of constitutional change, elect those who will decide the content of the revisions and/or vote on the reforms proposed by their representatives. I will not consider mechanisms of informal consultation in which ordinary citizens are part of the process in less direct ways, such as attending open meetings, participatory forums, or hearings; or participating in surveys and polls organised by constitutional commissions.

One relatively simple way to classify the different mechanisms of citizen participation in constitutional change is by identifying two dimensions: who makes the proposal and how popular participation is activated (see Kriesi 2012: 40–1). The first dimension enables a distinction between two general institutions; referendum and initiative. It is a referendum when state actors (executive, legislature, or both) make the proposal and an initiative when citizens themselves are the authors of the proposition (Leduc 2002; Kriesi 2012). Popular participation, in turn, can be activated in three different ways: by the request of state authorities, by the initiative of citizens, or by constitutional mandate. Table 3.1 summarises this typology.

*Table 3.1: Citizen participation in constitutional change*

| **Citizen participation required by** | **Constitutional proposal made by** | |
|---|---|---|
| | **State actors** | **Citizens** |
| State actors | State-initiated referendum (Authorising the election of a constituent assembly or ratifying a replacement or amendment) | – |
| Citizens | Citizen-initiated referendum (Abrogating or rejecting an amendment) | Popular initiative (Petitioning the election of a constituent assembly or proposing an amendment) |
| Constitution | Mandatory referendum (Authorising a replacement or ratifying a replacement or amendment) | – |

*Source:* Author, based on Kriesi (2012) and Leduc (2002).

The typical mechanism of citizen involvement in constitutional amendments is the mandatory referendum, where an amendment proposed by the legislature must be ratified in a popular vote before it comes into effect. American state constitutions have been pioneers in this type of procedure and most had established the popular ratification of legislative amendments by the early nineteenth century (Dinan 2009). Another mechanism is the popular constitutional initiative, which enables citizens to submit constitutional revisions to direct popular vote.[1] By the late nineteenth century, the federal constitution of Switzerland and several American states had incorporated this mechanism. A third procedure allows citizens to petition for a vote on whether a constitutional reform already passed by the legislature should be maintained or abrogated. This mechanism can be found in the 1946 Italian constitution and in some constitutions in Latin America, such as the 1991 constitution of Colombia, and the 1949 constitution of Costa Rica after the 2002 reform.

All these institutions are 'citizen-oriented' because in no case can state authorities mobilise citizens at their will to vote on constitutional amendments. Several constitutions, however, invest state authorities with the power to convene a referendum on an amendment proposed by them. In most of these cases the proposal is made by the legislature or by the executive with the consent of the legislature. Few democratic constitutions invest the executive with the sole authority to convene a referendum to approve a constitutional amendment. Examples of these rare cases are the 1999 Venezuelan Constitution and the 2008 Ecuadorean Constitution.

1. A more limited type of initiative allows citizens to submit amendment proposals to congressional approval.

In contrast to amendments, which are usually regulated in the constitution, wholesale replacements often occur outside the existing legal order. For this reason, procedural rules to replace a constitution tend to be established on an ad hoc basis. Nonetheless, comparative constitutional history shows that there are some common procedures implemented in these cases, usually oriented to obtaining the consent of the people to the new constitutional order. The most typical is submitting the final text to popular approval. As a matter of practice, the first constitutions to be ratified by referendum were the 1778 Massachusetts Constitution, the 1792 New Hampshire Constitution, and the 1793 French Constitution. During the nineteenth century the people ratified relatively few national constitutions. However, the use of this type of referendum increased significantly during the twentieth century.[2]

Referendums can also be used at the beginning of the process so that representatives obtain a popular mandate to replace the constitution or approve specific changes. Since the distinction between constituent and constituted powers prevents the latter from making fundamental changes to the constitution, initial popular approval may be required in principle. According to constitutional historians, it was based on this distinction that the state legislatures that created the first American constitutions after 1776 sought initial popular authorisation (Fritz 1997: 326). Later on, some constitutions formalised this procedure, such as the 1780 Massachusetts Constitution, and today fourteen state constitutions in the US require holding referendums after a certain number of years to ask citizens whether they would like to revise the constitution (Dinan 2006). Referendums asking for popular authorisation to replace the constitution were also recently implemented in Colombia in 1990, in Venezuela in 1998, and in Ecuador in 1997 and 2007. When a referendum seeks popular authorisation to replace the constitution in force, state authorities usually initiate it. However, citizens may also have the prerogative to petition for a new constitution.[3]

Although usually not listed as a mechanism of direct popular participation, the election of a representative body responsible for drafting and/or approving a new constitutional text is also linked to citizen involvement in constitution making. Most obviously, the election of such a body provides voters with the opportunity to consider alternative proposals of reform and elect its members based on their preferences about these proposals. In addition, just as referendums may be required to create a representative constituent body the latter may help citizens to have a more considered judgement about the reasons to support or reject the new constitution in case they are required to do so in a ratification referendum.

2. Using a sample of 413 episodes of constitutional change between 1800 and 2000, Ginsburg et al. (2008: 377) find that promulgation of the constitution through a popular referendum became the most common method of constitutional approval during the twentieth century, particularly after 1950.

3. The right to petition for replacement of the existing constitution may be implicit in existing mechanisms of popular initiative or explicitly regulated, as is the case of the Swiss Constitution and the new constitutions of Bolivia, Ecuador, Panama, Paraguay and Venezuela.

The two most common bodies where constitutional texts are deliberated, negotiated, and finally approved are constituent legislatures and constituent assemblies (see Elster 2006; Widner 2008; Ginsburg et al. 2009). Constituent legislatures are institutions responsible for both adopting a new constitution and enacting ordinary legislation. When a legislature assumes constituent tasks, a referendum may be required both to authorise and to ratify its work because this body may not have been elected or legally authorised to alter the constitution.[4] In the case of constituent assemblies or conventions, which are elected or appointed for the sole or primary purpose of adopting a new constitution, popular authorisation may be necessary when they are not regulated by the constitution.[5] Popular ratification, in turn, can be used to provide citizens with an ex post check on the work of their representatives.

## The challenge of popular participation in replacing democratic constitutions

The replacement of constitutions tends to be less structured than their amendment because the former is often not regulated in advance. The reason for this legal vacuum is obvious when the constitution is made at the time of creating a new state, after a revolution, or during a transition to democracy, because in those cases there is either no pre-existing constitution or the latter is considered illegitimate under the principles of the new regime. Yet it is also the case that most national constitutions within an already existing democratic regime do not include a procedure for their own replacement. The common position of Western constitutional thought on this issue is that although the people have the inalienable right to alter or abolish their government, this right should not be part of the constitution. The suppression of the constitution as a whole can only occur de facto, after a revolution that overthrows an oppressive government.[6]

A small group of constitutions in the world take the opposite position and attempt to regulate their own demise. Some of these constitutions authorise the legislative assembly to act as a constituent legislature. For instance, the Finnish and Swedish constitutions allow parliament not only to amend but also to replace the constitution by means of a constitutional act.[7] The same is true of the Swiss and Uruguayan constitutions, which regulate a process of total reform that enables the ordinary legislature to enact a new constitution, subject to a special procedure that includes popular ratification. This type of regulation may provide an exit option in the event of a popular demand for a new constitution. Yet it may not be a

4. On the different types of constituent legislatures, see Elster (2006), and Negretto (2016a).
5. I will refer to constituent assemblies and constitutional conventions interchangeably. For a distinction between the term 'constitutional convention', common in the American constitutional tradition, and 'constituent assembly', common in the French and Latin American legal traditions, see Elster (2006).
6. See Negretto (2016b) on the origins of this position in liberal constitutional thought.
7. See Oliver and Fusaro (2011) on these cases.

feasible alternative if citizens do not consider the ordinary legislature a legitimate body or if reform of this body is the main purpose of creating a new constitution (see Negretto 2012).

Another group of constitutions, also few in number and most of them located in Latin America, allow for the wholesale replacement (or total reform) of the constitution by a body different from the legislature, usually a constituent assembly. Currently, this procedure is regulated in the 1994 Argentine Constitution, the 2009 Bolivian Constitution, the 1991 Colombian Constitution, the 2008 Ecuadorean Constitution, the 1985 Guatemalan Constitution, the 1987 Nicaraguan Constitution, the 1972 Panamanian Constitution, the 1992 Paraguayan constitution, and the 1999 Venezuelan constitution. However, not only are these exceptions to the rule but several of the constitutions that now regulate their own replacement were themselves created in an extra-constitutional way.

Regardless of what the constitution says, constitutional replacements do occur within democratic regimes. A growing social demand for a new constitutional order is likely to emerge when the constitution in force loses legitimacy or becomes dysfunctional at a particular historical juncture. In such a situation, the political elite would sooner or later be forced to respond. Since social support for the existing constitution tends to decline in tandem with the discrediting of old governing elites and institutions, the constituent power of the people is often invoked in these cases (see Viciano Pastor and Martínez Dalmau 2010; Colon Rios 2012). Following this doctrine, it could be argued, as Jefferson or Condorcet once did, that each generation should have the right to decide whether they want to live under the constitution adopted by the past generation.[8] Or the case could be made, as Akhill Amar has proposed (1988, 1994), that the people should always have the legal right to revise or replace a democratic constitution, whether the constitution itself authorises the exercise of this right or not.

As Kalyvas has argued (2005: 235–9), to constitute a new order denotes the act of founding together, a collective act that should abide by the principles of participation and inclusion. The problem, however, is that since the people lack the spontaneous capacity to act collectively, activation of the constituent power very often depends on an elite that acts in their name (see Madison et al. 1987 [1788]: 40). Moreover, when a constitutional order already exists at the time of initiating a constitution-making process, the elite that invokes the constituent power of the people tends to be part of the constituted state powers.

If the constituted powers agree on creating a new constitution, the process can be organised in a relatively peaceful and legal (or at least not overtly illegal) manner (see Hoar 1917; Amar 1988; Ackerman and Katyal 1995). Several problems arise, however, when some of the constituted powers agree on the extra-constitutional revision while others disagree. Here is a (non-exhaustive) list of them:

8. See Thomas Jefferson, Letter to James Madison of 6 September 1789, in Jefferson (1984: 963) and Condorcet's 'On the need for the citizens to ratify the Constitution' (1789), in Condorcet (1994 [1789]).

1. What would happen if the legislature rejects the revisions and the executive supports them? Is the executive authorised to bypass the legislature and call a referendum to directly approve a constitutional change or to authorise the election of a special convention?
2. If a special convention is elected, who decides on the rules of election and the procedures of this body?
3. What powers should a constituent body have with respect to constituted powers?
4. What happens to the old constitution and the powers elected under it during the process of drafting the new constitution and until its final adoption?
5. What jurisdiction (if any) should the Constitutional Court (also created under the previous constitution) have over the process?

Not only does the doctrine of the constituent power not address these questions but it also complicates answering them. If the vote of the people can overcome any initial illegality, virtually any usurpation of power by a popular leader is possible with the 'consent' of the people (see Tierney 2012). Extra-constitutional revisions that invoke the superior constituent power of the people to justify unilateral decisions may and often do end up using citizen participation to mask a strategy aimed at concentrating power in the executive branch. The only way to prevent this outcome is by means of a consensual procedure in which direct popular voting on constitutional change is a complement, not a substitute, for inclusive elite negotiations and pluralistic public deliberation. As we will see, however, it may not always be feasible to reach such procedural agreement.

### *Alternative routes to constitution making in democratic constitutional orders*

Even if the constitution in force does not provide for its own replacement, the execution of a constituent process will inevitably adopt some institutional form.[9] There are four basic strategies of institutional regulation in this situation. This list of alternatives does not exhaust, of course, all the possible combinations but illustrates the range of general options.

The main option is whether to regulate the replacement of the constitution by means of amending the existing amendment procedure or by adopting a parallel procedure. Amendment of the amendment procedure usually implies providing for a form of general or total reform of the constitution that is different both from partial reforms and from individual amendments. If a parallel procedure is created, three new options become available. The first is to design a legal framework by means of an institutional agreement between the executive and the legislature, and

9. Even Carl Schmitt (1982: 93–103), who generally rejects the possibility of regulating the activation of the constituent power, admits that the execution of the popular will must be subject to procedures. See also Böckenförde (2000: 169) on this issue.

regulated by the latter. The second alternative is to design the process via an extra-institutional political agreement (that is, outside Congress) between the government and opposition forces. Lastly, the executive can adopt the parallel procedure in an extra-institutional manner and without any form of political agreement with other forces. This menu of options has precedents in various constitution-making episodes around the world and fits recent cases of constitutional rewriting in Latin America relatively well. Figure 3.1 illustrates these alternative routes to democratic constitution making in the absence of pre-existing regulation.

The first route attempts to preserve as much formal legal continuity with the previous order as possible. It also tries to subject the constituent process to constitutional principles in a way that is comparable to the use of an interim constitution in some cases of transitions to democracy.[10] Since amending the constitution usually requires qualified majorities, incorporating a procedure for its replacement means making the existing legislature the locus of negotiation among existing political forces. This route was followed in Bolivia when the constitution was amended in February 2004 to allow Congress to convene a constituent assembly and regulate its internal procedures. Based on this reform, Congress passed a law in 2006 regulating the election of constituent assembly delegates; the decision-making process of the assembly, which required a two-thirds majority to pass the constitution; the relationship between the constituent assembly and the Congress; and final ratification of the constitution by referendum (see Böhrt Irahola 2013).[11]

*Figure 3.1: Democratic constitution making in the absence of pre-existing regulation*

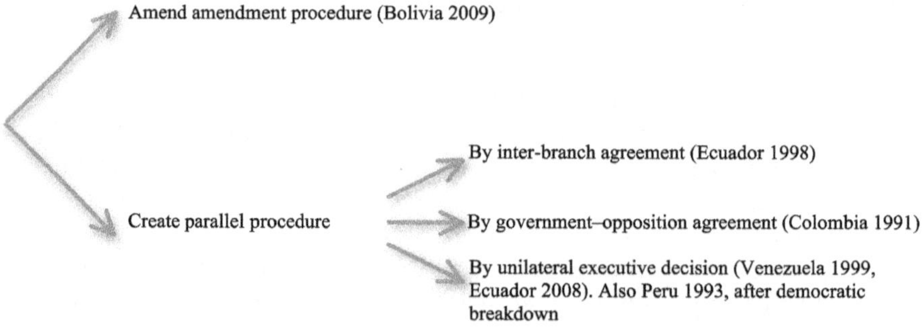


10. The most famous case of using an interim constitution to guide the constitution-making process (not only procedurally but also substantially) was that of South Africa from 1993 to 1996. Since then, however, the use of a provisional constitutional framework has inspired several cases of transitional constitution making. See Brandt et al. (2011).

11. Panama has also followed this path by amending the 1972 Constitution in 2004 to allow the election of a constituent assembly to write a new constitution. As of 2015, however, this process has not been implemented.

The second alternative has precedents in the constitutional tradition of the American states, where during the nineteenth century several constitutions were created in an extra-legal manner but with the consent or support of the existing legislature (see Hoar 1917: 52). In Latin America, we find a comparable process in Ecuador in 1997, where the interim president, using constitutional powers and in agreement with Congress, convened a referendum asking for authorisation to elect a constituent assembly (see Negretto 2013). As a result of popular support obtained in the referendum, Congress passed a transitory constitutional provision to regulate the election and tasks of the constituent assembly. In practical terms, although the existing amendment procedure was not itself amended, the addition of a transitory provision to the constitution had a similar effect to using the old constitution as a provisional legal framework to regulate the process.

The third option differs from the previous two in that neither is the process regulated through the constitution, nor is Congress the institutional forum where an agreement is reached among the different political forces. Rather, a political agreement is made between parties outside Congress in order to decide the basic procedures. In transitional settings, this route has some similarities to the round table negotiations that took place in certain eastern European countries, except that in these cases parliament was often used to formalise the agreement or define the procedure by which the final constitution would be made.[12] In Latin America, this alternative fits the case of Colombia between 1990 and 1991. After an unofficial referendum in the March 1990 congressional elections provided support for the election of a constituent assembly, President Barco issued a decree calling a new, but this time official, referendum in the May presidential election. As this referendum again supported the election of the constituent assembly, on 2 August, 1990, the president-elect, Cesar Gaviria of the Liberal Party, signed an agreement with the leaders of the main political forces on the procedures by which the constituent assembly would be elected and the aspects of the constitution that should be reformed (see Negretto 2013). In other words, although Congress did not formally acquiesce or participate in defining the rules of the constitution-making process, the legal framework that regulated it was made consensually.

The final option implies the most radical break with pre-existing legality, because in this case the executive acts unilaterally, not only without a formal agreement with the legislature but also without political negotiation with opposition parties. Due to the prominent role of the executive, this mode of constitution making has often occurred in an authoritarian or semi-democratic context. For instance, the making of Russia's 1993 constitution by an ad hoc constitutional commission appointed by Yeltsin and ratified by the people in a referendum fits this route (Partlett 2012). It also describes the making of the 1993 constitution in Peru by an irregular constituent congress convened by President Fujimori after suspending the constitution and dissolving the congress elected in 1990.

12. In the case of Poland, for instance, although substantive reforms were decided in round table negotiations, it was the parliament elected in 1991 that established the procedure by which the final constitution would be adopted. See Garlicki and Garlicka (2010).

However, this form of executive constitution making can also take place within an existing democratic regime, as was the case in Venezuela in 1998 and 1999, and Ecuador from 2007 to 2008. In both of these cases, the president unilaterally convened a referendum – without constitutional authorisation or forcing the interpretation of existing rules – so that citizens would vote on whether an elected constituent assembly should replace the constitution. Following this authorisation, a constituent assembly elected under the rules decided by the executive enacted a new constitution subject to final ratification by the people (see Bejarano and Segura 2013, Brewer Carías 2011, Landau 2013, Massüger and Welp 2013).[13]

### *Constitutional replacement, redistribution of power, and democracy*

Mapping the different alternatives for replacing a democratic constitution in the absence of regulation is conceptually and empirically useful because it facilitates tracing certain outcomes back to the characteristics of the process. However, this analysis begs an explanation of why a particular route is adopted at a given historical juncture. All recent cases of constitutional replacement in Latin America share some basic background factors: the old constitutional system was in crisis, the social discredit of traditional parties was high, and new political leaders and parties emerged as advocates of a new order. In addition, in these cases the existing constitution established a separation of powers system with two independent agents of popular representation: executive and legislature.

The exhaustion of the constitution as a governance structure and the emergence of social demand for its replacement do not occur in a vacuum. Deep crises of governability, representation, or both usually foster a widely shared perception that the existing legal order is obsolete. Political and institutional crises also tend to be associated with the discrediting of traditional parties as ineffective or corrupt organisations that benefited from the old system at the expense of the majority of the people. The delegitimation of traditional parties, in turn, favours the rise of new leaders and parties advocating radical reform. Why, then, was a dominant political group willing and able to organise the process unilaterally in some cases, while in others diverse actors reached an institutional or political agreement on procedures? I argue that the key factor to explain this variation is whether at the time of deciding the organisation of the process new parties win the presidency without achieving majority control of the legislature.

To provide empirical support for this hypothesis, I will make a comparative analysis of initial political conditions and procedural choices in the constitution-making episodes of Colombia 1990-1991, Peru 1992–1993, Ecuador 1997–1998, Venezuela 1998–1999, Ecuador 2007–2008, and Bolivia 2006–2009. All of these except Peru had a democratic political regime at the beginning. The case

13. *See* Wheatley, Chapter Four in this volume, for the analysis of what he calls 'power consolidation' referendums in cases of constitutional reform. This type of referendum is often used in cases of a radical legal break. *See* also the Power Struggle type of referendums in Welp and Ruth, Chapter Seven in this volume.

is comparable, however, because Peru was democratic until one year before the adoption of the new constitution and the constitution-making process in this country shared key features with those of the other countries. As I will show, the six cases show variation not only in terms of initial conditions and procedures, but also in relation to levels of democracy at the implementation stage of the new constitution. This provides a vantage point from which it is possible to explore the relationship between distribution of power, procedural rules, and democracy.

In the episodes of radical break (Peru 1992–3, Venezuela 1998–9, and Ecuador 2007–8), a deep transformation of the pre-existing party system was taking place in parallel with the decision to replace the constitution in force (see Roberts 2014). One way to capture these transformations is by looking at the level of popular support that candidates from new political movements or parties received in the immediately preceding presidential election. As shown in Table 3.2, the cases of executive constitution making coincided with the recent victory of the presidential candidate of a new party or movement. At the same time, however, the new political forces obtained only a minority of representatives in Congress.

The reason for the asymmetry between popular support in the presidential election and institutional support in Congress could be that the congressional election took place before the presidential election (Venezuela) or coincided with the first round of a run-off system (Peru and Ecuador). It could also be that traditional parties were more skilful or had more resources to keep support in the district-based congressional election than in the nation-wide presidential election. Whatever the reason, this asymmetry was bound to create polarisation and conflict because new presidents invariably advocated a radical programme of social and political reforms that was impossible to implement in Congress.

In Peru, Fujimori received more than 60 per cent of the vote in the run-off of the presidential election. Yet his party, Cambio 90, won only 18 per cent of the seats in the lower chamber, a situation that worked against the drastic economic and political reforms that the president embraced after his election. In the case of

*Table 3.2: Congressional support of the largest new party in the presidential election*

| **Cases** | **Initial regulation** | **Largest new party** | **Previous presidential election (% votes)** | **Congressional support (% seats)** | **Difference** |
|---|---|---|---|---|---|
| Bolivia | 2004 | MAS | 20.94 | 20.77 | –0.17 |
| Colombia | 1990 | MSN | 23.9 | 6.79 | –17.11 |
| Ecuador I | 1997 | Pachakutik | 20.61 | 9.76 | –10.85 |
| Ecuador II | 2007 | Alianza País | 56.57 | 0 | –56.57 |
| Peru | 1992 | Cambio 90 | 62.37 | 17.78 | –44.59 |
| Venezuela | 1998 | MVR | 56.20 | 17.24 | –38.96 |

*Source:* Author, based on Nohlen (2005) and Political Database of the Americas.

Venezuela, whereas Chávez won the presidential election with 56 per cent of the vote, his movement, Movimiento V República, attained only 17 per cent of the seats in the lower chamber. This situation was clearly unfavourable for the newcomers' goal of burying the old regime. In the case of Ecuador, Correa won the run-off of the presidential election with an ambitious programme for re-founding democracy in the country. However, his party Alianza País did not even field candidates in the congressional election.

In contrast to these scenarios, an institutional or political agreement to regulate the replacement of the constitution was reached when new parties were still a minority force in presidential elections and in Congress. In Colombia during 1989 and 1990 and Ecuador during 1997 and 1998, deep political and institutional crises left some of the old parties severely discredited, giving rise to new political options. Yet at the time of deciding the organisation of the process they still retained a significant influence and could not be marginalised. The same is true of Bolivia, when at the time of amending the constitution to regulate its replacement (2004) the largest new party advocating deep institutional transformations (Movimiento al Socialismo, MAS) was still a minority political group and had to form a coalition with the old parties to pass the reform.

To be sure, if reaching a procedural agreement hinged on the balance of power between established and new political forces, enforcing this agreement also depended on maintaining that balance over time. After winning the December 2005 presidential election by 53.7 of the vote and reaching almost an absolute majority in both chambers of the congress, Evo Morales and the MAS initially decided to abide by the replacement process that the constitution established. Yet after again winning the election of delegates to the constituent assembly but falling short of the two-thirds majority required for approval of the new text, the president and his party attempted substituting that decision rule for one of absolute majority (see Lazarte 2008; Lehoucq 2008). Although this bid for hegemony failed in the end, it shows how an alteration of the initial balance of forces can undermine the enforcement of the procedural rules.

Whether the government organised the replacement of the constitution unilaterally affected not only the degree of continuity with the pre-existing legal order but also certain important features of the process. Some of these features included the level of citizen involvement, the degree of representative pluralism in the constituent body, and the powers of the latter vis-à-vis the constituted powers. In all the cases of radical legal break, the level of citizen participation in the process was high, the degree of representative pluralism in the constituent body was low, and the constituent body replaced or intervened in constituted powers, in particular the legislature. These were all essential ingredients in a common strategy to give an aura of democratic legitimacy to a process oriented to redistributing power in favour of a particular political group.

There is a correlation between the existence of a procedural agreement and the level of direct citizen involvement in the constitution-making process. In two of the cases of radical break with the pre-existing constitutional legality (Venezuela 1998–9 and Ecuador 2007–8) the people voted first to authorise the election of the constituent assembly, then to elect this assembly, and finally to ratify the new constitution. In addition to voting, other formal channels of social participation were implemented during the drafting process, such as the submission of reform proposals to the constituent body by citizens and civil society organisations. Table 3 shows the relationship between the presence of a procedural agreement and the number of instances of popular participation.

There is also an association between single-party dominance of the constituent assembly and the powers assumed by this body during the drafting process. In all the cases of radical legal break the government party or coalition ended up being the dominant force in the constituent assembly. In addition, in the same cases this body proclaimed itself sovereign and successfully usurped legislative and other government functions. Table 3.4 summarizes the relationship between single-party dominance and the self-assumed powers of the constituent body.

It is not by chance that in the absence of a procedural agreement the level of citizen involvement was high, the degree of representative pluralism in the constituent body was low, and the constituent body usurped legislative functions. Without real and frequent citizen participation in the process, the government

*Table 3.3: Procedural agreement and popular participation in constitution making*

| **Cases** | **Procedural agreement** | **Authorisation referendum** | **Drafting participation** | **Ratification referendum** |
|---|---|---|---|---|
| Bolivia 2006–9 | Yes | No | Yes | Yes |
| Colombia 1990–1 | Yes | Yes | Yes | No |
| Ecuador 1997–8 | Yes | Yes | No | No |
| Ecuador 2007–8 | No | Yes | Yes | Yes |
| Peru 1992–3 | No | No | Yes | Yes |
| Venezuela 1998–9 | No | Yes | Yes | Yes |

*Table 3.4: Single-party control, constituent body powers and intervention in or usurpation of legislative functions*

| **Cases** | **Single-party control** | **Initial constituent body powers** | **Intervention in/ usurpation of legislative functions** |
|---|---|---|---|
| Bolivia 2006–9 | No | Drafting constitution | No |
| Colombia 1990–1 | No | Drafting constitution | No |
| Ecuador 1997–8 | No | Drafting constitution | No |
| Ecuador 2007–8 | Yes | Drafting constitution | Yes |
| Peru 1992–3 | Yes | Drafting constitution and enacting legislation | Yes |
| Venezuela 1998–9 | Yes | Drafting constitution | Yes |

could not make credible the claim that it was executing the will of the people. Without unilateral control over the constituent body, the constituent body could not be used as an instrument to redistribute power in favour of the president and his party.

It is clear that in all the cases of a radical break the government party enjoyed an important electoral advantage because it profited from the discrediting of traditional parties associated with the old regime. But the government also magnified this advantage by using state resources and/or designing electoral rules to favour the election of its allies to the constituent body. The most blatant example of this manipulation occurred in Peru, where the president organised the election of the constituent body after dissolving Congress, harassing opposition leaders, and intervening in the judiciary. As a protest against the government's authoritarian tactics, the two major opposition parties refused to participate in the elections, thus facilitating the victory of the government party, which obtained 55 per cent of the seats in the constituent body.[14] In Venezuela, the government adopted a personalised voting system in multi-member districts that worked in practice as a plurality formula.[15] This, in addition to the implementation of an informal strategy to signal to voters who the official candidates were in each district, led delegates from Movimiento Quinta Repúblicaublica and its allies to win 93 per cent of the seats in the constituent assembly (Carter Center Report 2001: 27–9). In the case of Ecuador, after convening a referendum in January 2007 in violation of the constitution and against the opposition of Congress, the government used state resources and official publicity to increase the electoral advantage of its candidates in the constituent assembly election, where they obtained 61 per cent of the seats (Carter Center Report 2007).

The organisation of the electoral process to secure unilateral government control over the constituent body was invariably presented as an expression of the will of the people. Following this logic, any criticism of the process by Congress, courts or opposition parties was portrayed as a conflict between the constituent power of the people, which incarnated the new democratic legitimacy, and the corrupt elite, which represented the old legality. In this perspective, voting to authorise the election of a special constituent body or electing it, using channels of public consultation during the drafting process, and referring to the people for the final approval of the constitution only reinforced the populist rhetoric of the government. In spite of their exclusionary nature at the representative level, these mechanisms created the appearance of a perfectly democratic process.

Using constitution making as a strategy to redistribute power in favour of a new political group required gaining control over the constituent body but also claiming that it had original sovereign power and was entitled to replace or take control of Congress, the judiciary, or other pre-existing state institutions. Heated

14. *See Latin American Weekly Report,* 16 April–3 December 1992.

15. There were 123 regional districts with numbers of seats varying from two to thirteen, and a national district with twenty-four seats.

political debates about the powers of the constituent body were central to all recent episodes of constitutional replacement in Latin America. In Colombia, the Supreme Court ruled that the constituent assembly was free to decide the content of the new constitution. Beyond its initial mandate, however, the assembly also decided that a new congress should be elected after the approval of the constitution (see Negretto 2013).[16] In the case of Bolivia, making the constituent assembly sovereign was one of the central demands of the government party, which in September 2006 managed to impose as the first rule of procedure that the constituent assembly was the holder of national sovereignty and 'above' constituted powers. Yet this rule did not authorise the assembly to replace or intervene in any of the constituted powers. Moreover, the final text of the constitution was negotiated with opposition forces in Congress after the government party failed to impose its own draft (Böhrt Irahola 2013).[17]

Only in Peru was the constituent body formally authorized to enact ordinary laws. After dissolving Congress and intervening in the judiciary, the government established that an assembly would be elected to act both as constituent body and ordinary legislature. In the cases of Venezuela and Ecuador 2007–2008, the constituent assembly went beyond its initial commission to draft a constitution and engaged in ordinary law making. Right after its election, the Ecuadorean convention issued a decree declaring its powers above any of the existing branches of government, including Congress and the judiciary. Based on this decision, the constituent assembly explicitly assumed the power to legislate and declared the existing congress in recess (Wray Reyes 2013).[18] In Venezuela, one of the first acts of the constituent assembly was to declare itself above the constituted powers, in violation of an explicit ruling of the Supreme Court in this regard. Following this declaration, it intervened in the judiciary and restricted the activities of Congress (Combellas 2003).

An irregular constitution-making process with high levels of citizen involvement and exclusionary political representation had an impact on the future performance of democracy. It is interesting to note that the Peruvian Constitution of 1993, the Venezuelan Constitution of 1999, and the Ecuadorean Constitution of 2008 incorporated radical instruments of popular participation. In some cases, as in Venezuela and to a lesser extent in Ecuador, the new constitution actually increased practices of citizen participation. At the same time, however, the enactment of the new constitution coincided with the erosion of representative institutions.

---

16. From July 15 to December 1, 1991, a 36-member commission appointed by the assembly was in charge of exercising legislative functions until the members of the newly elected congress took office. The constituent assembly, however, did not replace or intervene in Congress while it was in session.

17. It is for this reason incorrect to argue, as Levitsky and Loxton do (2013) that the case of Bolivia fits the pattern of using the constitution-making process to redistribute power in favour of the executive and his party.

18. As regards the judiciary the constituent assembly established that the Supreme Court, the Supreme Electoral Court and the Constitutional Court would continue in their functions unless it decided otherwise.

Indexes of representative democracy and evaluations of regime types are no doubt controversial. However, it is conventional in political science to use the Polity IV index for such evaluations (Marshall et al. 2015). Using this index, one can observe that although political conflicts associated with constitution making sometimes led to a decrease in the level of democracy, only in cases of a radical break did the country cease to be democratic at the time of or a few years after adopting the new constitution.[19] In this regard, whereas Bolivia remained democratic from 2006 to 2014, Colombia from 1991 to 2014, and Ecuador from 1979 to 2006, Venezuela ceased to be democratic in 2006, and Ecuador in 2007. Peru, in turn, which was democratic from 1980 to 1991, ceased to be democratic in 1992, one year before initiating the constitution-making process. This does not mean that some measure of legal continuity at the time of replacing the constitution immunised the country against future democratic backsliding. It means that the probability of representative institutions being eroded increased significantly when popular participation was used to replace public deliberation and inclusive negotiations during the creation of a new constitution.

## Conclusion

Popular participation may be considered a good in itself, particularly in constitution making. Yet both the goal and the means to achieve it are ambiguous. What seems clear is that direct citizen involvement (as most students of direct democracy currently acknowledge) can only strengthen democratic governance when it works in interaction with and as a complement of multiple instances of deliberation and negotiation within representative bodies. From this perspective, any attempt to implement mechanisms of direct popular participation to substitute for inclusive representation should be regarded with suspicion.

Replacing constitutions within an existing democratic constitutional order is a particularly risky scenario because most constitutions are silent about this process. As a result of social and political pressures to reform, one possible outcome is that different sectors of the political elite reach an institutional or political agreement to channel the process in a relatively institutionalised way. Yet it may also occur that in reaction to the legislature's opposition to reforms, a popular leader and his party are tempted to invoke the revolutionary theory of the constituent power of the people to bypass the legislature and opposition parties. This situation is likely to occur in a separation of powers system when at the time of implementing the process new parties advocating radical reform win the presidency without achieving majority control of the legislature. Such a process would be highly participatory, because citizens would be mobilised to vote in referendums aimed at authorising or ratifying the changes. At the same time, however, it would be highly exclusionary from the point of view of elite negotiations and public deliberation, anticipating the likely erosion of representative democracy in the future.

19. See Marshall et al. (2015).

**Acknowledgements**

I would like to thank David Landau, William Partlett, Julio Ríos-Figueroa, and Yanina Welp for their comments and suggestions on a previous version of this chapter.

**References**

Ackerman, B. and Katyal, N. (1995) 'Our unconventional founding', *University of Chicago Law Review*, 62(2): 478–573.

Amar, A. (1988) 'Philadelphia revisited: amending the constitution outside Article V', *University of Chicago Law Review*, 55(4): 1043–104.

—— (1994) 'The consent of the governed: constitutional amendment outside Article V', *Columbia Law Review*, 94: 457–508.

Banks, A. M. (2008) 'Expanding participation in constitution making: challenges and opportunities', *William & Mary Law Review*, 49(4): 1043–69.

Bejarano, A. M. and R. Segura (2013) 'Asambleas Constituyentes y Democracia: Una Lectura Crítica del Nuevo Constitucionalismo en la Región Andina', *Colombia Internacional*, 79: 19–48.

Böckenförde, E. (2000) *Estudios sobre el Estado de Derecho y la democracia*, Madrid: Trotta.

Böhrt Irahola, C. (2013) 'El Proceso Constituyente Boliviano', in C. Böhrt Irahola and N. Wray Reyes (eds) *Los Procesos Constituyentes Boliviano y Ecuatoriano: Análisis comparativo y prospectiva*, Stockholm: International IDEA.

Brandt, M., Cottrell J., Gai, Y. and Regan, A. (2011) *Constitution Making and Reform: Options for the process*, Geneva: Interpeace.

Brewer Carías, A. (2011) *Dismantling Democracy in Venezuela: The Chávez Authoritarian Experiment*, New York: Cambridge University Press.

Carter Center (2001) 'Observing the 2001 Guyana elections', available at https://www.cartercenter.org/documents/1036.pdf (accessed 15 April 2016).

—— (2007) Final Report on Ecuador's 30 September 2007 Constituent Assembly Election, available at https://www.cartercenter.org/resources/pdfs/peace/americas/Ecuador_Carter_Center_Electoral_Report_FINAL_website.pdf (accessed 15 April 2016).

Colon Rios, J. (2012) *Weak Constitutionalism: Democratic legitimacy and the question of constituent power*, New York: Routledge.

Combellas, R. (2003) 'El Proceso Constituyente y la Constitución de 1999', *Politeia*, 30(30): 183–208.

Condorcet, J.-A.-N. de Caritat (1994 [1789]) 'On the need for citizens to ratify the Constitution', in I. MacLean and F. Hewitt (eds) *Condorcet: Foundations of Social Choice and Political Theory*, Northampton, MA: Edward Elgar Publishing: 271–80.

Dinan, J. (2009) *The American State Constitutional Tradition*, Kansas: Kansas University Press.

Eisenstadt, T., LeVan, C. and Maboudi, T. (2015) 'When talk trumps text: the democratizing effects of deliberation during constitution making, 1974–2011', *American Political Science Review*, 103(3): 592–612.

Elster, J. (2006) 'Legislatures as constituent assemblies', in R. W. Bauman and T. Kahna (eds) *The Least Examined Branch: The role of legislatures in the constitutional state*, New York: Cambridge University Press: 181–97.

Fritz, C. (1997) 'Alternative visions of American constitutionalism: popular sovereignty and the early American debate', *Hastings Constitutional Law Quarterly*, 24(2): 287–357.

Garlicki, L. and Garlicka, Z. A. (2010) 'Constitution making, peace building, and national reconciliation: the experience of Poland', in L. E. Miller (ed.) *Framing the State in Times of Transition: Case studies in constitution making*, Washington, DC: United States Institute of Peace: 391–416.

Ginsburg, T., Elkins, Z. and Blount, J. (2008) 'The citizen as founder: public participation in constitutional approval', *Temple Law Review*, 81(2): 361–82.

—— (2009) 'Does the process of constitution-making matter?' *American Review of Law and Society*, 5: 201–23.

Hoar, R. S. (1917) *Constitutional Conventions: Their nature, powers, and limitations*, Boston: Little, Brown and Company.

Jefferson, T. (1984) *Writings*, New York: Library of America.

Kalyvas, A. (2005) 'Popular sovereignty, democracy, and the constituent power', *Constellations*, 12(2), 223–44.

Kriesi, H. (2012) 'The Swiss experience', in B. Geissel and K. Newton (eds) *Evaluating Democratic Innovations: Curing the democratic malaise?* New York: Routledge: 39–55.

Landau, D. (2013) 'Abusive constitutionalism', *UC Davis Law Review*, 47: 1–58.

Lazarte, J. (2008) 'La Asamblea Constituyente de Bolivia: De la Oportunidad a la Amenaza', available online at http://nuevomundo.revues.org/42663?lang=en (accessed 15 April 2016).

LeDuc, L. (2002) 'Referendums and initiatives: the politics of direct democracy', in L. Leduc, R. Niemi and P. Norris (eds) *Comparing Democracies 2: New challenges in the study of elections and voting*, London: Sage: 70–87.

Lehoucq, F. (2008) 'Bolivia's constitutional breakdown', *Journal of Democracy*, 19(2): 46–60.

Levitsky, S. and Loxton, J. (2013) 'Populism and competitive authoritarianism in the Andes', *Democratization*, 20(1): 107–36.

Madison, J., Hamilton, A. and Jay, J. (1987 [1788]) *The Federalist Papers*, London: Penguin.

Marshall, M., Jaggers, K. and Gurr, T. (2015) 'Polity IV project: political regime characteristics and transitions, 1800–2013', *Dataset Users' Manual*, Vienna, VA: Centre for Systemic Peace.

Massüger Sánchez Sandoval, N. and Welp, Y. (2013) 'Legality and legitimacy: constituent power in Venezuela, Bolivia, and Ecuador', in J. Wheatley and F. Mendez (eds) *Patterns of Constitutional Design: The role of citizens and elites in constitution making*, London: Ashgate: 103–18.

Negretto, G. (2013) *Making Constitutions: Presidents, Parties, and Institutional Choice in Latin America*, New York: Cambridge University Press.

—— (2012) 'Replacing and amending constitutions: the logic of constitutional change in Latin America', *Law & Society Review*, 46(4): 749–79.

—— (2016a) (forthcoming) 'Constitution making and constitutionalism in Latin America: the role of procedural Rules', in T. Ginsburg and R. Dixon (eds) *Comparative Constitutional Law in Latin America*, Northampton, MA: Edward Elgar.

—— (2016b) (forthcoming) 'El Poder Constituyente en la Tradición Constitucional Americana. El Legado Controvertido de los Federalistas', *Revista Chilena de Derecho.*

Oliver, D. and Fusaro, C. (2011) *How Constitutions Change: A comparative study*, Portland: Hart Publishing.

Paine, T. (1995 [1791]) *Rights of Man, in Thomas Paine: Collected writings*, New York: Library of America.

Partlett, W. (2012) 'The dangers of popular constitution making', *Brooklyn Journal of International Law*, 38(1): 193–238.

Roberts, K. (2014) *Changing Course in Latin America: Party systems in the neoliberal era*, New York: Cambridge University Press.

Schmitt, C. (1982) *Teoría de la Constitución*, Madrid: Alianza Universidad.

Tierney, S. (2012) *Constitutional Referendums: The theory and practice of republican deliberation*, London: Oxford University Press.

Viciano Pastor, R. and Martínez Dalmau, R. (2001) *Cambio Político y Proceso Constituyente en Venezuela (1998–2000)*, Valencia: Tiranto Lo Blanch.

—— (2010) 'Los Procesos Constituyentes Latinoamericanos y el Nuevo Paradigma Constitucional', *Revista del Instituto de Ciencias Jurídicas de Puebla*, 25: 7–29.

Widner, J. (2008) 'Constitution writing in post-conflict settings: overview', *William & Mary Law Review*, 49(4): 1513–41.

Wray Reyes, N. (2013) 'El Proceso Constituyente Ecuatoriano', in C. Böhrt Irahola and N. Wray Reyes (eds) *Los Procesos Constituyentes Boliviano y Ecuatoriano: Análisis comparativo y prospectiva*, Stockholm: IDEA International.

*Chapter Four*

# A Problem or a Solution? The Referendum as a Mechanism for Citizens' Participation in Constitution Making

*Jonathan Wheatley*

## Introduction

This chapter explores a constitutional referendum that is not well-recognised and is rarely discussed in the academic literature, a type of referendum that is far from democratic and in which citizens' votes are used instrumentally to alter the constitution to boost the power and authority of incumbent leaders. Far from being rare, this type of referendum is actually very common in authoritarian and semi-authoritarian settings. I refer to it as a 'power consolidation referendum'.

That referendums are not always about participatory democracy, but can instead be about the manipulation of power, has been commented upon by a number of observers. LeDuc argues that referendums do not always provide the high quality of democracy that they appear to promise. He observes that 'governments sometimes call referendums ... to advance their own political agendas' and the referendum can be 'a favoured tool of tyrants and dictators seeking to legitimise and sustain their rule' (LeDuc 2003: 46). Similarly Hamon (1995) identifies a subtype of referendum that he calls a 'referendum as the recourse of the prince', which he contrasts with the 'referendum as the recourse of citizens' and the 'referendum as the recourse of the parties', and which is implemented by a ruler to obtain public endorsement of a person, regime or programme (Hamon 1995: 197). The term 'referendum as a political weapon' was coined by Uggla (2008) to refer to instruments for the consolidation of presidential power, by parties in conflict, or by opponents as a weapon against the government. Although he does not define the term explicitly, he argues that such instruments often go beyond constitutional limits.

I define a 'power consolidation referendum' as a referendum that satisfies the following two criteria. First, the referendum must transfer power from one branch of government to another. As such it must involve a change to the constitution (or constitutional convention if no written constitution exists). Second, it is elite-initiated or 'top-down' and the de facto initiator of the referendum is the very same actor that is set to accrue power. In most cases nowadays that actor is the president.

In this chapter I argue that power consolidation referendums typically occur in the years following a period of civil war, revolution or other form of political turbulence. Following such a period, the new leadership initially has a rather tenuous grip on power and is often forced to share power, formally or informally, with potential 'spoilers'. It then works on consolidating power and gradually weakening its rivals until it senses an opportunity to make a bid for full hegemonic control over the polity. As soon as a window of opportunity opens, a power consolidation referendum, if successful, can change the rules of the game to make the uncontested exercise of power far more feasible. Using the referendum as a legitimising tool to do this helps convince actors both inside and outside the polity that the new status quo has the support of the people, despite any irregularities in the way in which the referendum is held. In this way, the new regime can become fixed, durable and more resistant to external shocks.

A referendum is therefore often used as a tactic to out-manoeuvre opposition from within the political elite. In a number of cases, this opposition comes from a parliament that jealously guards its sphere of influence against perceived encroachments from the president. Having gained control of most of the media and the election administration, a referendum is a relatively low-risk strategy used by the president and the presidential administration to win a power struggle with parliament. Lacking the capacity to organise autonomously and challenge the dominant narrative of the referendum, citizens are used instrumentally as a weapon in this power struggle.

As I argue later on in this chapter, the 'bid for hegemonic control' is not always successful. If 'spoilers' within the political elite still have access to sufficient levers of power they can scupper the referendum and either prevent it from taking place or prevent its outcome from entering into force. Similarly, if civil society can prove an effective counterweight to the ambitions of the executive, by instigating and framing a public debate around the proposals and by performing a watchdog function against fraud and voter manipulation, it can ensure that the proposal to increase the powers of the executive are defeated by the people.

Instances of the 'power consolidation referendum' have been observed across the world and in various epochs of time. Probably the best-known prototypes are the two constitutional referendums called by Napoleon in 1802 and 1804, the first of which made him High Consul and the second Emperor. In more recent years, as Europe gradually consolidated democracy, this type of referendum has become much rarer. It is also rare in most consolidated democracies in Latin America, although it still occurs sporadically in Latin American countries that have yet to fully consolidate democracy. Of this more will be said later in the chapter.

Power consolidation referendums are far more common in the authoritarian and semi-authoritarian states of the former Soviet Union and sub-Saharan Africa. Out of 140 referendums held in sub-Saharan African countries after independence thirty-four can be considered as power consolidation referendums, while in the former Soviet Union after the break-up of the USSR, sixteen out of forty can be considered as such (Wheatley 2013b).[1] Details of all these referendums can be found in the Appendix. What most of them had in common was that, according to the official result, either the percentage of voters supporting the motion being put to a referendum or the turnout was sufficiently high as to suggest that the referendum was neither free nor fair. The Napoleonic prototypes were trailblazers in this sense; purportedly 99.76 and 99.93 per cent of French voters voted for motions 'promoting' the future emperor in 1802 and 1804 respectively. In most cases the power consolidation referendum led to a further consolidation of power by existing power-holders.

This chapter focuses first and foremost on power consolidation referendums in the former Soviet Union and sub-Saharan Africa, but then goes on to explore the extent to which this mechanism is used in Latin America and whether it is used there in the same way. The rest of the chapter will proceed as follows. First I look at the sort of regimes and circumstances in which power consolidation referendums tend to occur, first by considering the extent to which democracy has (or has not) been established in the country in question and then by looking at the contextual background in which the event takes place. Second, I develop a number of hypotheses as to the circumstances in which they either do not occur, do not come into force, or are defeated, making reference to both the configurations of the political elite and to the strength of civil society. I argue that power consolidation referendums are more likely to be thwarted: (1) if political society is fragmented and (2) if civil society has developed the capacity to resist power grabs by political elites and that this capacity is at least on the way towards becoming institutionalised. I also argue that the (formal) institutional frameworks that determine the limits of executive power do not play the main role in determining whether power consolidation referendums occur. I illustrate these hypotheses with a few 'mini case studies' both from sub-Saharan Africa and from the former Soviet Union. I go on to explore the extent to which such referendums play a role in Latin America. I end the chapter with a short conclusion.

## Under what conditions do power consolidation referendums occur and are successful?

Following on from the earlier discussion, we would expect power consolidation referendums to be held and to achieve their aim of reinforcing the power of the executive in circumstances in which the balance of power, both among the political elite and among social forces, favours the incumbent elite. In other words, a power consolidation referendum is likely to be held and to be successful where

1. In this chapter I exclude two examples that I included in Wheatley (2013b), referendums held in 1995 in both Kazakhstan and Uzbekistan, to extend the term of the president, because they did not involve amendments to the constitution. However, I include the referendum to adopt the 1993 Constitution of the Russian Federation, which is not included in Wheatley (2013b), on the grounds that it represented a concentration of power over and above the constitutional provisions enshrined in the Basic Law of 1992.

pluralism is low, and where civil society is too weak to act as an effective check on the executive. Hence these referendums should occur more often in authoritarian and semi-authoritarian settings. This indeed seems to be the case. During the period between 1972 and 2012, new constitutions that were adopted by means of a referendum seem on average to have occurred in slightly less democratic settings than in cases where a new constitution was passed without a referendum. Drawing from data provided by the Comparative Constitutions Project (CCP) to identify constitutional replacements and summing the Freedom House (FH) scores for Political Rights (PR) and Civil Liberties (CL) in the country concerned for the year in which the new constitution is adopted, we find that the average FH score was 9.92 if a referendum was held (N=101), and 8.95 if a referendum was not held (N=149). As both PR and CL scores range from 1 (most democratic) to 7 (most authoritarian), our composite score ranges from 2 (most democratic) to 14 (most authoritarian).

Of course, only quite a small subset of power consolidation referendums occur in the context of full replacement of the constitution. Far more often, such referendums seek to recalibrate the separation of powers through constitutional amendments. It is beyond the scope of this chapter to identify all constitutional amendments that were associated with a redistribution of power in favour of the executive and compare cases in which a referendum was held to approve these amendments with cases in which a referendum was not held. Instead I look at the context in which power consolidation referendums were held in two regions of the world where they are particularly common: sub-Saharan Africa and the former Soviet Union. In both regions we see that the context was markedly undemocratic.

In sub-Saharan Africa since 1972, power consolidation referendums have been held when, on average, the FH index was 5.93 for PR and 5.25 for CL. In all cases the referendum passed and the constitutional changes were adopted. In the former Soviet Union the corresponding figures are 5.25 and 5.06, although if we discount the two cases in which the power consolidation referendum proved unsuccessful (Moldova in 1999 and Ukraine in 2000) the figures are 5.57 and 5.21. In almost 50 per cent of African cases (fourteen out of twenty-nine cases for which data was available) and in eight out of fourteen former Soviet cases (excluding the two ‘unsuccessful’ cases), the official turnout was 90 per cent or over (see Appendix), casting credible doubt over whether such referendums were free and fair. Overall, the power consolidation referendum is a formal democratic procedure implemented in an undemocratic context to achieve an undemocratic end.

The most common circumstances in which such a referendum is held is a certain time after a coup, period of conflict or major political upheaval. Initially constrained to co-opt rivals or potential spoilers, the executive often opts for a (formal or informal) power-sharing solution or even a form of limited democracy. However, over time, as the executive gradually begins to consolidate power, the power-sharing arrangement begins to feel like an unnecessary constraint. Keen to break free from earlier compromises with now enfeebled rivals, the executive spots a window of opportunity and initiates a constitutional change to cement its authority.

I will briefly illustrate how this works by focusing on a number of cases from sub-Saharan Africa and the former Soviet Union: Congo Brazaville, Cameroon, Tajikistan and Belarus.

In Congo-Brazzaville, a National Conference was set up in 1991 to oversee democratic reform. The Conference soon declared itself sovereign, stripping dictator Denis Sassou Nguesso of his executive powers. A new democratic constitution was passed in March 1992 and both parliamentary and presidential elections were held that year, leading to Sassou Nguesso's defeat and to victory for rival candidate Pascal Lissouba. However, Lissouba's presidency was marked by instability after an uprising by another rival in the 1992 presidential elections, Bernard Kolelas, left many dead. After a brief exile in Paris, Sassou Nguesso returned to Congo in May 1997 to contest the forthcoming presidential elections, but was promptly arrested. However, his forces rallied around him culminating in a brief civil war, from which Sassou Nguesso's forces emerged victorious by the end of the year with the help of Angolan troops and other foreign forces, and Sassou Nguesso was sworn in as president. Initially he promised to return to democracy within a three-year transition period. However, another round of fighting derailed the process and as soon as government forces once again gained the upper hand, Sassou Nguesso began to consolidate power. On 20 January 2002, he held a referendum on a new constitution that would extend the president's term of office from five to seven years, allowing him to appoint and dismiss ministers and remove the post of prime minister. The referendum was passed with 88 per cent of the vote amid allegations of vote rigging. Two months later Sassou Nguesso won presidential elections after his main rivals were disqualified. Although the 2002 constitution allowed the president just two seven-year terms in office, in October 2015 he won a further referendum (supposedly with 92 per cent of the vote) to amend the constitution and allow him to run for a third consecutive term as president, albeit once again reduced to five years.[2]

An earlier example is that of Cameroon. After independence from France in January 1960, French Cameroon (Cameroun) was led by President Ahmadou Ahidjo. In November 1961, the former British colony of the Southern Cameroons voted to join Cameroun, but retained an autonomous status (as West Cameroun) under Prime Minister John Ngu Foncha, who served as vice president under Ahidjo. Ahidjo was unable to consolidate power for a long time both as a result of West Cameroun autonomy and because of an insurgency by the Union des Populations du Cameroun (UPC), who had previously fought the French. The insurgency lasted until the arrest of UPC leader Ernest Ouandié in August 1970. After having Ouandié shot in January 1971 Ahidjo was able to consolidate power. The new constitution that was passed in a power consolidation referendum in April 1972 was supposedly approved by 99.99 per cent of voters on a turnout of 98.2 per cent, figures that stretch the limits of credulity. It effectively abolished

2. Philon Bondenga, 'Congo votes by landslide to allow third presidential term', Reuters, at http://www.reuters.com/article/2015/10/27/us-congo-politics-idUSKCN0SL0JW20151027#wgsdweLhMq5DVZjZ.97, accessed 30 November 2015.

West Cameroun's autonomy, established a centralised state and gave extensive new powers to the president, making him head of state and commander-in-chief, and allowing him to govern by decree.

Tajikistan is an example of a similar process in the former Soviet Union. Following the collapse of the USSR, Tajikistan became embroiled in a bloody civil war in which the main protagonists were 'government' forces, mainly former communist elites from the cities of Khujand (Leninabad) and Kulyab region (in the west), and an opposition (later known as the United Tajik Opposition) consisting of liberal reformers and Islamists from the Garm and Gorno-Badakhshan regions (in the centre and southeast of the country respectively). The war lasted from 1992 until an amnesty sponsored by the United Nations (UN) was brokered in 1997. The peace deal envisaged the incorporation of the United Tajik Opposition into the armed forces and government, but was short on specifics. This allowed the government forces, who anyway had the upper hand during the later stages of the war, thanks in part to support from Russia and Uzbekistan, to make good their advantage. Emomali Rahmon, a former communist apparatchik from the Kulyab region who had been nominal head of state since 1992 and president since 1994, won the presidential elections of 1999 with 97.6 per cent of the vote amid claims of voting irregularities, including multiple voting. While a constitutional reform, passed by referendum shortly before the elections, gave the president a single seven-year term of instead of two five-year terms, a second referendum on constitutional reform in 2003 increased this to two seven-year terms and discounted both the current and previous terms, effectively allowing Rahmon to remain in power until 2020. According to official results 93.82 per cent of voters supported the motion on a barely credible 96.38 per cent turnout.

Of course, it does not always require an event as dramatic as a coup or an armed conflict to begin the chain of events leading to a power consolidation referendum. Following the collapse of the former Soviet Union, it was common for established—or even occasionally new—power brokers to seize the reins of power in the newly independent republics with relatively little resistance and to give their position 'democratic' legitimacy by means of a referendum, while re-establishing the informal authoritarian dynamic of power that had been prevalent during the Soviet period. Such a scenario played out in both Kazakhstan and Uzbekistan, where in 1995 presidents Nursultan Nazarbayev and Islam Karimov, both of whom had been first secretaries of the Communist Party in their republics prior to the dissolution of the USSR, held referendums to prolong their presidential terms for five years without the need for elections. In both cases both turnout and the 'yes' vote exceeded 90 per cent (in Uzbekistan both ostensibly exceeded 99 per cent). This was followed up in Kazakhstan by a second referendum in the same year on a new constitution that provided for enhanced presidential powers, and in Uzbekistan a new referendum was held in 2002 extending the presidential term from five to seven years. According to official figures, both referendums were won with both a 'yes' vote and a turnout of more than 90 per cent. Nazarbayev remains in power at the time of writing, while Karimov held onto his position until his death in September 2016.

In some cases consolidation of power can occur with barely even a struggle. In Belarus a relative outsider, former collective farm boss Alexander Lukashenko, won the second round of the 1994 presidential elections on a populist anti-corruption mandate and immediately began to consolidate his authority with little resistance from other actors. In May 1995 he held a consultative referendum on a number of issues including restoring Soviet-era symbols and giving the president the power to dissolve parliament. After the parliament had half-heartedly tried to impeach him in the summer of 1996, he held (in November 1996) a more significant (and binding) referendum on another bundle of issues that included constitutional changes establishing a bicameral parliament, transferring many of the powers previously invested in the parliament to the president, including the appointment of key public officials, and allowing the president to serve a complete five-year term from the date these amendments were passed, in practice extending Lukashenko's current term of office from five to seven years. According to official figures he won this referendum with 88 per cent of the vote on an 84 per cent turnout. In 2004 he forced through a referendum on further constitutional changes allowing the president an unlimited number of terms of office, this time with 89 per cent of the vote on a 90 per cent turnout (according to official figures). For Gel'man, the critical factor in Lukashenko's consolidation of power was that the elite in Belarus was atomised without an organisational structure, rendering it incapable of resisting a power grab by the new president (Gel'man 2008: 168).

In the Central Asian and Belarusian cases described above, the (generally weak) resistance to the expansion of presidential powers came from the parliament. This was a common pattern in a number of former Soviet republics, including Russia. Following the collapse of the Communist Party of the USSR it was unclear in many republics who or what was the supreme political authority. Newly elected presidents therefore faced resistance from the parliament over who should control the main levers of government, such as local administrations, election commissions and courts. This led to an often bitter power struggle between president and parliament. In Russia, the Soviet-era 1978 constitution was amended several times during 1992 (the year after independence), providing strong parliamentary control over presidential appointments. President Boris Yeltsin fought to loosen these shackles and attempted to reframe his power struggle with parliament as a struggle between 'reformers' (the president) and 'hardline communists' (the parliament). This narrative appeared to win over most Western powers, as the West's support for Yeltsin in his power struggle against the Russian parliament in 1993 clearly shows. It also seemed to win over a significant section of the electorate; in the referendum held in December that year to approve a new constitution that enhanced presidential powers, official results suggested that over 58 per cent of voters supported the constitution. These figures need to be treated with a degree of scepticism given credible reports of manipulation (Sakwa 2008: 64).

If the logic for adopting a referendum as a means for consolidating power is to circumvent resistance from the legislature, the referendum is more frequently observed when the president lacks a 'ruling party' to ensure the loyalty of parliamentarians. Lacking a lever to ensure the loyalty of parliamentarians, which a party structure provides, presidents tend to turn to voters to confirm their new authority and undermine that of parliament. If at a later date they can once again count on a loyal parliament, by means of a new 'ruling party' to which most MPs are loyal, they are often able to dispense with a referendum in order to make constitutional changes. The case of the Russian Federation is a clear example of this. Faced with a hostile parliament, President Boris Yeltsin used a power consolidation referendum to force through a new constitutional order that bolstered presidential authority. However, in 2008 President Dmitri Medvedev, backed by the then prime minister Vladimir Putin, persuaded parliament to back a constitutional amendment that increased the presidential term from four to six years without a popular referendum. The amendments were passed by the required two-thirds majority thanks to the authority that the pro-government party United Russia had over the legislature. The amendment allowed Putin to return to the post of president in 2012 (a post he had vacated earlier in 2008) for a possible two further six-year terms.

### … And under what conditions are power consolidation referendums thwarted?

The Belarussian, Kazakh and Uzbek cases illustrate how under certain circumstances leaders can consolidate power rather quickly if they lack coherent rivals within the elite or, in Gel'man's words, the elite is 'atomised'. By the same token, it is more problematic to consolidate power either by a referendum or by other means if one's rivals' power remain undiminished. Under such circumstances a power consolidation referendum is likely to end in failure. A paradigmatic example here is that of Moldova. On 23 May 1999 a consultative referendum was held on the introduction of a presidential form of government in Moldova in which President Petru Lucinschi would have the right to form and lead the government. The referendum was held against a backdrop of growing conflict between the parliament and president. The former was dominated by the Communist Party, which controlled forty out of 101 seats and which had been resisting the president's nominees for prime minister. The 1994 Constitution had defined a mixed system of government that gave the president broad powers over matters of national defence, but made the government responsible to the parliament, which could pass a motion of no-confidence in it. In the referendum a majority (64 per cent) of those casting a valid ballot (58 per cent of registered voters) voted in favour of the president's proposal. However, as it was a consultative referendum it still required a two-thirds majority in parliament to confirm it. Such a majority was not forthcoming; instead parliamentarians from the Communist Party joined forces with other political factions and elaborated their own proposal for a parliamentary system of government with a president elected by members of parliament. On 5 July 2000 parliament approved a law on constitutional reform based on these proposals. Although the bill was vetoed by the president, on 21 July parliament was able to overturn the veto by a massive majority of eighty-seven votes to six.[3] Lucinschi's bid to consolidate power had failed and he left office in 2001 after the Communist Party won the 2001 election and communist parliamentarians elected their own president.

But it is not only rivals within the political elite who can derail a bid for consolidation of power; if civil society is strong enough to defend constitutional limits of executive power it can also put a stop to such attempts. Barry Weingast argues that if citizens can reach a consensus on the limits of state power and can coordinate their actions to defend these limits then they can depose any leader who violates them (Weingast 1997). Leaders and governments will then be bound to respect these limits as violations will be punished by citizens. Such limits could prevent leaders from concentrating power in their own hands in the manner described in this chapter.

A recent example of citizens defending constitutional limits on executive power is that of Senegal in 2012. In 2010, Senegal's president Abdoulaye Wade was coming towards the end of his second constitutionally madated five-year term of office (due to expire in 2012) and began to lobby for a third term. The following year he proposed reducing the electoral barrier for a run-off to allow first-placed presidential candidates to win the election with only 25 per cent of the vote. He also sought to establish the post of vice president, a post many observers thought to be earmarked for his son Karim. In June 2011 these moves triggered widespread protests with civil society groups such as Touche Pas à Ma Constitution! (Don't Touch My Constitution!) and Y'en a marre (Fed Up with It) forming an umbrella protest group called the '23 June Movement' (M23) and taking to the streets against the proposed constitutional amendments. The protests led Wade to retract his proposals, but in January 2012 he managed to cajole the Constitutional Court (made up mostly of his own supporters) into allowing him to stand for a third term on the grounds that the constitution had been amended since he was elected and the two-term limit only applied from the date of the amendment, rather than from the beginning of his first term. This led to a further wave of protests, which failed to reverse the Court's decision, but helped generate a wave of dissatisfaction towards Wade, who lost the elections to opposition candidate Macky Sall in a run-off held on 23 March 2012. In the end, civil society played a major role in preventing authoritarian entrenchment in the hands of Wade and his son.

Weingast (1997) argues that limits on government become self-enforcing when a basic consensus exists over what these limits are. Normally, in mature consolidated democracies, the sort of protests that we saw in Senegal are not necessary to ensure that a president complies with constitutional norms because there is an internalised set of norms and understandings that make such a scenario unthinkable. Irrespective of the character or ambition of the president of, say, France, the USA or Uruguay, we simply could not envisage in these countries today a situation in which he or she contemplated the kind of power grab that Abdoulaye Wade attempted.

3. RFE/RL Newsline, 21 July 2000, at http://www.rferl.org/content/article/1142200.html, accessed 30 November 2015.

However, it is not only in those countries that are normally assumed to be mature, consolidated democracies in which a set of norms that are shared by both political elites and society can prevent a leader from consolidating power. An interesting case in this respect is that of Benin, where a National Conference sat for ten days in February 1990 to oversee a transition to democracy and set clear constitutional limits on executive power. The Conference derived its legitimacy from the participation of diverse sectors of society including central and regional administrations, trade unions, churches, academia, political parties, the army, human rights associations and women's groups. The Conference provided broad legitimacy to the constitution, which set a maximum of two consecutive five-year terms for the president and high thresholds for constitutional amendments.[4] The constitution has not been amended since then, despite rumours that two incumbent presidents, former dictator Mathieu Kérékou and his successor Thomas Boni Yayi, were seeking to amend the constitution to give themselves a third term in office shortly before their second terms were due to end in 2006 and 2016 respectively. However, these rumours did not materialise into concrete actions, perhaps because of the sensitivities involved in amending a constitution that is seen to be a reflection of the will of the people as expressed in the National Conference.

The status of the Beninois constitution as somehow sacrosanct was underlined by a decision made by the Constitutional Court in 2006 overruling a vote by members of parliament, who had mustered the required four-fifths majority to amend the constitution to extend their mandates from four to five years. In their ruling the Constitutional Court judges decided that the constitutional article that limited the parliamentary mandate to four years was 'the result of a national consensus arrived at by the Conference of the bone and sinew of the nation in February 1990' and that parliamentarians' attempt to amend it represented an attempt at 'power confiscation' that did not conform to the principles embodied in the constitution (Wheatley 2013a: 82).

The Beninois case shows that it is not the letter of the constitution that counts, but rather the symbolism (or 'mystique') than embeds it. That the framing of the constitution as a document does not always provide a guarantee against power usurpation is illustrated by the case of Niger in 2009. The 1999 constitution of Niger, drafted to mark the return to democracy after a period of stability and civil war, contained within it an article that prevented the amendment of another constitutional article that determined that the president could serve a maximum of two five-year terms. However, this did not prevent Nigerien president Mamadou Tandja in May 2009 from attempting to amend the constitution in order to remain in office after his term expired later that year. After having his petition rejected by the Constitutional Court, Tandja dissolved the National Assembly, took to ruling by decree and announced a referendum that envisaged far-reaching constitutional amendments, including the removal of term limits for the president. His proposals

4. A three-quarters majority in parliament followed by a referendum or a four-fifths majority without a referendum.

were approved by the referendum, according to official results, but Tandja was deposed by a military coup the following year.

### *The power consolidation referendum in Latin America*

While power referendums are rare in consolidated democracies, they are not confined to the former Soviet Union and sub-Saharan Africa. Several such instances occurred in Latin America even after the so-called third wave of democratisation that engulfed the continent during the late 1970s and 1980s.[5] The classic Latin American case was the so-called 'auto-coup' (autogolpe) staged by Peruvian president Alberto Fujimori in April 1992 in which he dissolved the Congress of the Republic and used the military to arrest a number of opposition politicians. Having ruled by decree for a year, he put a new constitutional blueprint to a referendum in 1993, which he won. The new constitution centralised power through a new unicameral Congress (replacing the old bicameral parliament) and allowed the president to remain in office for two five-year terms (instead of one). Fujimori subsequently argued that this rule could not be applied to his first term as the old constitution was still in force when he was first elected and instead his two terms should begin from his re-election in 1995. With backing from the Constitutional Court he therefore stood for re-election again in 2000 (effectively for a third term) and won, allegedly with the help of electoral fraud. However, by the end of the year he had lost the support of Congress and was forced to resign.

A second example of a power consolidation referendums were those observed in Venezuela in 2007 and 2009. Both were motivated by President Hugo Chávez's desire to modify the constitution to abolish term limits for the president and both were mandatory referendums insofar as the existing constitution required any constitutional changes to be approved by a referendum. Chávez lost the 2007 referendum by a narrow margin, but remained determined to continue in his attempt and proposed further reforms, this time to remove term limits for all significant elected posts (including, of course, the presidency). In order to circumvent the constitutional requirement that a second constitutional reform cannot be submitted during a single legislative term (Article 345), Chávez presented this new modification as a constitutional amendment, rather than a reform. On this second occasion, he won the referendum with 55 per cent of the vote on a turnout of 70 per cent and ensured the abolition of term limits.

The 2007 Venezuelan referendum is neither the first nor the only case of a power consolidation referendum failing to pass. In 1980, the Uruguayan military sought to consolidate the newly established dictatorship by holding an ad hoc constitutional referendum to give more powers, as well as immunity from prosecution, to the military and to weaken the powers of the General Assembly and political parties. However the proposal was defeated, with only 41.86 per cent in favour of the changes and 55.95 per cent against. Despite later attempts

5. *See* Negretto, Chapter Three in this volume, analysing the role of citizen's participation in recent process of constitution making in the Andean countries.

by the military to strengthen its powers irrespective of the vote, these attempts were ultimately unsuccessful. As Welp and Ruth point out in Chapter Seven in this volume, the vote set the scene for a transition to democracy that came into being with the Uruguayan Naval Club Pact just four years later.

A much more recent example of a power consolidation referendum failing is that of Bolivia. On 21 February 2016 a mandatory referendum was held on the initiative of the governing party, the Movement Towards Socialism–Political Instrument for the Sovereignty of the Peoples (Movimiento al Socialismo–Instrumento Político por la Soberanía de los Pueblos, or MAS-IPSP), in order to amend Article 168 of the Bolivian constitution, which allows an incumbent president only to be re-elected once. The aim was to ensure that President Evo Morales would be able to stand for an extra term in office when his mandate expires in 2019. However, in a closely fought contest Morales and MAS-IPSP lost the referendum, garnering just 48.7 per cent of the vote.

These examples show that in Latin America, as in the former Soviet Union and sub-Saharan Africa, power consolidation referendums occur either in authoritarian regimes or in hybrid regimes where democracy is unconsolidated or deconsolidated. Venezuela in 2007 and 2009 and Bolivia in 2016 can best be described as hybrid regimes, with composite FH scores of 8, 9 and 6[6] respectively, while both Uruguay in 1980 and Peru in 1993 can best be described as authoritarian with a composite FH score of 10.

However, there are two features that stand out about power consolidation referendums in Latin America that distinguish these events from many (but not all) similar events in the former Soviet Union and sub-Saharan Africa. The first is that formal institutions and the rule of law matter. Even figures such as Hugo Chávez and Evo Morales have to play by the rules enshrined in the existing constitution. Thus, they were unable to bypass these rules by ignoring the constitution and using their overwhelming majorities in their respective parliaments to push through the changes without a referendum. Contrast this with the case of Niger where, although Tandja used a referendum to pass his new constitution, he did so by effectively tearing up the existing constitution.

The second is that in Latin America, holding a referendum is a high-risk strategy. Of all the power consolidation referendums held in sub-Saharan Africa and the former Soviet Union, not a single one has failed because of a rejection by voters. In the two (post-Soviet) cases (Moldova and Ukraine) where efforts at consolidating power failed, the failure was not because the referendum motion was unable to garner a majority of votes, but because a powerful section of the elite was able to thwart the attempt. In Latin America, despite the fact that power consolidation referendums, in recent years at least, have been few and far between, we can observe three cases in which the executive's proposal has been defeated in the ballot box. Probably the closest parallel in Africa is the above-mentioned case of Senegal, where President Wade was able to circumvent

6. In Bolivia figures for 2015 are taken, as the 2016 index was not available at the time of writing.

the need for a referendum by cajoling the Constitutional Court to accept his proposed constitutional amendments but was defeated by the people at the ballot box when he stood for a third term. In most of Latin America, as in a few isolated pockets in sub-Saharan Africa and the former Soviet Union, it is civil society that provides the main obstacle to power consolidation and can mobilise to defend the limits on executive power, and to ensure that any referendum is conducted freely and fairly. Much of Latin America, including Uruguay, Peru, Venezuela and Bolivia, have a history of social activism both through labour mobilisation and through social movements led by indigenous communities. In such a setting it can prove problematic even for the most dominant president to frame the referendum debate according to his or her narrative and win over a majority of voters.

Overall, therefore, due to the relative strength of civil society, consolidation of authoritarian control is a lot more difficult to achieve in Latin America than in the former Soviet Union and sub-Saharan Africa, even in countries such as Peru, Venezuela and Bolivia where democratic rule is not consolidated. It is noteworthy that within four months of being sworn in for his cherished third term, Fujimori was forced from office by his opponents in Congress. Moreover, the Uruguayan military in 1980, Chávez in 2007 and Morales in 2016 failed to get their way in the respective referendums, although Chávez succeeded late in a second attempt. Strong opposition from within Venezuelan society to his rule and to that of his successor, Nicolás Maduro, has continued unabated to this day and the opposition even gained control of the National Assembly in elections held in December 2015. Contrast this with the situation in Belarus or Congo-Brazzaville, where there appears to be no significant threat to the rule of the respective strongmen in the foreseeable future.

## Conclusion

Using a series of mini case studies to illustrate, this chapter has identified a type of constitutional referendum, the power consolidation referendum, which, despite being dressed up as an opportunity for citizens to decide their future, has nothing to do with democracy. Most often, the power consolidation referendum is used to approve proposals to augment the power of the president and the presidential administration at the expense of the legislative body. Frequently it is a defining moment in a power struggle between the president and parliament. This type of referendum is often marred by electoral fraud – especially to artificially inflate turnout figures – and very little time is devoted to public consultation for voters to consider the proposals they are voting on. It is particularly common in the former Soviet Union and sub-Saharan Africa but has been noted also in parts of Latin America. It tends to occur in authoritarian regimes or hybrid regimes in which democracy is yet to be consolidated. It tends not to occur either if the political elite is fragmented so that the leader lacks the authority to bring potential spoilers on board and unite most political, military and economic actors behind him/her, or if there is broad consent both among the political elites and across civil society on the desired limits of executive power and a capacity to mobilise in the event that those limits are breached.

The Latin American version of this instrument does, however, differ somewhat from its African and former Soviet counterparts both in terms of the context in which it occurs and in terms of its chances of success or failure. As mentioned earlier, calling a referendum in Latin America is a relatively high-risk strategy, insofar as the relative strength of civil society means that presidents and executives run a real risk that the referendum may not go their way. Given this risk, it would perhaps be more expedient for them to avoid a referendum altogether and find other means to alter the balance of power; however, many Latin American constitutions include strict stipulations that any transfer of competences between executive and legislature must be endorsed by a mandatory referendum. And herein lies a further difference between most of Latin America on the one hand, and much of Africa and the former Soviet Union on the other: constitutional law is (more or less) observed. It is virtually inconceivable that any Latin American president today could follow the path of Nigerien president Mamadou Tandja and tear up the existing constitution in order to remain in power. Both the strength of civil society and the long legacy of constitutionalism mean that constitutional law matters in Latin America, unlike in much of the former Soviet Union and sub-Saharan Africa where the communist legacy of prioritising goals over laws (former Soviet Union) or the legacy of weak or contested statehood (Africa) means that law is subservient to raw power. One could say therefore that direct democracy is only democratic if reinforced by the rule of law.

Overall, our discussion has implications for the role of popular participation in constitution making. 'One shot' participation in a referendum to approve constitutional changes that have already been proposed by a powerful political elite is neither an indicator of democracy nor a guarantee that limits on executive power will be observed. On the contrary, it is more often a sign of democratic malaise and an abusive relationship between rulers and ruled. Scholars should therefore be very wary of treating the constitutional referendum per se as an instrument of direct democracy. For citizens' participation in a constitution-making process to be meaningful it needs to be an ongoing process that generates broad consent among citizens as to what the limits of executive power are as well as a willingness to defend those limits. It is not even necessary that this ongoing process manifests itself as a formal constitution-making process, although in certain cases constitution making may be a part of it, as the Beninois case illustrates. More often, however, it is an incremental process in which limits – formal and informal – on executive power gradually become internalised among citizens and political elites. This is what we mean by the consolidation of democracy.

## References

Gel'man, V. (2008) 'Out of the frying pan, into the fire? Post-Soviet regime changes in comparative perspective', *International Political Science Review*, 29(2): 157–80.

Hamon, F. (1995) *Le Référendum: Étude Comparative*, Paris: LGDJ.

LeDuc, L. (2003) *The Politics of Direct Democracy: Referendums in global perspective*, Peterborough (Ontario): Broadview Press.

Sakwa, R. (2008) *Russian Politics and Society* (4th edn), Abingdon (UK): Routledge.

Uggla, F. (2008) 'Bolivia: Referéndums como armas políticas', paper presented at the conference '¿Hacia dónde va la democracia en América Latina?', Montevideo, Uruguay, 21 October.

Weingast, B. R. (1997) 'The political foundations of democracy and the rule of the law', *American Political Science Review*, 91(02): 245–63.

Wheatley, J. (2013a) 'Constitution-making in West Africa: keeping the President in check', in J. Wheatley and F. Mendez (eds) *Patterns of Constitutional Design: The role of citizens and elites in constitution-making*, Farnham: Ashgate: 69–86.

—— (2013b) 'The use of the power consolidation referendum: experiences from the former Soviet Union', in A. Good and B. Platipodis (eds) *Direkte Demokratie: Herausforderungen zwischen Politik und Recht* (Festschrift für Andreas Auer zum 65. Geburtstag). Bern: Stämpfli Verlag: 241–52.

# Appendix

*Table A4.1: National referendums in the Commonwealth of Independent States (CIS) and sub-Saharan Africa*

| Country | Date | Initiative | Issue | 'Yes' vote/ Turnout |
|---|---|---|---|---|
| Azerbaijan | 24 August 2002 | President/presidential administration | Constitutional change vesting the prime minister, rather than the chairman of parliament, with the power of acting president in the event of the current president's resignation (clearly favouring the president's son, Ilham Aliev, who was appointed prime minister the following year) | 96.79/ 88.47 |
| Azerbaijan | 18 March 2009 | New Azerbaijan Party (ruling party) | Twenty-nine proposals to amend the constitution, including a proposal to abolish the constitutional provision that a president can be elected for only two terms | 91.76/ 70.82 |
| Belarus | 24 November 1996 | President | Amending the constitution to bring about a significant shift in the balance of power from the Supreme Soviet to the president | 88.24/ 84.14 |
| Belarus | 17 October 2004 | President/presidential administration | Constitutional changes to remove term restrictions for presidential office | 88.91/ 90.28 |
| Benin | 31 March 1968 | Military Junta | New constitution introducing a presidential system in which the president could be re-elected an indefinite number of times | 92.21/ 81.88 |
| Burundi | 18 November 1981 | President Jean-Baptiste Bagaza and the ruling party UPRONA | New constitution establishing a presidential republic | 99.28/ 94.25 |
| Cameroon | 20 May 1972 | President | Constitutional changes marking transition from a federation to a centralised State and increased presidential powers | 99.99/ 98.25 |
| Central African Republic | 21 November 1986 | President | Constitution changes to make General Kolingba President for six years | 92.22/ 87.61 |
| Chad | 10 December 1989 | President/National Consultative Council | Constitution introducing a presidential republic, with a seven-year term of office for the president and unlimited re-eligibility | 99.94/ 93.04 |

*(Continued)*

Table A4.1 (*Continued*)

| **Country** | **Date** | **Initiative** | **Issue** | **'Yes' vote/ Turnout** |
|---|---|---|---|---|
| Chad | 6 June 2005 | President | Constitutional reform abolishing restrictions for the presidential term | 65.75/ 57.81 |
| Congo, Dem. Rep. of | 16 June 1967 | President | New constitution with strong presidential system | 98.44/ unknown |
| Congo, Rep. of | 8 July 1979 | President/Military Committee of the Party | New constitution with strong presidential system | 96.95/ 90.30 |
| Congo, Rep. of | 20 January 2002 | President | New constitution with strong presidential system | 88.19/ 77.98 |
| Congo, Rep. of | 25 October 2015 | President | Constitutional amendment to allow an extra presidential term | 92.27/ 72.44 |
| Côte d'Ivoire | 24 July 2000 | President | New constitution with a specific article to disqualify an opponent as a potential presidential candidate | 86.58/ 55.97 |
| Equatorial Guinea | 29 July 1993 | President | New constitution enshrining a presidential republic and a one-party state | 99.00/ unknown |
| Equatorial Guinea | 15 August 1982 | President | New constitution establishing presidential republic and appointing President Obiang as president for seven years | 95.79/ 93.47 |
| Equatorial Guinea | 13 November 2011 | President | Constitutional reform allowing the president a maximum of incumbent for a maximum of two more seven-year terms and the right to appoint a vice-president | 97.73/ 91.79 |
| Ghana | 31 January 1964 | President | Constitutional amendment to establish of a one-party state and allowing the president to nominate and dismiss judges | 99.91/ unknown |
| Guinea | 11 November 2001 | President | Constitutional amendments allowing President Lansana Conte to run for a third term in office | 98.36/ 91.28 |

*(Continued)*

Table A4.1 (*Continued*)

| Country | Date | Initiative | Issue | 'Yes' vote/ Turnout |
|---|---|---|---|---|
| Kazakhstan | 30 August 1995 | President/presidential administration | New constitution that gave significantly more powers to the president than the previous constitution | 90.01/ 90.58 |
| Kyrgyzstan | 22 October 1994 | President/presidential administration | Constitutional changes to introduce a bicameral parliament | 88.11/ 86.00 |
| Kyrgyzstan | 10 February 1996 | President/presidential administration | Constitutional changes to increase president's power | 98.56/ 96.62 |
| Kyrgyzstan | 17 October 1998 | President/presidential administration | Package of constitutional changes. The proposals included stripping the parliament of the right to discuss budgetary spending without government approval and allow deputies to be stripped of immunity in some cases | 95.38/ 96.44 |
| Kyrgyzstan | 21 October 2007 | President/presidential administration | Constitutional amendments giving the president the right to appoint and dismiss the heads of local administration, National Security Council, judges, prosecutors, board of directors of the National Bank and electoral commission | 95.44/ 81.58 |
| Madagascar | 8 October 1972 | Prime minister | Interim constitution with unrestricted powers for Prime Minister Ramanantsoa | 96.43/ 84.29 |
| Madagascar | 21 December 1975 | Supreme Revolutionary Council | New Constitution with a seven-year term as president for Captain Didier Ratsiraka | 95.57/ 91.77 |
| Madagascar | 17 September 1995 | President | Constitutional amendments allowing President to appoint new prime minister | 63.56/ 65.39 |
| Madagascar | 15 March 1998 | President | Constitutional amendments giving more powers to the president | 50.96/ 70.28 |
| Madagascar | 4 April 2007 | President | Constitutional amendments including one that would allow the President to govern by decree in a state of emergency | 75.33/ 43.68 |

*(Continued)*

Table A4.1 (*Continued*)

| Country | Date | Initiative | Issue | 'Yes' vote/ Turnout |
|---|---|---|---|---|
| Madagascar | 17 November 2011 | President of the 'Haute Autorité de la Transition' (HAT) | Constitutional amendments for a centralized state and reducing the age limit for the president to allow President of the 'Haute Autorité de la Transition' (HAT) to assume the post | 74.19/ 52.61 |
| Mali | 2 June 1974 | President | A new constitution with a president for a five-year term, who can be re-elected only once and a single-chamber parliament with restricted powers | 99.66/ 92.21 |
| Mauritania | 12. July 1991 | President | Constitution with unlimited re-eligibility for the President | 97.94/ 85.35 |
| Moldova | 23 May 1999 | President/presidential administration | Constitutional amendments proposed to introduce a presidential form of government. Subject to approval by the constitutional court and of two-thirds of members of parliament | 64.20/ 58.33 |
| Niger | 24 September 1989 | President/Supreme Military Council | New constitution based on a one-party presidential regime with two terms of seven years | 99.28/ 95.08 |
| Niger | 12 May 1996 | Coup leader and later president Ibrahim Baré Maïnassara | New constitution based on presidential Republic | 92.00/ 35.00 |
| Niger | 8 August 2009 | President | New constitution allowing extended term for president | 92.50/ 68.26 |
| Russian Federation | 12 December 1993 | President | New constitution establishing a presidential republic | 58.43/ 54.37 |
| Rwanda | 17 December 1978 | President | New constitution for a presidential republic with no term limits for the president | 89.00/ unknown |
| Senegal | 3 March 1963 | Parliament/ president | Abolition of the position of Prime Minister from the constitution | 99.45/ 94.29 |

(*Continued*)

Table A4.1 (*Continued*)

| Country | Date | Initiative | Issue | 'Yes' vote/ Turnout |
|---|---|---|---|---|
| Sierra Leone | 12 June 1978 | Parliament/ president | New constitution to provide a one-party Republican constitution with a strong presidency | 97.15/ 99.13 |
| Somalia | 25 August 1979 | President/Somali Revolutionary Socialist Party | Constitution based on a socialist one-party State with a presidential system of government. | 99.78/ unknown |
| Tajikistan | 26 September 1999 | Mandated by the peace deal, determined by presidential consent | Constitutional amendments creating a bicameral parliament, extending the president's term in office from five to seven years and allowing the formation of religious-based political parties | 75.32/ 92.54 |
| Tajikistan | 22 June 2003 | President/presidential administration | Constitutional changes including allowing the president to stand for two more seven-year terms | 93.82/ 96.38 |
| Togo | 9 April 1961 | Prime minister (later president) | Presidential constitution along the lines of the French Constitution | 99.62/ 89.95 |
| Togo | 5 May 1963 | Military | New constitution with a presidential republic and unicameral parliament | 98.53/ 91.05 |
| Togo | 30 December 1979 | President/military | New constitution with a presidential republic and a one-party system | 99.87/ 99.36 |
| Turkmenistan | 15 January 1994 | Parliament, under the direction of the president | Amendment to the constitution to extend President Niyazov's term to 2002 | 99.99/ 99.90 |
| Ukraine | 16 April 2000 | De jure, popular initiative. De facto, the initiative belonged to the president/presidential administration | Constitutional amendment to give the president the right to dissolve parliament | 85.92/ 81.08 |
| Uzbekistan | 27 January 2002 | Parliamentary majority | Constitutional amendments proposed to (1) establish a bicameral parliament, (2) extend the presidential term to from five to seven years. Supposedly approved by over 91% of those voting | 91.78/ 91.58 |

*Chapter Five*

# Plebiscites and Sovereignty: A Historical and Comparative Study of Self-Determination and Secession Referendums

*Matt Qvortrup*

> *L'existence d'une nation est (pardonnez-moi cette métaphore) un plébiscite de tous les jours, comme l'existence de l'individu est une affirmation perpétuelle de vie.*
>
> Ernest Renan (Qu'est-ce qu'une nation? Conference, Sorbonne, 11 March 1882, Sorbonne, Paris, p. 27)

*Lex est quod populus iubet atque constituit*
Gaius, *Institutiones*, I, 3, AD 161

## Introduction

The relationship between democracy and secession has been a sore point in constitutional theory and practical politics since the sixteenth century when French King Francis I (1494–547) held a plebiscite in Burgundy on whether to transfer the area to the Spanish king in 1527 as he had agreed to in the Treaty of Madrid. Yet while plebiscites (or referendums – I will use the words interchangeably) were also employed to add legitimacy to the French annexation of Avignon in 1793, it was not until the nineteenth century that the referendum was used to resolve matters of sovereignty in a way reminiscent of today (Mattern 1921: 118).[1]

Using direct democracy to resolve diplomatic and international issues is a rarity. The default position has been that such matters be left to the people's representatives – whether elected or not. Somehow, the people were not trusted to make enlightened decisions and many raised the fear that the use of direct democracy more generally would result in strife, discord and conflict. As Laurence Whitehead (Chapter Two in this volume) notes, the contention from James Madison onwards has been that referendums and direct democracy have the potential to create factions. This would appear to be a particular concern in cases of votes on ethnic and national issues such as secession referendums. But it is one thing to hypothesise in the abstract, it is quite another to consider the matter empirically. This chapter takes an empirical look at the history of independence referendums with an emphasis on plebiscites held since the 1860s.

1. For a history of the earlier referendums see Qvortrup 2015.

## The earlier history of referendums on independence

Referendums on independence are more common than we think. While there had been referendums in Europe since the early sixteenth century, the first referendum in America was held in 1788 in Massachusetts, when voters were consulted on whether they wanted to give up their independence and join the newly minted United States. By the mid-1850s it had become commonplace to consult the citizens on major issues of constitutional importance. It was natural, therefore, that Arkansas, Texas, Virginia and Tennessee submitted the decision to secede from the Union to the voters in 1860. What is perhaps interesting is that the support for secession was not unanimous. In Arkansas, 27,415 voted for a convention to sever the ties with Washington, while 15,826 voted against. In Tennessee 104,019 voted for secession while 47,238 voted against, and in Texas the figures were 34,794 for and 11,235 against (Mattern 1921: 118).[2] These were not endorsements of epic proportions – and perhaps this should have caused the confederate leaders to think again. The less than unanimous support perhaps suggested the nuclear option favoured by the confederate elites was not supported by the Dixie voters.

After the American Civil War referendums on independence were almost forgotten. There were debates about plebiscites to resolve the border dispute between Denmark and Germany, but these came to naught (Mattern 1921: 106). It took a full forty-five years before the next referendum on independence was held. This was a vote on whether Norway should secede from Sweden in a referendum in 1905, which more than 99 per cent supported (Bjørklund 2003: 66). In the Norwegian case the referendum was the brainchild of Norwegian Prime Minister Christian Michelsen, who wrong-footed the Swedish Unionist elite by calling a surprise referendum after the Swedish king had refused to appoint a government that had a majority in the Norwegian *Stortinget* (parliament) (Bjørklund 2003: 66).

But although the principle of self-determination of the people was much espoused in the wake of the First World War – especially by US President Woodrow Wilson, who had campaigned for the use of more referendums in America while he was governor of New Jersey – no referendums were held on independence for the newly established countries (e.g. Czechoslovakia or Yugoslavia) or the secession of states from established ones (e.g. Hungary and Finland). To be sure there were several referendums on the drawing of borders in Europe, e.g. in Schleswig and in Tyrol in 1920 (Wambaugh 1920: 55), but referendums on outright independence were not held. It was very much the case that, as Mattern put it, 'the rules governing the intercourse of states [did] neither demand nor recognize the application of the plebiscite [referendum] in the determination of sovereignty' (Mattern 1921: 171).

In the period between the two World Wars, only two referendums were held. One was in 1933, on whether Western Australia should secede from Australia, and the other was in 1935, on whether the Philippines should become independent from the United States. In the former, a majority voted for independence, but as the National Party, which campaigned for independence, lost the election held on the

2. We do not have figures for Virginia.

same day, nothing came of it (Musgrave 2003: 95). In the latter case, a successful referendum was held on a new independence constitution after the Philippine Congress had rejected the US Congress' Hare–Hawes–Cutting Act (enacted in 1933), which granted independence for the erstwhile overseas dependency.

However, it was not after the Second World War that referendums began to be used when areas seceded from their parent states. Of the fifty-eight referendums on independence since 1860, fifty-one were held after 1944, and the vast majority of these were held after 1990.

As shown in Table 5.1 there were only thirteen independence referendums in the four decades after the Second World War. As we shall see shortly, these referendums followed different logics and different paths.

There are few common denominators between these referendums. Given the differences it is instructive to go through the cases individually.

The Faroe Islands – formally a municipality of Denmark – were under British protection during the Second World War. After the War the Independence Party (*Folkaflokkurin*) – having proved that it could govern without Copenhagen – organised a referendum. This resulted in a yes vote for independence. However, the Danish government demanded that new elections to the *Lagtinget* (the assembly) were held. When these resulted in a majority for the Unionist parties the independence referendum was forgotten (Qvortrup 2014: 52).

The case of Malta was a different kettle of political fish. Having voted for integration into the United Kingdom in 1956, London had done little to honour its promises and in 1964 a referendum was organised on a new constitution for an independent country (Fenech 2003).

*Table 5.1: Secession referendums (1944–80)*

| Parent country | Seceding country | Year | Turnout | Yes (%) |
|---|---|---|---|---|
| Denmark | Iceland | 1944 | 98 | 99 |
| China | Mongolia | 1945 | 98 | 64 |
| Denmark | Faroe Islands | 1946 | 50 | 64 |
| UK | Newfoundland | 1948 | 52 | 88 |
| France | Cambodia | 1955 | 100 | – |
| France | Guinea | 1958 | 97 | 95 |
| New Zealand | Western Samoa | 1961 | 86 | 77 |
| West Indian Federation | Jamaica | 1961 | 46 | 60 |
| France | Djibouti | 1967 | Na | 40 |
| UK | Malta | 1964 | 50 | 80 |
| UK | Rhodesia | 1964 | 61 | 90 |
| Spain | Equatorial Guinea | 1963 | 62 | N/A |
| UK | Canada | 1980 | 85 | 40 |

*Source:* www.c2d.ch (accessed 2 January 2015).

Newfoundland was an altogether different case. It is one of the rare examples of a multi-option referendum – though one with a twist. Formally under Britain, Newfoundland had the option of remaining under the United Kingdom rule, becoming an independent country or becoming a Canadian Province (Warntz 1955). After the status quo option received the lowest number of votes, a run-off referendum between the two remaining options was held a few months later. After a surprisingly bitter campaign characterised by sectarian divisions between Protestants and Catholics, the confederate option (favoured by the Loyal Orange Association) secured a majority of 52.3 per cent (Qvortrup 2014: 69).

As if these referendums were not different enough already, the plebiscite held in Jamaica in 1962 provides yet another example of a seemingly idiosyncratic referendum. Having been part of the newly established West Indies Federation, Jamaica – the largest state in the union – was aggrieved that it had to bear the brunt of the costs of the smaller territories and felt it was not given due recognition (Wallace 1962). Formally, the federation was under the sovereignty of the United Kingdom but the aim was that the new federation would gradually become fully independent. This prospect did not appeal to Alexander Bustamante, the leader of Jamaica's Labour Party. He advocated independence. In an attempt to call his opponent's bluff, Norman Manley, the Premier of Jamaica, called a referendum, which he expected to win. To his surprise, a majority of 54 per cent voted for independence (Nohlen 2005: 430).

These referendums – as we have seen – shared few common denominators except that they were used ad hoc and served opportunistic purposes. The elites who fought for and won independence were not, in most cases, willing to risk the political victories gained in negotiations by submitting declarations of independence to an unpredictable electorate. Indeed, the only colonies to submit the declarations of independence to referendum were Cambodia, Western Samoa and Guinea (three out of twelve cases listed). The three cases – while similar in certain regards – followed different trajectories.

In the early twentieth century, international lawyer, L. F. L. Oppenheim considered it 'doubtful whether the Law of Nations will ever make it a condition of every cession that it must be ratified by plebiscite' (Oppenheim 1912: 274). The secessions without referendum in the post-Second World War era suggest that he had a point. This makes it all the more remarkable that Western Samoa was pressured by the international community to follow democratic procedures, i.e. the UN demanded the independence referendum. As Caroline Morris writes: 'Samoa obtained its independence from New Zealand as a result of a referendum supervised by the UN … . the 1961 referendum also asked Samoans to approve a draft constitution … the driver behind the holding of the referendum was international pressure' (Morris 2014: 239).

But other referendums followed different paths. In Cambodia the referendum was organised by King Sihanouk, as an attempt to prove his popularity and to secure support for his regime in an ethnically divided nation. The plebiscite – according to a Canadian diplomatic observer – was 'orderly but completely unsecret' (cited in Chandler 1993: 77). In many ways, perhaps, the referendum in Cambodia follows the pattern identified by Johnathan Wheatley as power consolidation referendum (*see* Wheatley's Chapter Four in this volume). Referendums in autocracies tend to take place if there is a high level of ethnic fractionalisation, as this diversity necessitates token 'proofs' of the passion for unanimity, which can be secured through 'difference eliminating referendums' (Qvortrup 2014: 110). In short, dictators hold referendums to prove that the 'people' are united behind them, the ethnic diversity notwithstanding.

In Guinea, the only country to opt for independence from France in 1958, the referendum was held as an act of defiance by Ahmed Sékou Touré who wanted to prove that he could govern independently of France. This referendum – while inconsistent with ideal democratic practices – was not held to paper over differences between domestic forces (as was the case in Cambodia). Rather the vote was held to show Paris that the country could govern without their help. The plebiscite was the symbolic culmination of an anti-colonial struggle (Schmidt 2009: 1). The Guinean referendum was held on the same day as eleven other referendums in other French colonies, on whether to take part in the new *communauté française* established by Charles de Gaulle. The Guineans defied Paris and voted to become independent (with 95 per cent of the voters supporting independence). France retaliated by withdrawing all aid. However, within two years Mali, Niger, Upper Volta (now Burkina Faso), Côte d'Ivoire, Chad, the Central African Republic, the Republic of Congo and Gabon – all territories that had returned huge majorities for maintaining links with France in their referendums in 1958 – became independent states. But none of the new states submitted the decision to become independent to the voters. It was almost as if referendums on independence were anathema to the independence movements.

Generally, the reasons for holding referendums in the aftermath of the Second World War were varied. In the case of Mongolia, the vote was held for geopolitical reasons at the instigation of Stalin; the referendum was held after an agreement with Chiang Kai-shek that the Soviet Union would not support Mao if they were allowed to keep Mongolia as a satellite state (Radchenko 2015).

The vote in Algeria was held after a lengthy war of independence and negotiations, and served the function of pacifying anti-gaullist forces in France proper. The referendum was in many ways a reflection of the domestic political constraints facing President de Gaulle. The president did not have a majority in parliament and submitted the Evian Agreement (the accord reached with the Algerians) as a means of bypassing the elected representatives. Yet the President's motivation was not merely opportunist. Ideologically, President Charles de Gaulle was strongly in favour of the referendum – an instrument pioneered by his political idol Napoleon. As he put it in his posthumously published *Mémoires d'Espoir* ('Memories of Hope'): 'I was convinced that sovereignty belongs to the people, provided that they express themselves directly and as a whole' (de Gaulle 1971: 6). Hence the President should be entitled to 'submit to a referendum any government bill dealing with the working of the country's institutions; that in the event of a grave crisis, internal or external, he [the president] should be able be empowered to take the measures demanded by the circumstances' (de Gaulle 1971: 7). This explanation seems accurate in the case of Algeria – about which it was written. But the referendum in Guinea followed a different pattern, as indeed did the vote in 1967 in Djibouti, which was more a plebiscite to give legitimacy to France's attempt to keep 'a strategic toehold in Africa' (Marks 1974).

And, as if to cement the view that each referendum follows an idiosyncratic pattern, the referendum in 1964 on South Rhodesia, in which an overwhelming majority of the white-only electors endorsed the question 'Are you in favour of or against Southern Rhodesia obtaining independence on the basis of the 1961 Constitution of Southern Rhodesia?', shows yet another pattern. The vote was an example of how a referendum can be used to communicate unity to a recalcitrant external world. Ian Smith's government was unwilling to accept British Prime Minister Harold Wilson's terms for independence, and a referendum was held to communicate this unity to the British (Onslow 2005).

Overall, therefore, it would be difficult to find a general pattern of when referendums were held after the Second World War. Not all social science phenomena follow a law-like pattern, or as Karl Marx put it, 'world history would have been a rather mysterious thing if chance didn't play a role' (Marx 1946: 309).

In the 1970s there was only one referendum on independence, the decision of the Trust Territory of the Pacific Islands, to become independent from the USA under the name of the Federated States of Micronesia in 1975. In the 1980s there was a similar paucity of plebiscites. The only one in the latter decade was the 1980 vote in the Francophone Canadian province of Quebec, in which 59 per cent, on a 85 per cent turnout, rejected the secessionist Parti Québécois' proposal for 'sovereignty association' – a veiled description of independence.

It was only after the fall of Communism in 1989 and the collapse of the Soviet Union in 1991 that the floodgates of independence referendums opened. Again the reasons seem to have been varied. But, in many cases, referendums were held because the international community – especially the major European powers – insisted upon referendums in order to recognise the new states. In particular the *Badinter Commission* – set up by the European Communities (soon to become the European Union) – stressed that referendums were a *conditio sine qua non* for recognising new states. There is historical and anecdotal evidence to suggest that it was this requirement that prompted a large number of successor-states to hold referendums, especially in the former Yugoslavia (Radan 2000: 47). The referendums in Yugoslavia have been described as 'an anarchy of referendums' (Brady and Kaplan 1994: 206).

Contrary to the view of Oppenheim and other international lawyers some ninety years earlier, the referendum had 'become a condition of every secession' (Oppenheim 1912: 274) – indeed, it seemed that it was the *only* condition. With scant regard for minority rights, ever smaller population enclaves declared their independence after referendums characterised by fraud and based on dubious legal grounds – or, in most cases, no constitutional provisions whatsoever. The plebiscites in the former Yugoslavia gave referendums a bad name, although the reference to *vox populi* remained a powerful political slogan. Much as the plebiscites in Yugoslavia can be criticised on legal and constitutional grounds, the continued use of referendums – for example in self-proclaimed Donetsk and Luhansk People's Republics in Eastern Ukraine in 2014, suggests that appeals to the people are still the gold standard of legitimacy, even by rulers who are less than enthusiastic about democracy.

Irrespective of the constitutional legality of the votes, the referendum displays a kind of symbolic national manifestation of a newly found freedom. By voting – often almost unanimously – in an independence referendum, the new state made the plebiscite a symbolic representation of the nation itself; a mirror image of the *demos* and the *ethnos* merged into one indivisible unity. Ernest Renan's often cited remark, quoted at the beginning of this chapter, that a 'nation is a daily plebiscite' is an accurate description of these referendums (Renan 1996).

But the referendums are also held for more prosaic reasons, namely when a new elite was under threat from external and internal powers and wanted to prove that it had popular support and the requisite legitimacy to govern (Qvortrup 2014: 12). The celebrations of independence through referendums had ulterior motives and often displayed that 'violent passion for assent, for unanimity' that Carl Friedrich and Zbigniew Brzezinski famously made the hallmark of totalitarian dictatorship (Friedrich and Brzezinski 1965: 132).

*Table 5.2: Secession referendums (1991–2014)*

| Parent country | Seceding country | Year | Percentage turnout | Yes vote | New state formed |
|---|---|---|---|---|---|
| USSR | Lithuania | 1991 | 91 | 84 | Yes |
| USSR | Estonia | 1991 | 77 | 83 | Yes |
| USSR | Latvia | 1991 | 74 | 88 | Yes |
| USSR | Georgia | 1991 | 98 | 90 | Yes |
| USSR | Ukraine | 1991 | 70 | 85 | Yes |
| Georgia | South Ossetia | 1991 | 98 | 90 | No[a] |
| Georgia | Abkhasia | 1991 | 99 | 58 | No[a] |
| Yugoslavia | Croatia | 1991 | 98 | 83 | Yes |
| Croatia | Serbs | 1991 | 98 | 83 | No |
| Yugoslavia | Macedonia | 1991 | 70 | 75 | Yes |
| USSR | Armenia | 1991 | 95 | 90 | Yes |
| Bosnia | Serbs | 1991 | 90 | – | No |
| Serbia | Sandjak | 1991 | 96 | 67 | No |
| Serbia | Kosovo | 1991 | 99 | 87 | Yes |
| USSR | Turkmenistan | 1991 | 94 | 97 | Yes |
| USSR | Karabagh | 1991 | | | No |
| USSR | Uzbekistan | 1991 | 98 | 94 | Yes |
| Macedonia | Albanians | 1991 | 99 | 93 | No |

*(Continued)*

Table 5.2 (*Continued*)

| Parent country | Seceding country | Year | Percentage turnout | Yes vote | New state formed |
|---|---|---|---|---|---|
| Moldova | Transnistie | 1991 | | | No |
| Yugoslavia | Bosnia | 1992 | 99 | 64 | Yes |
| Yugoslavia | Montenegro | 1992 | 96 | 44 | No |
| Georgia | South Ossetia | 1992 | N/A | N/A | No[a] |
| Bosnia | Krajina | 1992 | 99 | 64 | No |
| Russia | Tartarstan | 1992 | 61 | 81 | No |
| Bosnia | Serbs | 1993 | 96 | 92 | No |
| USA | Puerto Rico | 1993 | 48 | 73 | No |
| Georgia | Abkhasia | 1995 | 96 | 52 | No |
| Quebec | Cris | 1995 | 95 | 75 | No |
| Canada | Quebec | 1995 | 49 | 94 | No |
| St Kitts and Nevis | Nevis | 1998 | 57 | 61 | No |
| USA | Porto Rico | 1998 | 50 | 71 | No |
| Indonesia | East Timor | 1999 | 78 | 94 | Yes |
| Somalia | Somaliland | 2001 | – | 97 | No |
| New Zealand | Tokelau | 2006 | | 95 | No |
| Yugoslavia | Montenegro | 2006 | 55 | 86 | Yes |
| Sudan | South Sudan | 2011 | 97 | 98 | Yes |
| UK | Scotland | 2014 | 84 | 43 | No |
| Ukraine | Luhansk | 2015 | 74 | 89 | No |

*Source:* www.c2d.ch (accessed 2 January 2015)
a Recognised by the Russian Federation.

Not all the states, of course were recognised, and not all the referendums were conducted in accordance with internationally recognised standards of free and fair voting. In addition to referendums in former Soviet and Yugoslav entities, a proliferation of plebiscites were held in subnational territories, such as Abkhazia in Georgia and Krajina in Bosnia, where minorities sought to win approval for independence from recently declared independent states. None of these subnational referendums succeeded (Brady and Kaplan 1994).

While most referendums were held in former communist countries, a few polls were held in Western democracies as well. In 1995 voters in Quebec again rejected independence, this time by a whisker, and so did voters in Puerto Rico in a multi-option referendum in 1993. And in 1998, voters in Nevis failed to meet the required threshold of 66 per cent necessary to secede from St Kitts and Nevis (Qvortrup 2014: 153). Interestingly, the only unsuccessful referendums on independence have been held in countries with established democratic traditions. In regions such as Quebec and Scotland, support for independence has been at best lukewarm.

Their parent states are rich countries with established democratic traditions. Consequently, their citizens have much to lose if they opt for an uncertain future as an independent nation. Conversely, citizens in developing countries or countries with a short democratic history have less to lose. Some of these countries – whether South Sudan, Montenegro or East Timor – had been ruled by regimes who showed scant regard for the rights of the national minorities living in these regions. Hence, these regions could afford to experiment; things could only get better!

Given that most referendums are held in territories with less than impeccable democratic records, it is difficult to establish what determines the outcome of a referendum. But if we broaden the category to include referendums on autonomy and devolution there seems to be a tendency that voters are more inclined to support propositions if the government proposing the change or the secession has been in power for a relatively short period of time. In other words, it is easier to win a referendum on devolution or independence during the honeymoon period immediately after an election – something proved perhaps by the devolution referendums in Britain in 1997. Conversely the longer you have been in office the greater the risk of losing the referendum. Why is this? One possible and credible explanation was advanced by Key who in a classic analysis observed that 'to govern is to antagonize' (Key 1968: 30). All governments break promises, fail to deliver and enact unpopular laws. A referendum can be a proxy for a vote on the record of the government. Hence, a no vote in a referendum is often a positive function of the years in office, a fact perhaps most clearly shown in the Canadian referendum on a new constitution in 1992, in which Prime Minister Brian Mulroney's personal disapproval rating was the determining factor of the negative outcome. However, it should be noted that Milo Đukanović, the Prime Minister of Montenegro, had served as premier since 1991 when he succeeded in winning the independence referendum in 2006 (Qvortrup 2014: 66). The main factor behind winning an independence referendum is the voters' support for the proposition. Given these factors, it was perhaps not surprising that the Scots rejected independence – though it should be stressed that the Scottish National Party (SNP) achieved a considerable feat in almost closing the gap (*see* Tierney, Chapter Six in this volume). At the risk of simplifying matters; the nationalists lost the referendum but they won the campaign.

## Balloting to stop bullets?

As was shown in the case of Bosnia, referendums on independence have sometimes resulted in civil war and conflict. Yet at other times the political split has been amicable. But despite horroific examples like the former Yugoslavia, independence referendums relatively rarely result in wars. To wit, in Aleksandar Pavkovic and Peter Radan's much cited *Creating New States: Theory and Practice of Secession* (2007), the authors use six case studies to uncover the logic of secession; three violent secessions or session-attempts (Biafra, Bangladesh and Chechnya) and three peaceful ones (Norway, Slovakia and Quebec) (Pavkovic and Radan 2007). Interestingly, the former three all have one thing in common; no referendum was held. Conversely referendums were held only in the peaceful examples. Of course this does not prove that referendums are conducive to peaceful political divorce settlements. If we use the cases of secession cited by Pavkovic and Radan (1900–2010), we find that forty-four of the sixty secessions or secession attempts were preceded by referendums. Of forty-four referendums war broke out in six cases. In other words, the secession was achieved peacefully in thirty-eight (86 per cent) of the cases. Examples such as Bosnia and East Timor are the exceptions to the rule.

## Special majority requirements

Given the momentous importance of the vote it seems reasonable that 'if the approval rate of a referendum is too low, it ought to be discredited. A nearly simple majority does not provide sufficient legitimacy' (Beogang 2002: 77). Without passing judgement as to the fairness of such a requirement, it is worth outlining a few comparative examples of when such stipulations have been introduced. Turnout and quorum requirements are relatively common in referendums on independence and other referendums on ethnic and national issues. Of course, this is not just the result of a concern for fairness and democratic legitimacy. Far from it. In politics, opportunism and ulterior motives are often presented in the guises of what we might call democratic appropriateness. Special majority requirements are no exception. A special majority quorum is often a mechanism of obstructionism. This was arguably the case in the late 1970 when the Callaghan Labour government's proposal for Scottish and Welsh devolution was obstructed by the Labour MP George Cunningham who introduced an amendment to the effect that devolution had to be supported by a majority that represented at least 40 per cent of eligible voters. This meant that devolution in Scotland was rejected although a majority of those voting voted yes in the referendum in 1979.

This type of obstructionism, albeit in a different setting, was also the motivation behind Soviet leader Mikhail Gorbachev's insistence that a two-thirds majority should be required for secession in Latvia. The Soviet leader was not the only one seeking to use obstructionist tactics. A similar rule was passed by the Israeli Knesset to the effect that a peace deal with the Palestinians must be supported by a supermajority. Tellingly the law was introduced by parties opposed to returning the occupied territories to the Palestinians. In the light of these examples, it was unsurprising that one of the demands made by the Khartoum government before the independence referendum in South Sudan in 2011 was that at least 60 per cent turned out to vote.

The Canadian Clarity Act, passed in response to a court ruling that a referendum in Quebec would have to be decisive for the result to stand, is often (but inaccurately) cited as a precedent for supermajority requirements. However, the Canadian Act does not provide a specific percentage, but merely states that:

> [The House of Commons shall consider] whether, in the circumstances, there has been a clear expression of a will by a clear majority of the population of that province that the province ceases to be part of Canada. Factors for House

of Commons to take into account include (2) (a) the size of the majority of valid votes cast in favor of the secessionist option; (b) the percentage of eligible voters voting in the referendum; and (c) any other matters or circumstances it considers to be relevant. (Clarity Act 2000).

A better example of a supermajority requirement, albeit a small one, was used in 2006 in Montenegro. The law stipulated that independence would be approved if supported by 55 per cent of those eligible to vote. The total turnout of the referendum was 86 per cent – 55.5 per cent voted in favour and 44.5 were against breaking the state union with Serbia.

Another – perhaps more exotic – example is St Kitts and Nevis in the Caribbean. Under the constitution, Nevis has considerable autonomy and has an island assembly, a premier and a deputy governor general. Under certain specified conditions, it may secede from the federation. In June 1996, the Nevis Island Administration under the Concerned Citizens' Movement led by Premier Vance Amory – a former international cricketer with a batting average of 23.2 – announced its intention to become independent. Secession requires approval by two-thirds of the assembly's five elected members and by two-thirds of voters in a referendum in accordance with Art. 38.1 (b) of the Constitution. After the Nevis Reformation Party blocked the bill of secession, Amory called for elections on 24 February 1997. Although the elections produced no change in the composition of the assembly, the Premier pledged to continue his efforts towards independence. A referendum – which could be regarded as ultra vires – was held in 1998, but only 61 per cent voted in favour of the proposition, and hence the referendum failed.

A similar mechanism exists in tiny Tokelau, where a self-determination referendum also failed to reach the required quorum. Yet these examples are – given the small size of the countries – not likely to create precedent in the sense of an international norm with the force of international law. In most other referendums (e.g. East Timor in 1999, Malta in 1964, and the referendums on independence for former Soviet states in 1991), there were no special majority requirements. While it is certainly possible to cite examples of special majority requirements, it cannot in fairness be said that the simple majority requirement in the Scottish referendum was at odds with international norms (*see* Tierney's contribution in this volume).

## Do biased questions in referendums affect the outcome?

There has been a considerable debate about the wording of the question on the ballot in referendums on independence. The Scottish government's decision in 2012 to include the word 'agree' in the proposed question on the ballot in the 2014 referendum led to criticism that they were trying to influence the result by using positive language that could sway voters. The argument – credibly enough – was that a biased and one-sided question could prompt the voters to vote yes to a question which they – had they understood it – would have rejected. This has always been a charge against referendums on divisive issues. But is it a real danger in referendums on independence? Will the voters be swayed by rhetorical questions? Or is the question on the ballot of minor importance as the voters know the question from the debate? It is difficult to answer this question with any degree of mathematical certainty but we can – perhaps – draw some conclusions if we compare some of the recent examples of wordings in the referendums on independence held in peacetime in the past twenty years.

Referendum questions have come in many shapes and sizes, from the blatantly biased to the bland. In Northern Ireland, in 1998, the voters were asked to approve (or otherwise) the rather neutral question 'Do you support the agreement reached in multi-party talks on Northern Ireland and set out in Command Paper 3883?': The result was that 71.2 per cent did. Command Paper 3883 was a coded reference to the official document containing the Belfast Agreement. There are several examples of similar questions that have not created a bias. For example in 1999, in East Timor, the voters were asked the question: 'Do you *accept* the proposed special autonomy for East Timor within the Unitary State of the Republic of Indonesia?' (emphasis added). A majority of the voters – close to 75 per cent – *rejected* the proposal, with the result that East Timor became independent. In this internationally monitored referendum that value-laden word 'accept' did not swing the voters.

A similar conclusion could be drawn from the referendum in Quebec in 1995. In this referendum the voters were asked a question that included the word 'agree', namely, 'Do you *agree* that Quebec should become sovereign after having made a formal offer to Canada for a new economic and political partnership within the scope of the bill respecting the future of Quebec and of the agreement signed on 12 June 1995? (emphasis added)'. While the result was very close (the proposal was defeated by 51 per cent), there was no indication that the wording of the question swayed the voters. The citizens had learned about the pros and cons of the proposed 'sovereignty association' during the campaign. In both East Timor and Quebec, it seems that an attempt to hoodwink the voters to support a proposition by using positive language failed.

So what other type of questions have been asked? There is no standard format, but a quick look at recent examples may be illustrative. In 2006, 55.5 per cent of the voters in Montenegro opted for independence by supporting the proposition, 'Do you want the Republic of Montenegro to be an independent state with a full international and legal personality?' The question was drafted with the help of the EU. As in Montenegro, the question on the ballot on Eritrean independence from Ethiopia in 1993 was drafted by an international committee. Having been advised by the United Nations, the parties opted for the question 'Do you want Eritrea to be independent?'

Another example of a simple question was provided by the UN-organised referendum in South Sudan in 2011. In this referendum the voters – many of whom were illiterate – were presented with two images and the text in both Arabic and English saying either 'separation' or 'unity'. During negotiations between the Sudanese government in Khartoum and the pro-independence Sudan People's Liberation Movement (SPLM), the latter expressed reservations about the positive connotations of the word 'unity' and the negative connotations of the word 'separation'. However, on polling day, these 'positive' words did not sway the voters. Independence was supported by 99 per cent in a reasonably fair referendum that was monitored by the United Nations.

These examples do not conclusively prove that referendum questions have no effect on the outcome, but it is noteworthy that the attempts to use positive language in both Quebec and East Timor – and to a lesser degree in South Sudan – failed to sway the voters in massive numbers. Needless to say, the results do not tell us anything about the motives of the individual voters. But we have no evidence from qualitative or quantitative research that suggests that the question mattered, if anything, the result in East Timor and South Sudan show that those who attempted to use value-laden words went down to conclusive defeats.

**Who should be allowed to vote?**

As Zoran Oklopcic has noted 'if a democratic referendum purports to detect the will of "the people", this, however, only begs the logically preceding question: who is the people?' (Oklopcic 2012: 22). Who is a member of the *demos*? Who is a voter? Are you still a part of the demos if you leave the country, or are you then merely a part of the *ethnos*? It is questionable whether those living outside a jurisdiction have thereby forfeited their right to vote.

Some litigation in Europe suggest as much. For example, in an *obiter dictum* in *Matthews v United Kingdom*, the European Court of Human Rights found that: 'persons who are unable to take part in elections because they live outside the jurisdiction ... have weakened the link between themselves and the jurisdiction, and can consequently not claim a right to vote' (*Matthews v United Kingdom* 1999: 64). This ruling was recently reinforced by *Schindler v United Kingdom*, Though in the latter case, the European Court of Human Rights held that, 'the matter may need to be kept under review in so far as attitudes in European democratic society evolve'. It continued that 'the margin of appreciation enjoyed by the State in this area still remains a wide one', and as a consequence citizens of countries that are signatories to the European Convention of Human Rights do not have a right to vote in national elections and referendums. But the law may change as 'there is a clear trend in favour of allowing voting by non-residents, with forty-four States granting the right to vote to citizens resident abroad otherwise than on State service' (*Schindler v United Kingdom* 2013: 115). However, it is still permissible to deny non-residents the right to vote. This might justify the exclusion of Montenegrins living in Serbia at the time of the 2006 referendum. Conversely, there are examples of voters in the Diaspora being entitled to vote. In both East Timor in 1999 and in Eritrea in 1993, voters living outside the country were allowed to vote. However, in the both cases this inclusion of expats was, arguably, justified on account of the displacement that had taken place due to violent conflict. Given recent litigation and the precedent from the recent referendum in Montenegro, it seems consistent with international norms that Scots living in England, Wales, Northern Ireland, or other parts of the world were not entitled to vote in the 2014 referendum.

## Conclusion

'The necessities of international policy may now and then allow or even demand a plebiscite [but] in most cases they will not allow it' (Oppenheim 1912: 274). Thus wrote the international lawyer Oppenheim in 1912. It is testament to the changes in international politics that referendums now seem to be the norm rather than the exception. However, we should not jump to the conclusion that Oppenheim's view is bound to be obsolete in perpetuity. Referendums on secession have come in waves. Beginning in the 1860s when several of the confederate states seceded from the Union in the United States (and hence precipitated the Civil War), secessionist referendums were held in Norway (1905), the Philippines (1935), and unsuccessfully in Western Australia in 1933.

Generally referendums on independence only became common after the fall of the Soviet Union, possibly because a number of Western states insisted on the ratification of declarations of independence in referendums. But referendums were also held as a kind of national celebration of the newly established unity. If anything can be concluded from the *tour d'horizon* of the fifty-nine cases of independence referendums in this chapter, it is this; all cases seem to follow unique patterns and trajectories. Despite superficial similarities (as reported by Qvortrup 2014), there is little that links the South Rhodesian referendum in 1964 with the Ukrainian plebiscite in 1991. And these two votes have little in common with the independence referendums in, respectively, Jamaica in 1961 and in Quebec in 1995.

Most referendums have been held in countries with relatively weak democratic institutions. The often huge yes majorities suggest that the votes are not always free and fair. But in the few independence referendums that have been held in democratic countries, it seems that governments have tended to win the plebiscites if they have taken office recently and only if there is broad popular support for independence before the campaign. Given the SNP has been in office since 2007 and that support for independence before the campaign stood at 33 per cent, this was not a good omen for those supporting Scottish independence, although the margin of 'victory' for the opponents was much narrower than many had expected prior to the vote.

Referendums have on occasion resulted in the exacerbation of ethnic conflict, as occurred in Bosnia-Herzegovina and in East Timor. However, generally speaking referendums are not correlated with civil war. Most of the debate about the referendum has revolved around procedural questions, such as should there be a special majority requirement? Who should be allowed to vote? Independence is an irreversible event. For this reason, it could be argued there should be a special majority requirement in such a plebiscite. While there are examples of special majority requirements in countries with impeccable democratic records – such as Canada – these are rare. More often than not such requirements have been introduced as an obstructionist tactic, such as in Israel or the Soviet Union. Given that most referendums on independence have not been subject to a supermajority requirement, to demand a special majority in the Scottish referendum would not have been warranted. As a general rule, only voters living in the jurisdiction are allowed to vote. To be sure expats and displaced voters were allowed to vote in the independence referendums in Eritrea and South Sudan. But in Montenegro in 2006 only those living in the country, no matter what ethnicity they were, were entitled to vote. This precedent and recent case law from the European Court of Human Rights suggested that the Scottish government was justified in only allowing voters living in Scotland to vote. However the issue of voting rights for non-resident citizens is, as the European Court of Human Rights noted in *Schindler v United Kingdom*, to be 'kept under review' as 'there is a clear trend in favour of allowing voting by non-residents'. Referendums on independence seem likely to keep constitutional and international lawyers as well as their political scientist colleagues busy for years to come.

## Legal references

*Clarity Act* (2000) c. 26 [assented to 29 June 2000].
*Matthews v United Kingdom* (1999) 28 ECtHR 361.
*Schindler v United Kingdom* [2013] ECHR 19840/09.

## References

Beogang, H. (2002) 'Referenda as a solution to the national-identity-identity/boundary question: an emperical assessment of the theoretical literature', *Alternatives*, 27(1): 67–97.

Bjørklund, T. (2003) *Om Folkeavstemninger: Norge og Norden 1905–1994*, Oslo: Universitetsforlaget.

Brady, H. E. and Kaplan, C. S. (1994) 'Eastern Europe and the former Soviet Union', in D. Butler and A. Ranney (eds) *Referendums around the World: The growing use of direct democracy*, London: Macmillan: 174–217.

Chandler, D. P. (1993) *The Tragedy of Cambodian History: Politics, war, and revolution since 1945*, New Haven, Yale University Press.

De Gaulle, C. (1971) *Memoirs of Hope*, London: Weidenfeld & Nicolson.

Fenech, D. (2003) 'The 2003 Maltese EU referendum and general election', *West European Politics*, 26(3): 163–70.

Friedrich, C. J. and Brzezinski, Z. K. (1965) *Totalitarian Dictatorship*, Cambridge, MA: Harvard University Press.

Key, V. O. Jr (1968) *The Responsible Electorate: Rationality in presidential voting 1936–60*, New York: Vintage Books.

Marks, T. A. (1974) 'Djibouti: France's strategic toehold in Africa', *African Affairs*, 73(290): 95–104.

Marx, K. (1946 [1871]) 'Brief an L. Kugelmann', in *Werke Karl Marx and Friedrich Engels Werke, Vol. 33*, Berlin: Dietz, 205–6.

Mattern, J. (1921) *The Employment of the Plebiscite in the Determination of Sovereignty*, doctoral thesis, Baltimore, MD: Johns Hopkins University.

Morris, C. (2014) 'Referendums in Oceania', in M. Qvortrup (ed.) *Referendums around the World: The continued growth of direct democracy*, Basingstoke: Palgrave, 218–45.

Musgrave, T. (2003) 'Western Australian Secessionist Movement', *Macquarie Law Journal*, 3: 95–110.

Nohlen, D. (2005) *Elections in the Americas: A data handbook*, Oxford: Oxford University Press.

Oklopcic, Z. (2012) 'Independence referendums and democratic theory in Quebec and Montenegro', *Nationalism and Ethnic Politics*, 18(1): 22–42.

Onslow, S. (2005) 'A question of timing: South Africa and Rhodesia's Unilateral Declaration of Independence, 1964–65', *Cold War History*, 5(2): 129–59.

Oppenheim, L. F. L. (1912) *International Law*, London: Longman, Green & Co.

Pavkovic, A and Radan, P. (2007) *Creating New States: Theory and practice of secession*, Aldershot: Ashgate.

Qvortrup, M. (2014) *Referendums and Ethnic Conflict*, Philadelphia PA: University of Pennsylvania Press.

Radan, P. (2000) 'Post-secession international borders: a critical analysis of the opinions of Badinter', *Melbourne Law Review*, 50(1): 47–64.

Radchenko, S. (2015) 'The truth about Mongolia's independence 70 years ago', *Diplomat*, available at http://thediplomat.com/2015/10/the-truth-about-mongolias-independence-70-years-ago/ (accessed 15 April 2016).

Renan, E. (1996) *Qu'est-ce qu'une Nation?: et autres écrits politiques*, Paris: Imprimerie nationale.

Schmidt, E. (2009) 'Anticolonial nationalism in French West Africa: what made Guinea unique?' *African Studies Review*, 52(02): 1–34.

Wallace, E. (1962) 'The West Indies Federation: decline and fall', *International Journal*, 17(3): 269–88.

Wambaugh, S. (1920) *A Monograph on Plebiscites: With a collection of official documents*, New York, Oxford University Press.

Warntz, W. (1955) 'A methodological consideration of some geographic aspects of the Newfoundland referendum on confederation with Canada, 1948', *Canadian Geographer/Le Géographe canadien*, 2(6): 39–49.

*Chapter Six*

# The Scottish Independence Referendum: A Model of Good Practice in Direct Democracy?

*Stephen Tierney*

## Introduction

On 18 September 2014, 55 per cent of Scots voted no to the proposition: 'Should Scotland be an independent country?' Inevitably during the campaign attention was focused upon the outcome of the vote and major substantive issues of contention such as currency relations between an independent Scotland and the United Kingdom, and the ease or difficulty with which an independent Scotland would achieve membership of the European Union. What was often overlooked was the fact that the credibility of the outcome would ultimately depend upon the legitimacy of the referendum process itself. Given the heat that the debate generated in the last few weeks of campaigning, it was of the highest importance that the process of the referendum itself be fair and be seen to be so by both sides: in short, that the result was agreed to, even if it was not agreed with, by losers as well as winners.

In this chapter I will assess the referendum process. I will do so in light of the legislation passed by the Scottish Parliament to regulate the referendum but also against the broader context of UK-wide referendum law within which the Scottish law was made. I will begin by outlining broader work that considers whether referendums in general are capable of offering an environment within which ordinary citizens can make a reasoned and deliberative decision about matters of the highest constitutional importance. This will offer a theoretical framework with which to assess the Scottish referendum process. The ultimate question that the chapter poses is this: did the regulatory regime for the Scottish referendum help create a platform for the meaningful participation of citizens?

### *The referendum pathology: practice not principle?*

Referendums are paradoxical. For some, they represent an ideal model of democracy. The voters are called upon to speak as one unified people, deciding on an issue directly without the mediation of politicians. The referendum gives a directly determining voice to the demos in a way that captures neatly both the people's popular sovereignty and the political equality of all citizens. What could be more democratic? For others, however, the referendum is a dangerous device because it in fact imperils democracy, which can only be properly effected through exclusively representative institutions, and as a result the referendum is best excluded from processes of constitutional change (*see* Qvortrup, Chapter Five in this volume).

Elsewhere I have identified three main objections that inform the scepticism of the latter position: that referendums lend themselves by definition to elite control and hence manipulation by the organisers of the referendum ('the elite control syndrome'); that there is an in-built tendency of the referendum process merely to aggregate preformed opinions rather than to foster meaningful deliberation ('the deliberation deficit'); and that referendums consolidate and even reify simple majoritarian decision making at the expense of minority and individual interests ('the majoritarian danger') (Tierney 2012). I have argued, however, that these are problems of practice not principle, and that they can be overcome by good practice in the design and regulation of the referendum based upon principles of popular participation, public reasoning and pluralism in decision making. In particular, properly constructed electoral law and models of regulation can help construct a 'deliberative referendum' (Tierney 2013).

The referendum in Scotland offers an ideal case study with which to test this hypothesis for the following reasons. First, it was organised within a healthy and fully functioning democracy. Second, it was long in the planning: the Scottish Government announced its intention to hold a referendum in January 2012 (see Scottish Government 2012), some two-and-a-half years before the vote itself, thus offering a lengthy span of time within which channels of deliberative participation might be fostered. Third, the UK already had in place a model of detailed regulation of referendums (Political Parties, Elections and Referendums Act 2000, see UK Government 2000) which, inter alia, created an independent Electoral Commission and invested it with a detailed oversight role in UK referendums; the existing UK legal regime was very influential in the framing of the Scottish referendum process. Fourthly, the referendum process was framed against, and given additional legal authority and political credibility by, the Edinburgh Agreement between the UK and Scottish governments (UK Government and Scottish Government 2012), the aim of which was to ensure the referendum delivered 'a fair test and a decisive expression of the views of people in Scotland and a result that everyone will respect' (see Scottish Government 2012). And finally, the referendum was regulated by two statutes passed by the Scottish Parliament – the Scottish Independence Referendum (Franchise) Act 2013 ('the Scottish Franchise Act', see UK Government 2013b), and the Scottish Independence Referendum Act 2013 ('the Scottish Referendum Act', see UK Government 2013a) – which together offered a comprehensive framework of rules and constraints.

I will, therefore, assess how well this legislation has served first, to constrain elite control, and second, to help foster meaningful deliberation, particularly among citizens. Scotland is not a divided society with readily identifiable minorities whose interests are clearly imperilled by an exercise in majoritarian decision-making. Therefore, I will not discuss the third criticism of referendums ('the majoritarian danger') further here. In passing though, it is notable that the referendum decision was reached upon the basis of a simple '50 per cent plus one' majority rule. This has been a controversial issue elsewhere, particularly in Canada (Tierney 2004), but it was never a focus of debate in the Scottish context, and again for this reason I will not address it further here.

### *The Scottish Referendum: constraining elite control?*

The 'elite control syndrome' is generally the main objection to referendums. The charge is that referendums are organised by governments to effect political goals and are therefore only staged when the prospects of a successful outcome (from the government's viewpoint) are favourable. To this end an executive is able to shape – indeed manipulate – the various elements of process design to achieve this result. As well as the initiation power they can also set the question, choose the date, fix the franchise, decide whether and if so how the referendum will be regulated, and determine the funding and spending rules for the campaign.

### How did the Scottish process measure up in response to this problem?

In a sense any referendum is 'elite-controlled', as indeed is any electoral process, if this is taken to mean organised by the established institutions of the state. The central issue is how this power is allocated among institutions. The feature that tends to set alarm bells ringing is when the organisation power in a referendum, or indeed any election, rests exclusively in the hands of the executive without a meaningful role for the legislature or for any level of independent oversight.

The first issue is the decision to set the referendum itself. Some countries, for example Australia and Ireland, offer constitutional regulation of the initiation power; a referendum is a legally required part of the constitutional amendment process. By contrast the UK leaves the initiation of referendums to the discretion of the central government as we have seen in the referendums of 1975, 1979, 1997, 1998 and 2011 (*see* Table 6.1).

There is of course no explicit constitutional recognition of referendums in an unwritten constitutional system, although there has been some move towards making future referendums a legal requirement in the devolution context (e.g. Northern Ireland Act 1998, section 1; Government of Wales Act 2006, Part IV). No such reference to referendums appears in the Scotland Act 1998 and indeed when the Scottish Government announced its intention to hold a referendum in January 2012 a dispute ensued as to whether the devolved institutions of government in Scotland had the power to do so (Anderson et al. 2012). There was an immediate rebuttal by the United Kingdom Government which challenged the legislative competence of the Scottish Parliament to pass this bill (Secretary of State for Scotland 2012). For a time the disagreement over the meaning of, in particular, section 29(3) of the Scotland Act, was intractable and it seemed as though this issue might find its way to the United Kingdom Supreme Court for adjudication. But in the end, and to the surprise of many, on 15 October 2012 a deal was reached between the two governments (UK Government and Scottish Government 2012). This, and the associated 'memorandum of agreement',

*Table 6.1: Referendums in the United Kingdom*

| Place | Date | Issue | Turnout | Result |
|---|---|---|---|---|
| Northern Ireland | 8 March 1973 | Remain part of the UK | 58.7 | Approved: 98.9 |
| Northern Ireland | 22 May 1998 | Belfast Agreement | 81.1 | Approved: 71.1 |
| Scotland | 1 March 1979 | Creation of a Scottish Assembly | 33 | Approved: 52 (did not meet threshold) |
| Wales | 1 March 1979 | Creation of a Welsh Assembly | 58.8 | Not approved: 79.7 |
| Scotland | 11 September 1997 | 1. Creation of a Scottish Parliament.<br>2. Devolution of limited tax-varying powers | 60.4 | 1. Approved: 74.3<br>2. Approved: 63.5 |
| Wales | 18 September 1997 | Creation of a National Assembly | 50.1 | Approved: 50.3 |
| England (London) | 7 May 1998 | GLA and Mayor | 34.6 | Approved: 72 |
| England (North East) | 4 November 2004 | North East England regional assembly | 47.8 | Not approved: 78 |
| Wales | 3 March 2011 | Devolution of further powers to the National Assembly | 35.4 | Approved: 63.5 |
| Scotland | 18 September 2014 | Independence | 84.7 | Not approved: 55.3 |
| United Kingdom | 5 June 1975 | Continued EC membership | 64.5 | Approved: 67.2 |
| United Kingdom | 5 May 2011 | Electoral system: Alternative Vote | 42.2 | Not approved: 67.9 |

provided that the referendum should have a clear legal base; be legislated for by the Scottish Parliament; and be conducted so as to command the confidence of parliaments, governments and people. This was formalised by an Order in Council (per Scotland Act 1998, section 30) which devolved to the Scottish Parliament the competence to legislate for a referendum on independence which had to be held before the end of 2014 (UK Government 2013c: para 3).

The result therefore was an intergovernmental agreement on the initiation power, which also outlined further elements of the referendum process and the pathway by which these were to be drawn up. In this respect the Scottish referendum bears healthy comparison with other UK referendums which were instigated solely by the central government, on occasion for political purposes. For example, in the early 1970s the Labour Party feared that a damaging split could emerge over membership of the European Economic Community (EEC) and decided that a referendum would help avoid this by allowing a free vote for MPs including ministers. James Callaghan described the referendum as a 'lifeboat' into which the party was climbing in order to see off the danger of fission (Butler and Kitzinger 1976: 282). Labour returned to the referendum in similar circumstances in relation to devolution. Proposals put forward in 1976 for assemblies for Scotland and Wales were widely opposed within the party. Vernon Bogdanor comments that the promise of a referendum which accompanied these proposals 'was a device that would enable Labour backbenchers opposed to devolution nevertheless to vote for it in the House of Commons while campaigning against it in the referendum' (Bogdanor 1981: 42). The bill was in the end withdrawn in March 1977. But when it was revived in 1977–8, referendums were again proposed and these were held in 1979. Again Bogdanor points to how the 1979 referendums were used 'to defuse an issue' (Bogdanor 1981: 45).

The AV (Alternative Vote) referendum in 2011 was also instigated for party political purposes. The decision to hold a referendum on this issue was the result of a political deal by the two parties forming the coalition government in 2010. One consequence of using a constitutional referendum as a political fix in this way (which also tightly circumscribed the model of electoral system that would be presented as an alternative to first-past-the-post in the referendum) is that the issue to be put to the people is not subjected to wider deliberation; instead of a detailed discussion of electoral reform and the opportunity for all of the options to be fully aired, only one model, which proved to be difficult to understand and indeed to support, was put to the people.[1] This process came in for criticism from a number of people giving evidence to the House of Lords inquiry on referendums (House of Lords 2009). And again we must also see the prospective EU referendum in this light. The promise to hold an in/out vote in 2016 is also a political device to confront the UKIP threat and to shore up a potential split in the Conservative Party; in the latter respect this proposal bears parallels with the 1975 referendum.

The initiation power is of course not the only issue within the elite control criticism. A second charge is that with this power the executive also has carte blanche in framing the process for the referendum itself: determining the timing of the referendum, the setting of the question, defining the franchise, regulating the campaign and ballot procedure, setting funding and spending rules, etc., and also determining the extent, if any, of independent oversight of these different components. But in fact when we look to the UK experience there is a growing body of legislation and good practice that now operates to regulate these various process components and in doing so to overcome the risks of elite manipulation.

For over a decade UK referendums have operated on the basis of a dedicated referendum law (the Political Parties, Elections and Referendums Act 2000, or PPERA), which emerged as a result of the report by the Committee on Standards

1. This can be contrasted with the way in which New Zealand used referendums to test the popularity of different electoral models (see Vowles et al. 1995).

in Public Life ('Neill Report', 1998). In addition there tends also to be tailored legislation that sets further rules specific to a particular referendum (e.g. the Parliamentary Voting System and Constituencies Act 2011). Notably the PPERA 2000 applies only to referendums organised by the Westminster Parliament and so did not regulate the proposed referendum in Scotland. However its terms acted as an important benchmark for the Scottish Government in drafting the Scottish Franchise Bill and the Scottish Referendum Bill,[2] and for the Scottish Parliament deliberating upon these.

PPERA also created the Electoral Commission which was another recommendation of the Neill Committee, while the Commission's supervisory and investigatory powers were extended by the Political Parties and Elections Act 2009. The Commission has various duties mostly related to funding and spending rules but also in relation to the intelligibility of the referendum question. This body is again central in the constraint of illegitimate elite control. As a creature of PPERA however, the Electoral Commission had no automatic role in relation to the Scottish referendum. Nonetheless such a role was in time guaranteed by the Scottish Franchise Act and Scottish Referendum Act, and by the actions of the Scottish Government. The Commission's role will be discussed particularly in the next section of this chapter, and from this it will be clear that it played a hands-on role across a number of areas including the setting of the question, the provision of information to citizens, the regulation of funding and spending, and the management of the mechanics of registration and voting. For now it might be noted that early on in the process (September 2013) the Commission also conducted a full review to highlight any risks 'while there is still time to address them'. It concluded: 'preparations are on track to deliver a well-run poll' (Electoral Commission 2013b).

And finally, in discussing the regime of regulation in broad terms it should be noted also that the Scottish Referendum Act includes sanctions for violations of the referendum rules, both civil sanctions (Schedule 6) and criminal offences (Schedule 7) in relation to various categories of electoral malpractice; and once again the Electoral Commission was given an important role in enforcing the former.

In concluding this section we find that in general a great deal of discretion exists within the UK as to when and on what issues referendums should be held. But this is particularly the case in relation to the powers of the UK Government as we saw with the AV referendum and in relation to a referendum on EU membership. One of the recommendations of a House of Lords inquiry on referendums was

2. The Edinburgh Agreement provided: 'Both governments agree that the principles underpinning the existing framework for referendums held under Acts of the UK Parliament – which aim to guarantee fairness – should apply to the Scottish independence referendum. Part 7 of the Political Parties, Elections and Referendums Act 2000 (PPERA) 2, provides a framework for referendums delivered through Acts of Parliament, including rules about campaign finance, referendum regulation, oversight and conduct' (UK Government and Scottish Government 2012: para 2).

that, if referendums are to be a feature of British democracy, there should be legal regulation of the types of issue that ought to be subject of referendums and of how and when these issues might be brought directly before the people (House of Lords 2009).

By dint of the limited competence of the Scottish Parliament and the subsequent uncertainty concerning its power to hold a referendum, the initiation power for the Scottish referendum was in fact regulated more fulsomely and by a more plural array of actors than would an equivalent process organised by the UK Government. The result was a complex regime of regulation encompassing three distinct elements: the first was the primary role of the Scottish Government in initiating the proposal and the Scottish Parliament, which was required to pass the key legislation. The second was the Scotland Act 1998 which delimits the powers of these two bodies, ensuring that each of these roles was circumscribed by the boundaries of devolved competence. And the third was a significant role for the UK Government and Parliament through a combination of the Edinburgh Agreement and the section 30 Order, with the latter, for the avoidance of any doubt, transferring any necessary powers to the Scottish Parliament to legislate for the holding of the referendum. As we will see in the next section, this combination of regulatory elements served significantly to constrain the powers of the Scottish Government.

## Facilitating deliberation?

The second main criticism of referendums, by which they are often held in contrast to the purported merits of representative democracy, is that public reasoning, which allows for the informed reflection and discussion of ideas before decisions are reached, is absent from referendum processes. Various assumptions underpin this idea: referendums tend to be held quickly by way of a snap poll organised at the behest of the government; voters are presented with an issue that is itself confusing and can be made worse by an unintelligible question; voters themselves lack the time, sufficient interest in the matter at stake or the competence to understand or engage properly with the issue, and in effect turn up at the polling station, if indeed they bother to do so at all, in an unreflective manner, often following party cues in determining how to vote.

In this section I will consider a number of elements in the regulatory design of the Scottish referendum, assessing these against the benchmark of deliberative participation: the franchise (by which the inclusiveness of the poll can be assessed) and the participation of citizens in the referendum; the question, both its intelligibility and how the determination of this was overseen; the time and information available to voters to deliberate upon the issue; the sixteen-week 'referendum period' and twenty-eight-day purdah period within which the activities of political actors were regulated; and the spending and funding rules, designed to ensure that the campaign was not dominated by one campaign or powerful interests.

## Franchise

In a mass popular engagement with democracy both participation and deliberation are vital. It is not enough that those who make the decision do so in a reflective and discursive way, it is also essential that the process should generate the widespread engagement of citizens across the polity if the exercise is to be truly legitimate. That the franchise is defined in a properly inclusive way is therefore the first step in achieving this goal. The body of voters in the Scottish referendum was largely uncontroversial. The franchise for the referendum was the same as for Scottish Parliament elections and local government elections (UK Government 2013b: section 2), mirroring the franchise used in the Scottish devolution referendum in 1997. One consequence is that EU citizens who are resident in Scotland would be able to vote in the independence referendum.

One major difference from the 1997 franchise, however, was the provision in the Scottish Franchise Act extending the vote to those aged sixteen and seventeen (UK Government 2013b: section 2(1)(a)). This was a radical departure; never before have people under the age of eighteen been entitled to vote in a major British election or referendum (UK Government 1983: section 1(d)). Another notable provision of the Scottish Franchise Act excluded convicted persons from voting in the referendum if they are detained in a penal institution (UK Government 2013b: section 3). This has been a controversial topic in the United Kingdom ever since the European Court of Human Rights ruled that the blanket ban on prisoner voting in UK elections violated Article 3 of Protocol 1 of the European Convention on Human Rights (*Hirst v the United Kingdom (No 2)* [2005] ECHR 681). It seemed clear, however, that section 3 of the Franchise Act did not violate the Convention since, A3P1 guarantees 'the free expression of the opinion of the people in *the choice of the legislature*' (emphasis added), which is generally taken to refer exclusively to parliamentary elections and to exclude referendums (Tierney 2013). This view has been endorsed by Lord Glennie in the Outer House of the Court of Session (*Moohan and others, Petitioners* [2013] CSOH 199), and subsequently by the Inner House (*Moohan and others v Lord Advocate. Reclaiming Motion* [2014] CSIH 56) and the UK Supreme Court (*Moohan and Another v Lord Advocate* UKSC 2014/0183 (24 June 2014).

Franchise is one thing, citizen engagement quite another. If citizens are simply not interested in the referendum then the very legitimacy of the process comes into question. It may simply be that the subject matter of the referendum is an issue that most people think fit for an exercise in direct democracy. It is clear from the turnout and result in 2011 that many people did not view the AV proposition to be an important issue (turnout of 42.2 per cent; 68 per cent voted no and 32 per cent voted yes). The referendum in Wales in 2011, with a turnout of 35.4 per cent, also failed to mobilise public interest.

The level of debate and subsequent turnout demonstrate that the Scottish referendum did not suffer from this fate. Astonishingly 4,285,323 people (97 per cent of the electorate) registered to vote and in the end 84.7 per cent turned out, the highest figure for any UK electoral event since the introduction of universal suffrage, significantly trumping the 65.1 per cent who voted in the 2010 UK general election and the 50.6 per cent who bothered to turn out for the 2011 Scottish parliamentary elections. This is even more remarkable when we consider that the franchise was extended to sixteen- and seventeen-year-olds, which created a significant logistical task for those registering new voters while taking care of data protection and other issues in relation to young people (UK Government 2013b: section 9).

Turnout is of course only one marker of participation. The story we now hear time and time again from voters and campaigners alike is that citizens felt greatly empowered by the referendum and the role they had in making such a huge decision. Evidence is emerging of the extent to which people sought out information about the issue at stake and engaged vociferously with one another at home, in the workplace, in pubs and public meetings, and to an unprecedented degree in British politics, on social media through online newspaper comment sections, Twitter, Facebook, blogs, etc. (Henderson et al. 2014).[3] My own evidence is merely anecdotal, but as someone who lived through the referendum campaign I can say that in the month before the vote I experienced a level of public engagement with a major political issue the like of which I have never known.

## Question: the intelligibility test

Do citizens understand the question? If not, then meaningful deliberation in any referendum is not possible. PPERA gives the Electoral Commission an important role in overseeing question setting in referendum processes organised by the Westminster Parliament. Where a bill is introduced into Parliament that provides for the holding of a referendum, and this bill specifies the wording of the referendum question, the Commission 'shall consider the wording of the referendum question, and shall publish a statement of any views of the Commission as to the intelligibility of that question' (UK Government 2000: section 104(2)). Notably the Electoral Commission goes about its task of assessing intelligibility by addressing what people really understand, convening focus groups to test the question empirically, assessing how well it is understood by people, etc. (Electoral Commission 2010, 2013a).

Despite the fact that PPERA does not regulate the Scottish process, and therefore the Electoral Commission has no legally guaranteed role in relation to the 2014 referendum, the Scottish Government decided to send its proposed question for review by the Electoral Commission. This process was concluded quickly and the Commission reported back suggesting a change to the question.[4]

3. See also Applied Quantitative Methods Network project (AQMeN, http://aqmen.ac.uk, accessed 15 April 2016).

4. The Scottish Government's proposed question was: 'Do you agree that Scotland should be an independent country? Yes/No'. The Electoral Commission took the view that 'based on our research and taking into account what we heard from people and/organisations who submitted their views on the question, we consider that the proposed question is not neutral because the phrase 'Do you agree ...?' could lead people towards voting "yes".' They therefore recommended the following question: 'Should Scotland be an independent country? Yes/No' (see Electoral Commission 2013a).

This was accepted by the Scottish Government and this new question was included in the Scottish Referendum Act (UK Government 2013a: section 1(2); Black 2013).

The Electoral Commission also offered the view that the clarity of the question hinged not only on its syntax but upon the content of the independence proposal: 'clarity about how the terms of independence will be decided would help voters understand how the competing claims made by referendum campaigners before the referendum will be resolved' (Electoral Commission 2013a: para 5.43).[5] This is an interesting comment, reflecting as it does the requirement that a fully deliberative process is only possible if citizens know what they are voting for.[6] The Scottish Government published a White Paper in November 2013, which set out its vision of independence (Scottish Government 2013), followed by a White Paper and draft Scottish Independence Bill, which sought to lay out proposals for an interim and permanent constitutions for an independent Scotland (Scottish Government 2014). Each of these was of course heavily criticised by the UK Government and by the Better Together campaign. The November White Paper in particular led to a series of papers by the UK Government contesting many of the claims made in the White Paper. In the end, and surely inevitably, citizens were left with a debate in the context of the referendum campaign, rather than any agreed set of 'facts' about what independence would look like.

## Time to understand the issue?

Another prerequisite of serious deliberation is that people have time to consider the issue upon which they are being asked to vote. An element of control that was left to the Scottish Government by the Edinburgh Agreement was the timing of the referendum and in January 2012 it set its course for a referendum some two-and-a-half years hence. This timing was of course strategic. The Scottish Government saw the autumn of 2014 as a propitious time. It allowed the SNP sufficient time to make the case for independence and it would coincide with a number of significant events: the anniversary of the Battle of Bannockburn, the Commonwealth Games, and even the Ryder Cup in Gleneagles. It would also come shortly before a UK general election that it was anticipated would distract the UK parties and perhaps make them less inclined to work together.

5. See generally paras 5.41–5.44, e.g. 'We recommend that both Governments should agree a joint position, if possible, so that voters have access to agreed information about what would follow the referendum. The alternative – two different explanations – could cause confusion for voters rather than make things clearer' (Electoral Commission 2013a: para 5.43).

6. One of the main criticisms of the Quebec referendum in 1995 was that the proposal of sovereignty and partnership was not well understood by citizens (see Tierney 2004: 293–9).

But, from the perspective of deliberative participation, a beneficial side-effect of this procrastination was that the election debate was conducted over a very long period of time, allowing each side to make its case in full and giving citizens time and space to consider the issues.

A related issue is how fixed the date is. One controversy that arose in the Quebec referendum in 1995 was that the date was changed in the course of the campaign from June to October as opinion polls in the spring showed that the measure would likely fail (Young 1999). In fact the date of 30 October was not fixed until 7 September, and not formally adopted by the National Assembly until 20 September. Similarly, the French referendum in 2005 on the EU Constitutional Treaty was brought forward as the government sensed support for the no side was growing (EU Business Partners 2015, see also Marthaler 2005). Originally planned for the second half of 2005, on 4 March it was announced that the French referendum would be brought forward to 29 May. These are examples of how elites with too much power can manipulate the timing of the vote to their advantage.

This issue did not arise in Scotland. The timing of the Scottish referendum was in part regulated by the Edinburgh Agreement and subsequent section 30 Order, which set a condition that the referendum must be held before the end of 2014. The actual date of 18 September 2014 was announced by the Scottish Government on 21 March 2013 and included in the Scottish Independence Referendum Bill. This was then passed into law and there was no suggestion at any stage that it might be changed. Other important timing issues included in the legislation are the sixteen-week 'referendum period' (UK Government 2013a: Schedule 4, Part 3) and the four-week purdah period (UK Government 2013a: Schedule 4, para 25), discussed below.

To conclude, one of the standard criticisms of referendums from the perspective of deliberation is that they are held too hastily without time for proper deliberation of the issues. This was clearly not a problem in the Scottish context where the referendum was proposed some thirty-three months before it was held and where both campaigns had almost two years from the conclusion of the Edinburgh Agreement to explain their respective cases to the voters. The timing was also regulated by both the Edinburgh Agreement and subsequent legislation, which fixed the date and gave certainty to both campaigns and to citizens as to when the referendum would take place.

## Information: is there evidence voters understood the issue?

Citizens cannot deliberate properly without access to sufficient, reliable information. In many ways such an environment depends more upon the health of a particular democracy and of its civil society than it does upon legal regulation. Indeed, excessive regulation can in fact serve to inhibit the free flow of ideas.

In the Scottish referendum there were many sources of information: both governments,[7] each campaign group, other registered participants in the referendum campaign, and various other sources in civil society,[8] including the media, and academia.[9] As observed above, a particularly notable source of information was also social media, with Twitter, Facebook and blogs playing a major role in the dissemination of ideas and also in discussion and debate.

The provision of information by the two campaigns has been touched upon in the context of the November White Paper, but other related issues include the provision, and indeed the very possibility, of providing independent or neutral information to voters through the Electoral Commission, and second, the provision of a state subsidy to the main referendum campaigns to provide a mail-shot to households. In the UK both practices have become standard practice.

Taking the second issue first, PPERA contains the option of allowing each of the main campaign organisations in a referendum – if the campaigns register themselves as such – one free mail-shot setting out their views; this can be adopted by the enabling legislation for a particular referendum (UK Government 2000: Schedule 12, para 1). The section 30 Order extended this power from PPERA, thereby allowing the Scottish Parliament to offer such a free mailing to each of the two main organisations (UK Government 2013c: Article 4(1)).

As regards the provision of neutral information, during the AV referendum campaign the Electoral Commission sent an information booklet to all 27.8 million households in the UK explaining what elections were taking place, the referendum question, how to take part in the referendum and giving 'an independent explanation of the "first past the post" and "alternative vote" systems'. The booklet was also supported by a multi-media advertising campaign (Electoral Commission 2011b). But this raises the question about how much the Electoral Commission can in fact say. The booklet set out briefly what the two models of voting on offer were, but did not engage with the arguments for and against each. Instead it simply stated: 'Campaigners in the referendum will explain why they think you should vote "yes" (to use the "alternative vote" system) or "no" (to continue using the "first past the post" system). Look out for information from them' (Electoral Commission 2011a).[10]

The Scottish Referendum Act builds upon this practice. Among a number of statutory duties, the Commission was given the task of promoting public awareness and understanding in Scotland about the referendum, the referendum question,

7. We have noted 'Scotland's Future' above (Scottish Government 2013). In June 2014 the UK government sent a sixteen-page booklet called 'What staying in the UK means for Scotland' to every household in Scotland, setting out the case for the no side (Macnab 2014).
8. See for example on the franchise and mechanics of voting issued by the National Association of Citizens Advice Bureaux (http://adviceguide.org.uk, accessed 15 April 2016).
9. For example, see the major ESRC 'Future of the UK and Scotland' project (http://esrc.ac.uk, accessed 15 April 2016).
10. This has been criticised by Richard Wyn Jones for its lack of content (see Scottish Parliament 2013a).

and voting in the referendum (UK Government 2013a). This was always going to be a very challenging duty in light of the deep disagreement between the two campaigns about what was meant by independence (Tierney 2014). It was always hard to see how the Electoral Commission could attempt to produce an objective account of a number of highly technical and fiercely contested issues, concerning not only international relations but also defence, economic relations, the question of a currency union, the disentanglement of the welfare state, national debt, etc., particularly when so many features of the post-referendum landscape would be contingent upon negotiations between the two governments in the event of a majority yes vote. Indeed it was argued in evidence before the Scottish Parliament Referendum Bill Committee that it was simply not possible to perform such a role in a neutral way.[11]

In the end the Electoral Commission intimated that it would 'not seek to explain to voters what independence means' but would offer information 'aimed at ensuring that all eligible electors are registered and know how to cast their vote' (see evidence of John McCormick (Electoral Commissioner for Scotland) to the Scottish Parliament Referendum (Scotland) Bill Committee, Scottish Parliament 2013b). The Electoral Commission also concluded that both governments had a duty here to help explain the implications of either a yes or a no vote, and that a joint position on this would benefit voters. This was a brave attempt to improve the deliberative environment for citizens, even if in political terms such a joint position was never likely to be achievable.

And so on 18 June the Commission announced the publication of a booklet that would go to all households with information on the voting mechanics. Rather than seek to explain the issue of independence the booklet instead contained campaign statements from both the designated lead campaigners, and a joint statement by the Scottish and UK governments on the process that would follow the referendum (Electoral Commission 2014b). Electoral Commissioner for Scotland, John McCormick, said about the booklet: '[it] provides important, factual information for voters in advance of polling day and we have tested it with the public to ensure it gives them the information they need'. With regard to the joint statement by the UK and Scottish governments included in the booklet, John McCormick noted:

> During our question assessment process people told us they wanted impartial information about the referendum before they voted. Although we said we did not expect the terms of independence to be agreed before the vote, we called for clarity from both governments about what would happen in the event of a yes or a no vote.

And in the end this is all that was achievable in the document launched on 11 August 2014 (Electoral Commission 2014f). The two page joint statement at

11. See William Norton's evidence before the Referendum (Scotland) Bill Committee (Scottish Parliament 2013a).

the end of the document does however set out a useful summary of what would happen following a yes or a no vote. It does not try to explain what independence means but it does discuss the need for negotiations in the event of a yes vote, and the balance of devolved and reserved competences in the interim period.

## Referendum period and purdah

The greatest threat to a deliberative referendum in which citizens can consider the issues calmly and without undue influence arises in the period immediately preceding the vote. Inevitably this is also the period of greatest intensity in campaigning, and so, just as voters are taking more interest in the issue there is a particular risk of misinformation being fed to the public in part through distortions brought about by excessive, and potentially lop-sided, campaign spending.

The Scottish Referendum Act addressed this problem by two devices. First, it introduced a 'referendum period' (UK Government 2013a: Schedule 8) of sixteen weeks before the referendum within which the statutory regime of campaign regulation took effect, the main purpose of which was to impose limits on campaign expenditure (UK Government 2013a: Schedule 4, Part 3). The length of the period could perhaps be criticised on the grounds that it still left a substantial period of time following enactment of the legislation but before the referendum period began within which the two main referendum campaigns were not subject to these detailed provisions. And indeed PPERA offers flexibility here. It does not fix a specific length of time for every referendum period, provided it is more than ten weeks and less than six months (UK Government 2000: Section 102). The regulated period for the 1997 Scottish devolution referendum (held before PPERA was passed of course) was 119 days (seventeen weeks) and for the AV referendum in 2011 it was only eleven weeks. Sixteen weeks is therefore within the normal period for UK referendums. In addition, there was an additional practical concern. The sixteen-week period commenced shortly after the European parliamentary elections and it was felt by some that it would not have been practical to have two regulated periods operating at the same time in relation to different electoral processes.

Second, the Act also provided for what is commonly known as a 'purdah' period; called by the Act the 'relevant period'. This is common in UK elections. Again the Scottish Referendum Act reflected the existing UK legal regime. Under PPERA there is to be no promotional activity by government, local authorities or public bodies during the twenty-eight day relevant period prior to an election poll (UK Government 2000: section 125). This provision is largely replicated in the Scottish Referendum Act (UK Government 2013a: section 10 and Schedule 4, para 25) in relation to the Scottish Government and a wide range of other public bodies that must not engage in promotional activity in the four weeks prior to the referendum. The UK Government also committed to be bound by equivalent restrictions in the Edinburgh Agreement.[12] In general the purdah period was well respected, although it is open to debate whether the promise of more powers for Scotland in the event of a no vote, which was made repeatedly in the final weeks of the campaign violated the UK Government's obligations (Ross 2014). The argument was that these promises came from the UK political parties, in the most prominent case presented by former Prime Minster Gordon Brown (Johnson 2014), and not by the UK Government.

## Funding and spending

Funding and spending is such a central part of any electoral event, and so potentially destabilising to the deliberative participation of citizens, that it requires to be addressed as a separate category. The primary aim of the Scottish Referendum Act was to arrive at some degree of parity between the two campaigns. In this endeavour, as in its detailed provisions, the Scottish Referendum Act again largely reflects the PPERA regime.

PPERA is a serious attempt to address the funding and spending issue in detail with a view to a level playing field, while allowing for these rules to be tailored further from referendum to referendum. It contains a highly elaborate set of financial provisions (in fact the degree of elaboration has come in for some criticism, see Ghaleigh 2009). The fact that the Electoral Commission oversees the setting and implementation of these spending and funding limits, as well as other aspects of the process, also goes a long way to satisfying crucial conditions for effective deliberation.

Building upon the UK regime, the Scottish Referendum Act sought to ensure equality of arms between the two campaign groups. Each side in the campaign was able to apply to the Electoral Commission to be appointed as one of two 'designated organisations', and both the Yes Scotland and Better Together campaign groups intimated their respective intention to do so. They were designated as such in April 2014 (Electoral Commission 2014c). Notably the Act sought to deal with a criticism of PPERA relating to designation. PPERA does not permit the Electoral Commission to designate only one campaign organisation; either both (or more) must apply for designation or neither can (UK Government 2000: Section 108). In the referendum in Wales in 2011 the no campaign 'True Wales' did not apply, which led to a criticism that this was 'gaming', to prevent the yes campaign from attracting public funding and the other benefits of designation (see Scottish Parliament 2013a, Tierney and Suteu 2013). By contrast, the Scottish Referendum Act allows for designation by one side alone (UK Government 2013a: Schedule 4, para 5(3)), thereby avoiding this problem. In the end this was not an issue in practice as the two campaigns applied for official status, but it does illustrate that the Scottish Parliament addressed PPERA in detail and was keen to adopt its advantages and tinker with its potential disadvantages. This might well be a lesson for future UK-wide referendums.

Another difference from the PPERA model is that the Scottish Referendum Act did not provide for any public funding for designated organisations. This again

12. For a comment on this by Deputy First Minister Nicola Sturgeon, see Scottish Parliament (2013c: cols 554 and 560).

was a conscious departure from PPERA which does offer grants to designated organisations (UK Government 2000: section 110). The decision not to fund the 2014 referendum was a political one taken by the Scottish Government. It did not lead to any opposition either within the Scottish Parliament, or by either of the two main campaign groups perhaps because both campaigns expected to be amply funded by private donors.

Turning to the rules in detail, a 'Campaign Rules' provision within the Act created a regulatory regime through which funding, spending and reporting were administered (section 10 and Schedule 4). This is generally in line with standard PPERA rules. A 'Control of Donations' provision (Schedule 4, Part 5) indicates what types of donations were allowed and what constituted a 'permissible donor' (Schedule 4, para 1(2)). Under these provisions an application must be made for this status. There are also reporting requirements, which meant that reports on donations received required to be prepared every four weeks during the referendum period (Schedule 4, para 41).

## Spending limits

Within the Scottish Referendum Act there were four categories of actor entitled to spend money during the campaign period: Designated Organisations (which could each spend up to £1.5 million) (Schedule 4, para 18(1)); political parties as 'permitted participants' (see below) (Schedule 4, para 18(1)); other 'permitted participants' who could spend up to £150,000 (Schedule 4, para 18(1)); and any other participants spending less than £10,000, which means they did not require to register as permitted participants.

Political parties, as 'permitted participants', had a spending limit of either £3 million multiplied by their percentage share of the vote in the Scottish Parliament election of 2011, or £150,000 (whichever was greater). By this formula the spending limits for political parties represented in the Scottish Parliament are as follows:

Scottish National Party: £1,344,000
Scottish Labour Party: £834,000
Scottish Conservative & Unionist Party: £396,000
Scottish Liberal Democrats: £201,000
Scottish Green Party: £150,000

The Referendum Act also defined 'campaign expenses'. These included campaign broadcasts, advertising, material addressed to voters, market research or canvassing, press conferences or media relations, transport, rallies, public meetings or other events. This also extended to notional expenses such as use of/sum of property, services or facilities etc. (Schedule 4, paras 9 and 10). There were also detailed rules on reporting of expenditure (Referendum Act, Schedule 4, paras 20–4). The Electoral Commission had a power to issue guidance on the different kinds of expenses that qualify as campaign expenses: Schedule 4, para 10).

It seems that these rules led to a generally level playing field in terms of expenditure within the referendum period (also called the regulated period). For example, the total spending limit for the two pro-independence parties (SNP and Greens) was almost equal to that for the three unionist parties – Labour, Conservative and Liberal Democrat. It should also be observed that these rules reflect the spending limits recommended by the Electoral Commission (2014a) by which they were overseen, and which issued statements on the four weekly reports (Electoral Commission 2014d, 2014e). Prior to the referendum there was some concern among commentators with 'splintering', whereby a larger group sets up a number of permitted participants to get round its own limited spending power (see Adams 2014, Riley-Smith 2014).

An indication of the Electoral Commission's oversight can be seen from two interventions concerning the CBI (Confederation of British Industry). In May 2013 the Electoral Commission did not permit this body to register as a permitted participant on the basis that the person signing the application form was not authorised to do so. The CBI director general, John Cridland, accepted that the attempt to register had been a mistake and no further attempt was made to do so (see Carrell 2014). Second, the Commission ruled that the CBI annual dinner held in August 2014 did constitute an election expense in part because it was to be addressed by the prime minister, but since it cost less than £10,000 it did not require the CBI to register as a campaigner in the referendum (Electoral Commission 2014g).

## Conclusion

Law can only do so much. Deliberative participation depends primarily upon the interest of citizens in the issue before them, their civic education, the health of broader civil society and the responsibility of the private media. Each of these elements will be assessed in retrospect following the referendum. But law does have a role to play. The Scottish Referendum Act is an instrument which, in building upon the Edinburgh Agreement principles and in modifying the PPERA regime both to meet the specific needs of the Scottish process and to correct some of the negative side-effects of PPERA that were evident from the two referendums of 2011, has helped set the conditions for a fair, lawful and democratic referendum. A significant task for the Electoral Commission once the regulated period began was to monitor how well the legislation in the Scottish Referendum Act and Scottish Franchise Act was implemented and how responsibly all of those engaged in referendum campaigning behaved. So far the evidence is that it has approached its regulatory role in a vigorous way.

As we cast the Scottish process into wider perspective it is indeed notable that the leading strategist from the yes campaign in the Quebec referendum of 1995, a referendum which suffered from a rancorous relationship between the two campaigns and the absence of agreed and independently overseen process rules, has written recently commending the UK for the way in which the Edinburgh Agreement fostered a mutually acceptable referendum process. And he sees this breakthrough to be of great significance to other countries facing similar referendum processes: 'Nations that have been through this wrenching debate recently or who, especially in Catalonia, will navigate these waters soon, need the British government to keep offering a template of fair play and respect for democracy' (Lisée 2014). The Scottish referendum is indeed an opportunity to provide a model of citizen engagement at a time when the referendum is proliferating around the world like never before (LeDuc 2003: 29). In the end the quality of Scottish, and indeed British, democracy will be gauged not only by how each side reacts to the outcome, but by the process through which that outcome is reached.

## Legal references

*Hirst v the United Kingdom* (No 2) [2005] ECHR 681.
*Moohan and others, Petitioners* [2013] CSOH 199.
*Moohan and others v Lord Advocate. Reclaiming Motion* [2014] CSIH 56.
*Moohan and Another v Lord Advocate* [2014] UKSC 0183.

## References

Adams, L. (2014) 'Scottish independence: questions raised over campaign spending rules', *BBC News*, 1 May, available at http://www.bbc.co.uk/news/uk-scotland-scotland-politics-27228971 (accessed 15 April 2016).

Anderson, G., Bell, C., Craig, S., McHarg, A., Mullen, T., Tierney, S. and Walker, N. (2012) 'The independence referendum, legality and the contested constitution: widening the debate', *UK Constitutional Law Association Blog*, 31 January, available at https://ukconstitutionallaw.org/2012/01/31/gavin-anderson-et-al-the-independence-referendum-legality-and-the-contested-constitution-widening-the-debate/ (accessed 15 April 2016).

Black, A. (2013) 'Scottish independence: SNP accepts call to change referendum question', *BBC News*, 30 January, available at http://www.bbc.co.uk/news/uk-scotland-scotland-politics-21245701 (accessed 15 April 2016).

Bogdanor, V. (1981) *The People and the Party System: The Referendum and Electoral Reform in British Politics*, Cambridge: Cambridge University Press.

Carrell, S. (2014) 'Electoral Commission voids CBI listing as no campaigner in Scotland vote', *Guardian*, 1 May, available at http://www.theguardian.com/business/2014/may/01/electoral-commission-voids-cbi-listing-no-campaigner-scotland-independence-referendum (accessed 15 April 2016).

Committee on Standards in Public Life (1998) *The Funding of Political Parties in the United Kingdom* ('The Neill Report'), Chairman: Lord Neill of Bladen, London: HMSO (Cm. 4057).

Electoral Commission (2010) *Referendum on the UK Parliamentary Voting System: Report of views of the Electoral Commission on the proposed*

*referendum question*, available at http://www.electoralcommission.org.uk/__data/assets/pdf_file/0006/102696/PVSC-Bill-QA-Report.pdf (accessed 15 April 2016).
—— (2011a) *Local elections and Referendum on the voting system used to elect MPs to the House of Commons*, Booklet, available at http://www.electoralcommission.org.uk/__data/assets/file/0005/109877/Eng-web.pdf (accessed 15 April 2016).
—— (2011b) 'Voting referendum confirmed', news release, 17 February, available at http://www.electoralcommission.org.uk/news-and-media/news-releases/electoral-commission-media-centre/news-releases-referendums/voting-referendum-confirmed (accessed 15 April 2016).
—— (2013a) *Electoral Commission, Referendum on independence for Scotland: Advice of the Electoral Commission on the proposed referendum question*, available at http://www.electoralcommission.org.uk/__data/assets/pdf_file/0007/153691/Referendum-on-independence-for-Scotland-our-advice-on-referendum-question.pdf (accessed 15 April 2016).
—— (2013b) 'Referendum plans on track to deliver for voters', news release, 25 September, available at http://www.electoralcommission.org.uk/i-am-a/journalist/electoral-commission-media-centre/news-releases-referendums/referendum-plans-on-track-to-deliver-for-voters (accessed 15 April 2016).
—— (2014a) 'Electoral Commission advice on spending limits for the referendum on independence for Scotland', report, available at http://www.electoralcommission.org.uk/__data/assets/pdf_file/0004/153697/Report-on-spending-limits-for-the-referendum-on-independence-for-Scotland.pdf (accessed 15 April 2016).
—— (2014b) 'Electoral Commission publishes its information booklet for the Scottish Independence Referendum', news release, 18 June, available at http://www.electoralcommission.org.uk/i-am-a/journalist/electoral-commission-media-centre/news-releases-referendums/electoral-commission-publishes-its-information-booklet-for-the-scottish-independence-referendum (accessed 15 April 2016).
—— (2014c) 'Electoral Commission designates "Yes Scotland" and "Better Together" as lead campaigners at Scottish Independence Referendum', news release, 23 April, available at http://www.electoralcommission.org.uk/i-am-a/journalist/electoral-commission-media-centre/news-releases-referendums/electoral-commission-designates-yes-scotland-and-better-together-as-lead-campaigners-at-scottish-independence-referendum (accessed 15 April 2016).
—— (2014d) 'First pre-poll donations and loans report at Scottish Independence Referendum published', News Release, 8 July, available at http://www.electoralcommission.org.uk/i-am-a/journalist/electoral-commission-media-centre/news-releases-referendums/first-pre-poll-donations-and-loans-report-at-scottish-independence-referendum-published (accessed 15 April 2016).

—— (2014e) 'Second pre-poll donations and loans report at Scottish Independence Referendum published', News Release, 5 August, available at http://www.electoralcommission.org.uk/i-am-a/journalist/electoral-commission-media-centre/news-releases-donations/second-pre-poll-donations-and-loans-report-at-scottish-independence-referendum-published (accessed 15 April 2016).

—— (2014f) 'Every household in Scotland to get impartial voting guide', news release, 11 August, available at http://www.electoralcommission.org.uk/i-am-a/journalist/electoral-commission-media-centre/news-releases-campaigns/every-household-in-scotland-to-get-impartial-voting-guide (accessed 15 April 2016).

—— (2014g) 'Electoral Commission statement on the CBI Scotland's annual dinner', News Release, 27 August, available at http://www.electoralcommission.org.uk/i-am-a/journalist/electoral-commission-media-centre/news-releases-referendums/electoral-commission-statement-on-the-cbi-scotlands-annual-dinner (accessed 15 April 2015).

EU Business Partners (2015) 'Chirac accelerates EU referendum after gains for no camp', *EUBusiness.com*, 18 February, available at http://www.eubusiness.com/europe/france/050218132610.w1ahja90/ (accessed 15 April 2016).

Ghaleigh, N. S. (2009) 'Sledgehammers and nuts? Regulating referendums in the UK', in K. G. Lutz and S. Hug (eds) *Financing Referendum Campaigns*, London: Palgrave Macmillan, 180–200.

Henderson, A., Delaney, L. and Liñeira, R. (2014) 'Risk and attitudes to constitutional change', *ESRC Scottish Centre on Constitutional Change, Risk and Constitutional Attitudes Survey*, 16 August, available at http://www.centreonconstitutionalchange.ac.uk/sites/default/files/news/Risk%20and%20Constitutional%20Attitudes%20Full%20Survey%2014%20Aug.pdf (accessed 15 April 2016).

House of Lords (2009) *Referendums in the United Kingdom: Report with evidence*, Select Committee on the Constitution, HL Paper 99, 12th Report of Session 2009–10.

Johnson, S. (2014) 'Gordon Brown unveils cross-party deal on Scottish powers', *Telegraph*, 8 September, available at http://www.telegraph.co.uk/news/uknews/scottish-independence/11082930/Gordon-Brown-unveils-cross-party-deal-on-Scottish-powers.html (accessed 15 April 2016).

Lisée, J.-F. (2014) 'Well done, Britain, for a fair referendum – it's a shame Canada didn't manage it', *Guardian*, 9 September, available at http://www.theguardian.com/commentisfree/2014/sep/09/britain-referendum-canada-scottish-independence-vote (accessed 15 April 2016).

LeDuc, L. (2003) *The Politics of Direct Democracy: Referendums in global perspective*, Calgary: Broadview Press.

Macnab, S. (2014) 'UK "fact booklet" to be sent to Scots households', *Scotsman*, 12 June, available at http://www.scotsman.com/news/politics/uk-fact-booklet-to-be-sent-to-scots-households-1-3442518 (accessed 15 April 2016).

Marthaler, S. (2005) 'The French Referendum on ratification of the Constitutional Treaty', Referendum Briefing Paper No. 12, *European Parties Elections and Referendums Network*, 29 May.

Riley-Smith, B. (2014) 'Scottish independence: Yes campaign accused of using "dummy" organisations to get around spending rules', *Telegraph*, 28 April, available at http://www.telegraph.co.uk/news/uknews/scottish-independence/10792157/Scottish-independence-Yes-campaign-accused-of-using-dummy-organisations-to-get-around-spending-rules.html (accessed 15 April 2016).

Ross, J. (2014) 'Scottish independence: Osborne's further powers plan "not against purdah rules"', *BBC News*, 7 September, available at http://www.bbc.co.uk/news/uk-scotland-29100372 (accessed 15 April 2016).

Scottish Government (2012) *Your Scotland – Your Referendum – A Consultation Document*, paper, 25 January, available at http://www.scotland.gov.uk/Publications/2012/01/1006 (accessed 15 April 2016).

—— (2013) *Scotland's Future*, White Paper, 26 November, available at http://www.scotland.gov.uk/Publications/2013/11/9348 (accessed 15 April 2016).

—— (2014) *Scottish Independence Bill: A consultation on an interim constitution for Scotland*, White Paper, June 2014, available at http://www.scotland.gov.uk/Publications/2014/06/8135/downloads (accessed 15 April 2016).

Scottish Parliament (2013a) Scottish Parliament Referendum (Scotland) Bill Committee Official Report, 9 May, available at http://www.scottish.parliament.uk/parliamentarybusiness/report.aspx?r=8286&mode=pdf (accessed 15 April 2016).

—— (2013b) Scottish Parliament Referendum (Scotland) Bill Committee Official Report, 23 May, available at http://www.scottish.parliament.uk/parliamentarybusiness/report.aspx?r=8326&mode=pdf (accessed 15 April 2016).

—— (2013c) Scottish Parliament Referendum (Scotland) Bill Committee Official Report, 13 June, available at http://www.scottish.parliament.uk/parliamentarybusiness/report.aspx?r=8413&mode=pdf (accessed 15 April 2016).

Secretary of State for Scotland (2012) *Scotland's Constitutional Future: A consultation on facilitating a legal, fair and decisive referendum on whether Scotland should leave the United Kingdom*, Command Paper 8203, January 2012, available at https://www.gov.uk/government/uploads/system/uploads/attachment_data/file/39248/Scotlands_Constitutional_Future.pdf (accessed 15 April 2016).

Tierney, S. (2004) *Constitutional Law and National Pluralism*, Oxford: Oxford University Press.

—— (2012) *Constitutional Referendums: The theory and practice of republican deliberation*, Oxford: Oxford University Press (OUP 2008).

—— (2013) *Possible vires issue in relation to section 3 of the Scottish Independence Referendum (Franchise) Bill*, Advice to the Scottish

Parliament, Scottish Referendum Bill Committee Paper, 21 March 2013, available at http://www.scottish.parliament.uk/S4_ReferendumScotlandBillCommittee/20130321_Letter_to_DFM_on_prisoners_voting_rights.pdf (accessed 15 April 2016).

—— (2014) 'Why is Scottish Independence unclear?' *UK Constitutional Law Association Blog*, 25 February, available at https://ukconstitutionallaw.org/2014/02/25/stephen-tierney-why-is-scottish-independence-unclear/ (accessed 15 April 2016).

Tierney, S. and Suteu, S. (2013) 'Towards a democratic and deliberative referendum? Analysing the Scottish Independence Referendum Bill and the Scottish Independence Referendum (Franchise) Bill', *ESRC Report*, 21 August.

United Kingdom Government (1983) Representation of the People Act 1983, available at http://www.legislation.gov.uk/ukpga/1983/2/introduction/enacted (accessed 15 April 2016).

—— (2000) Political Parties, Elections and Referendums Act 2000, available at http://www.legislation.gov.uk/ukpga/2000/41/contents/enacted (accessed 15 April 2016).

—— (2013a) Scottish Independence Referendum Act 2013, available at http://www.legislation.gov.uk/asp/2013/14/enacted (accessed 15 April 2016).

—— (2013b) Scottish Independence Referendum (Franchise) Act 2013, available at http://www.legislation.gov.uk/asp/2013/13/contents/enacted (accessed 15 April 2016).

—— (2013c) Scotland Act 1998 (Modification of Schedule 5) *Order 2013*, Statutory Instrument 2013 No. 242, available at http://www.legislation.gov.uk/uksi/2013/242/made (accessed 15 April 2015).

United Kingdom Government and Scottish Government (2012) Agreement between the United Kingdom Government and the Scottish Government on a referendum on independence for Scotland, 15 October 2012, available at: http://www.scotland.gov.uk/About/Government/concordats/Referendum-on-independence (accessed 15 April 2016).

Vowles, J., Aimer, P., Catt, H., Lamare, J. and Miller, R. (1995) *Toward Consensus? The 1993 election in New Zealand and the transition to proportional representation*, Auckland: Auckland University Press.

Young, R. A. (1999) *The Struggle for Quebec: From referendum to referendum?* Montreal: McGill-Queen's University Press.

*Chapter Seven*

# The Motivations Behind the Use of Mechanisms of Direct Democracy

*Yanina Welp and Saskia P. Ruth*

## Introduction

Mechanisms of direct democracy (MDDs) have been put on the agenda by both political actors and political scientists as a potential solution to the crisis of representation that plagues both established and new democracies in recent years (Dalton et al. 2001). Nevertheless, some researchers contend that the consequences of MDDs for the quality of representative democracy vary greatly depending on the type of mechanisms introduced, specifically if they can be triggered by the authorities (top-down), automatically (mandatory) or by the citizens themselves (bottom-up) (Setälä 1999). With respect to the Latin American region, the first is negatively associated with the concentration of power in the hands of political actors (e.g. the president), while the last are positively associated with an increased influence of citizens on decision making (Altman 2010, 2011; Lissidini 2015; Zovatto 2014; Breuer 2011; Durán-Martínez 2012).

However, the binary distinction between top-down and bottom-up MDDs is not able to explain the variety of effects different mechanisms may have on representative democracy for several reasons. First, evidence from established democracies shows that top-down mechanisms may serve different political goals, like the legitimation of controversial political decisions or to settle conflicts between political actors (Bjørklund 1982; Morel 2001; Qvortrup 2006). Consequently, the same mechanism can have different effects on the quality of representative democracy. Second, bottom-up mechanisms are not necessarily associated with the empowerment of citizens, since on many occasions, these processes are highly influenced by political actors, such as governments or political parties, both with respect to the organisational feasibility of the process and the potential to set the political agenda (Serdült and Welp 2012; Wheatley 2008; Uleri 2002). Finally, in Latin America scholarly research on the potential consequences of MDDs, to the best of our knowledge, focuses exclusively on the institutional design of these instruments and usually only on the type of actor that triggers it (Zovatto 2014). Moreover, while the study of direct democracy has made great advances with respect to distinctions between different mechanisms and the analysis of the reasons for their various uses (Altman 2010, 2011; Breuer 2009; Lissidini 2015), only a few studies engage in the systematic analysis of the consequences of MDDs in Latin America. Altman (2011) and Durán-Martínez (2012) are two exceptions in this respect. The former analyses the consequences of the use of direct democratic instruments based on the highly aggregated distinction between top-down, mandatory, and bottom-up instruments mentioned above (Altman 2011). Durán-Martínez (2012), on the other hand, takes into account different MDDs, but focuses only on how they affect the concentration of executive power.

To systematically analyse the consequences of the use of MDDs in a more generalist way we argue that it is important to focus not only on the institutional design of these mechanisms but also on their normative function and the political motivations of the actors involved in these processes. This chapter, hence, proposes an actor-centred approach to the study of the consequences of MDDs for representative democracy. Due to our main focus on the motivations of political actors for triggering direct democratic mechanisms, our study *per definitionem* excludes automatically triggered referendums. To systematise the political motivations of the involved actors, we merge information on the institutional settings and the normative functions of MDDs.

With respect to the former, we build on the classification of MDDs proposed by Tsebelis (2002) and Hug and Tsebelis (2002). This classification is based on the veto player theory which allows us to account for both the institutional design of individual mechanisms (i.e. agenda-setting rules) as well as the specific political context in which an instrument is triggered (i.e. the veto player constellation).[1]

With respect to the second criteria, we build on the distinction proposed by Uleri (2002) and Durán-Martínez (2012) of the political scope of direct democratic mechanisms, i.e. whether decisions are aimed at changing institutions or policies (or both). If a direct democratic decision aims at changing the institutional structure of a political system (either its constitution or the power constellation of individual political actors) such a decision has a different quality than a decision directly aimed at policy change. Combining these two criteria allows us to systematically structure the different motivations behind the use of MDDs, and enables us to reach more fine-grained conclusions with respect to their consequences for representative democracy.

The chapter is structured as follows: in the next section we will provide an overview of the literature on which we build our own classification of political motivations of MDDs. We then provide a detailed discussion of our classification, followed by a first empirical mapping of direct democratic mechanisms in Latin America from 1900 to 2014. Finally, we provide some conclusions and avenues for future research.

## Institutional design and political functions of MDDs

### *Institutional classifications*

MDDs are defined as a set of procedures allowing citizens to take political decisions directly through a vote beyond regular election of representatives

1. A veto player is defined as a political actor (individual or collective) whose agreement is required for a change of the status quo (Tsebelis 2002).

(Altman 2011). This definition covers a variety of different mechanisms like mandatory referendums, abrogative referendums, or popular initiatives. In general, these mechanisms introduce the citizens (or more specifically the median voter) as an additional veto player in the decision-making process. Under some circumstances, however, MDDs may also reduce the number of veto players in the decision-making process, for example, if a classical veto player (e.g. a president) can circumvent other veto players by triggering a MDD (see Hug and Tsebelis 2002; Serdült and Welp 2012).

Of the three types of MDDs mentioned above, mandatory referendums are used to ratify new constitutions, constitutional amendments or international treaties. The citizens are added as an additional veto player in these cases, which is why mandatory referendums are often labelled as mechanisms of control or democratic accountability (Auer 2008; Uleri 1996). Top-down down referendums – i.e. MDDs in which an institutional veto player can trigger the process – are the most frequently used types of MDDs worldwide (IDEA 2008) and at the same time the most controversial ones, especially if we consider their use in hybrid regimes (Wheatley 2008) and new democracies (Barczak 2001; Durán-Martínez 2012). In presidential systems, like those in Latin America, we need to distinguish these mechanisms further according to the fragmentation or concentration of the agenda-setting process (see Breuer 2007; Durán-Martínez 2012). Breuer (2007) delimits *proactive* from *reactive* veto player referendums. In the former the agenda-setting power is concentrated in the hands of one political actor – e.g. the president can both trigger the process and formulate the question to be put to a vote – while for reactive referendums the agenda-setting power is shared between two (or more) political actors – e.g. the president can trigger the process but Congress has the power to formulate the question, or vice versa.

Finally, citizen-initiated mechanisms may be distinguished with respect to their law-rejecting (popular veto or recall) or law-promoting (popular initiative) quality (see Hug and Tsebelis 2002; Breuer 2007; Uleri 1996). Law-rejecting initiatives, on the one hand, give citizens the power to veto pending bills or enacted laws (i.e. abrogative and derogative initiatives) as well as recall the mandates of elected representatives. Law-promoting initiatives, on the other hand, give citizens the means not only to trigger a direct democratic vote but also to formulate the question to be asked (both with respect to ordinary legislation and constitutional amendments).[2] Hence, this differentiation mirrors the distinction made between reactive and proactive veto player referendums (Breuer 2007).

While the previous paragraphs help us to systematise the institutional design of MDDs we still need more information to judge the incentives and political motivations of political actors who use these instruments.

2. Additionally, Uleri (2002) distinguishes between regulated (optional) and non-regulated (ad hoc) top-down referendums.

### *Functional and motivational classifications*

Beyond studies based on institutional design, researchers investigated the political functions and (elite) motivations of MDDs around the world. However, the literature on political functions and motivations of MDDs remains scattered and a consensus on how to systematise them has yet to emerge. We structure our literature overview in two parts: on the on hand, we discuss studies that centre on defining the scope of MDDs focusing on their normative function. On the other hand, we review studies that focus on the motivations for triggering these events.

With respect to the scope of MDDs, Durán-Martínez (2012) distinguishes MDDs in Latin America according to their normative aim, i.e. whether they set out to change institutions or policy. This qualitative distinction is crucial to evaluate the consequences of MDDs for democracy since it highlights the dimensionality of direct democratic decisions. While MDDs on policies are usually one-dimensional and their outcomes easier to predict, MDDs on constitutional reforms are multi-dimensional since they impact how power is accessed and exercised in the first place. Therefore, their outcomes are both highly consequential and much more difficult to predict (see Hug and Tsebelis 2002: 470–1).

With respect to potential motivations for triggering MDDs, Serdült and Welp (2012) focus on bottom-up procedures and differentiate them according to the influence of political actors in the agenda-setting process. In their classification, bottom-up procedures serve to *concentrate power* if the government drives the agenda-setting process, they serve to *increase competition* if opposition parties drive the agenda-setting process, and they serve to *empower citizens* if civil society actors take on the role of agenda setter (Serdült and Welp 2012: 92). We build on their distinction and extend it to a broader range of MDDs in this chapter.

An earlier study by Bjørklund (1982), focused on top-down referendums, identifies three motivations for using MDDs based on the Nordic countries. First, referendums may be used as a *weapon of the parliamentary minority*. Second, if a government coalition is divided concerning a political issue they may consult the public and use a referendum as an *instrument of mediation*. Third, referendums may be used to resolve highly sensitive issues (*lightning rod*). In a similar way, Rahat (2009) proposes three elite motivations for using MDDs based on the Israeli experience. The first motivation is *avoidance*, which addresses politicians' fear that a decision on a certain issue might lead to a split within the party or party voters whose cohesion they wish to sustain. The second motive is *addition*, which refers to a situation where politicians who trigger a referendum actually have the necessary majority to adopt change without turning to the public but call for the referendum anyway. The referendum then serves two goals, to legitimise a decision through public support and to empower the politician or party who initiated it. The third motive is *contradiction*, which brings an issue to the agenda that was rejected in the conventional decision-making forum (Rahat 2009: 102–3).

In her study on government-initiated referendums, Morel (2001) identifies several motivations for using referendums such as mediation (to resolve internal conflicts), agenda (to remove an issue from the electoral agenda), legislative (used by minority governments to bypass the normal parliamentary process), legitimation (to solve a crisis) and power reinforcing (to increase authority). To analyse the UK, Quortrup (2006) extends these elaborations by Morel (2001) distinguishing five types of referendums according to the motivations driving them: (1) decision-solving referendums, which address popular consultation in the case of internal government dissent on a specific topic; (2) legislative referendums, initiated by a legislative minority to surpass the legislative majority; (3) strategic referendums, which serve to mobilise political support in favour of the actor that triggers the event; (4) legitimation referendums, through which elites seek popular consultation on controversial issues to directly legitimise them; (5) politically obligatory referendums, which touch upon controversial topics on the electoral agenda that incline political actors to call for a direct vote by the citizens.

This literature overview indicates that there is still a gap between the analysis of the institutional design of MDDs and the conceptualisation and systematisation of political motivations that might explain and predict their use in different contexts. While studies on political motivations of MDDs usually focus on explaining either experiences in individual countries or specific types of instruments they do not enable us to make generalising accounts as to how different MDDs complement or contradict representative democratic decision-making procedures cross-nationally (or even over time). To address this gap, we propose a systematic classification of the motivations for triggering non-obligatory MDDs – transcending their distinction in top-down or bottom-up mechanisms – by focusing on the position of the agenda setter in the veto player constellation and the normative function they serve (i.e. their scope). Hence, our proposal is based on an actor-centred approach and combines institutional and functional classifications to systematise the incentives relevant actors have in these processes to trigger them. Such a classification enables us to theorise and better understand the consequences of MDDs for representative democracy and, ultimately, develop generalisable and testable hypotheses.

### *A classification of political motivations*

In this section we propose a classification of MDDs that infers the political motivation of the use of these instruments based on a combined analysis of the political actor constellation and the normative function they serve.

With respect to the first criterion, we argue that it is not only important to know who promotes the mechanism, i.e. who can trigger it, but also what this actor's position is within the broader constellation of important political players in the political system – in other words, whether the agenda setter of a MDD is a veto player – the president or a majority in congress – or a minority actor without institutionalised power to veto legislation apart from triggering a

MDD. This distinction allows us to differentiate political motivations against the background of potentially changing political actor constellations within a political system.

For example, the political actor constellation plays a decisive role with respect to the distinction Breuer (2007) draws between proactive and reactive referendums in presidential systems. The distinction is based on the logic of the separation of power between a president and congress in a presidential system – which facilitates the fragmentation of the agenda-setting power. Nevertheless, the distinction plays a secondary role in situations of unified government, where both the president and the congress are dominated by the same political party or a coherent coalition of parties (see Mainwaring and Shugart 1997). In such an actor constellation, the agenda control – both the activation of a mechanisms and the formulation of the question to be asked – is unified in the hands of one veto player. Hence, the actor constellation may actually extenuate or attenuate specific aspects of the institutional design of MDDs, which should also translate into different motivations for triggering such mechanisms.

Following this reasoning, we observe three constellations an agenda setter might face that we judge as important in analysing the political motivation for triggering MDDs: whether the agenda setter is a single veto player (unified government), a veto player in a constellation with several veto players (divided government), or does not hold formal veto power (i.e. a parliamentary minority or an extra-parliamentary actor).

With respect to the second criteria of our classification – the normative function – we argue that political motivations should differ depending on whether MDDs are oriented towards the change or protection of constitutional rules or towards the change or protection of public policies (see Durán-Martínez 2012). MDDs aimed at changing the institutional equilibrium (either through constitutional change or through shifting power between institutional veto players) entail higher stakes for the political actors involved in these processes than MDDs aimed at influencing the political decision-making process with respect to a single issue (see Uleri 1996; Hug and Tsebelis 2002). Combining these two criteria we arrive at six different political motivations, which are shown in Table 7.1.

*Table 7.1: Classification of the political motivations behind MDDs*

| **Actor constellation** | **Institutional change** | **Policy change** |
|---|---|---|
| Agenda setter = single *veto player* | (I) Power legitimation | (II) Policy delegation |
| Agenda setter = *veto player* among others | (III) Power struggle | (IV) Policy struggle |
| Agenda setter = without *veto player status* | (V) Empowerment | (VI) Policy responsiveness |

*Source:* Author's elaboration.

**Power legitimation (I):** If the agenda setter of a referendum forms part of a unified government, this actor does not need the MDD to initiate institutional change. Hence, we assume that in such contexts the purpose of triggering such an event anyway is to additionally legitimise the existing power distribution through popular consultation. This category relates to the motivation conceptualised by Rahat (2009) as addition as well as Morel's power-reinforcing referendums (2001).

**Policy delegation (II):** Similar to category (I), policy delegation referendums are triggered by an agenda setter within a constellation of unified government. Hence, according to the veto player theory the political actor would not need to put the topic up for a vote to change the policy. But as mentioned above, even powerful political actors may fear the consequences of deciding on controversial or highly polarised topics without the consent of the people. Additionally, the delegation of policy decisions to the citizens may also serve to externalise internal policy struggles within the government party or coalition.[3] Circling back to other classifications of motives to call for MDDs this category is in line with Bjørklund's (1982) instrument of mediation, Rahat's (2009) motive of avoidance, Morel's (2001) mediation referendums and Qvortrup's (2006) decision-solving referendums.

**Power struggle (III):** Referendums aiming at institutional change that are activated by one veto player among others fall into this category. For example, a president who faces an opposition-led parliament at a time of divided government might have an incentive to bring the people in to circumvent the legislature and potentially concentrate power in the executive branch (e.g. Pérez-Liñán 2007). Hug and Tsebelis (2002), for example, indicate that such referendums serve to reduce the number of veto players in the decision-making process to facilitate institutional change, which otherwise would not have been possible. Serdült and Welp (2012) refer to this category in their classification under the label of power-concentrating referendums and Morel (2001) refers to these instances as power-reinforcing referendums.

**Policy struggle (IV):** Similarly to category (III), policy struggle referendums between the government and an opposition-led legislative branch appeal to the citizens as a moderating power to solve policy conflicts (see Hochstetler 2006). Additionally, (divided) governments may call for popular consultation on highly controversial issues, and in this way remove them from the electoral

3. Institutional veto players in presidential systems may be absorbed into one veto player due to the partisan context, i.e. cohesive political parties or party coalitions in the legislature backing a president. Hence, unified governments in presidential systems depend on the ongoing support of a parliamentary majority. But since both the cohesion and discipline of political parties is lower in presidential systems than in parliamentary regimes, policies that divide the political coalition between presidents and the parliamentary majority pose a special threat to their unity, and consequently, their governability.

agenda where they might harm the future electoral prospects of the political actor (see Morel 2001). This category is captured in Bjørklund's (1982) lightning rod, Morel's (2001) agenda referendums, and Qvortrup's (2006) politically obligatory referendums.

However, depending on the institutional design and the political actor constellation, MDDs do not always serve to reduce the number of veto players since they bring the citizens in as an additional veto player in the political system (Tsebelis 2002; Hug and Tsebelis 2002). This is especially the case if these mechanisms can be triggered by the citizens themselves (i.e. as a bottom-up process).

**Empowerment (V):** Referendums on institutional issues that can be triggered by actors without formal veto power in the political process may serve to empower political minorities or civil society groups to increase their political rights vis-à-vis the national majority, e.g. through the introduction of autonomy rights for regional minorities. This category relates to Serdült and Welp's (2012) competition-increasing referendums – since these processes potentially empower additional political actors in the system – and to Bjørklund's (1982) minority weapon.

**Policy Responsiveness (VI):** MDDs that provide actors without formal veto power in the system – like civil society groups or minority parties in Congress – with the power to trigger policy responsiveness referendums enable them to influence the political decision-making process in line with their policy preferences. Such bottom-up processes aim at increasing the responsiveness of political elites to the preferences of the citizens (beyond electoral campaigns) building a safeguard against representation gaps (*see* also Annunziata, Chapter Eight in this volume, on the relationship between responsiveness and MDDs). This category covers referendums aiming at the empowerment of citizens (Serdült and Welp 2012), or Rahat's (2009) contradiction motive and Qvortrup's (2006) legislative referendums.

To put our classification to a first empirical test, we map the direct democratic experience in Latin America from 1900 until 2014 in line with our six categories in the following section.

## Direct democracy in Latin America

### *Case selection*

We confine our analysis of the use of MDDs in the Latin American region from 1900 until 2014 with respect to four criteria: First, since we are interested in the political motivations that drive political actors to trigger MDDs we exclude mandatory referendums from our sample. Second, we exclude informal referendums not recognised by the state (e.g. the electoral body) from the sample. Third, we exclude closely related mechanisms like legislative agenda-setting instruments from our sample, since they do not lead to a popular vote on either institutional or policy issues. Finally, we restrict our analysis to the national level of government.

With respect to the coding of individual cases, we count MDDs aimed at different topics but asked at one point in time as one single case if they have been triggered by the same political actor. Similarly, we count MDDs as separate events if they aimed at *different issues* but took place on the same date and were triggered by different political actors. Finally, we count MDDs aimed at *the same topic* and asked at one point in time but triggered by different political actors as one single case.

Including mandatory referendums (for now), we count seventy-nine MDDs in Latin America, covering 154 topics that have been put to a vote by the people in the period under study. However, the frequency of the use of MDDs varies vastly within the region. El Salvador, Honduras, Mexico, Nicaragua and the Dominican Republic did not activate any MDDs throughout the whole period, and Argentina, Costa Rica, Paraguay, Peru, Guatemala and Brazil only used them on very few occasions. From the 1990s onwards we find both an increased use of MDDs and a wider range of topics on which citizens have been consulted. Of the seventy-nine MDDs in the region, twenty-two were mandatory referendums (which we exclude from our final sample), forty-four were initiated by the authorities (so-called top-down referendums) and thirteen were activated through bottom-up signature collection processes (of which ten took place in Uruguay). Unfortunately, we had to exclude the case of Uruguay in 1950 from our analysis, since we did not find sufficient information on this referendum. Hence, in the remainder of the chapter we analyse fifty-six non-mandatory MDDs (for a detailed overview *see* Table 7.3 in the Appendix).

### *Descriptive analysis*

Table 7.2 gives an overview of the fifty-six MDDs studied here and assigns them to the six categories presented above. At first sight, we can see that most of the MDDs intentionally triggered in the region have been activated by political actors with some form of veto power (i.e. only fourteen referendums, or 25 per cent, have been triggered by a non-veto player). Moreover, we can find different types of MDDs – according to their institutional design – within each of these categories.

## Power legitimation

With sixteen MDDs this category covers the second highest number of cases from our sample. Interestingly, most of the power legitimation referendums in the region took place in authoritarian or transitional contexts, e.g. Chile in 1978 and 1980, Guatemala in 1954, or Venezuela in 1957 (which is in line with the observations made by Qvortrup (Chapter Five) or Wheatley (Chapter Four) in this volume). Nevertheless, we can also find some cases that took place under democratic rule, as in Ecuador in 2011. Some of these MDDs aimed at legitimising political actors

*Table 7.2: Political motivations of MDDs in Latin America (1900–2014)*

| **Actor constellation** | **Institutional change** | **Policy change** |
|---|---|---|
| | *Power legitimation (16)* | *Policy delegation (5)* |
| Agenda setter = single *veto player* | Bolivia 1931<br>Chile 1980, 1978<br>Colombia 1957<br>Ecuador 2011*, 1978<br>Guatemala 1954, 1935<br>Panama 1940<br>Paraguay 1940<br>Peru 1993, 1939, 1919<br>Uruguay 1980, 1917<br>Venezuela 1957 | Argentina 1984<br>Ecuador 2011*<br>Paraguay 1938<br>Uruguay 2009<br>Venezuela 2000 |
| | *Power struggle (20)* | *Policy struggle (7)* |
| Agenda setter = *veto player* among others | Bolivia 2006, 2008<br>Brazil 1963<br>Chile 1925<br>Colombia December 1990, May 1990**, 2003*<br>Ecuador 2007, 1997, 1995*, 1994*, 1986<br>Uruguay 1971, 1966, 1962, 1958, 1946, 1938, 1934<br>Venezuela 1999 | Brazil 2005<br>Bolivia 2004<br>Colombia 2003*<br>Costa Rica 2007**<br>Ecuador 2006, 1995*, 1994* |
| | *Empowerment (2)* | *Policy responsiveness (12)* |
| Agenda setter = without *veto player status* | Colombia May 1990**<br>Venezuela 2004 | Costa Rica 2007**<br>Peru 2010<br>Uruguay 2009, 2004, 2003, 1999a, 1999b, 1994a, 1994b, 1992, November 1989, April 1989 |

*Source:* Author's elaboration.

*Notes:*
* these cases refer to both institutional and policy change at the same time;
** these cases involve proposals on the same topic by two agenda setters.

in power and some at legitimising the political regime in general. The Chilean referendum of 1978 serves as a classical example for this category within an authoritarian setting. The referendum was put forward during the dictatorship of President Augusto Pinochet to address international accusations of human rights abuses in the country. The question that was asked perfectly reflects the power legitimising purpose of the referendum: 'In the face of the international aggression against the Government of our fatherland, I support President Pinochet in his defence of Chile's dignity, and I reconfirm the legitimacy of the government of the Republic and his leadership of the sovereign, institutional process in this country' (authors' translation, emphasis added). Despite high levels of repression against opponents of the regime 22 per cent of the citizens voted against the proposition (Gonnet 2009). Similarly, the two referendums in 1957 – in Colombia and in Venezuela – were activated ad hoc by military juntas to legitimise elite pacts between themselves and most of the political parties in the countries (with the exception of the left). However, considering their control over the media system and limited civil liberties enjoyed by the population the favourable outcomes of these events are highly questionable from a democratic standpoint. Nevertheless, even MDDs in autocratic or transitional contexts entail at least some degree of uncertainty, as the example of Uruguay in 1980 shows. In this case, the citizens rejected the proposal made by the autocratic regime, opening the way for a swift and far-reaching reaching democratic transition (Altman 2011).

## Policy delegation

This category covers five of our cases and in line with our expectations all the cases refer to government-initiated referendums delegating the decision on controversial policies to the citizenry. Examples range from the ratification of important agreements – like the peace agreement in Paraguay in 1938 or the agreement about the Beagle Canal (between Argentina and Chile) in Argentina in 1984 – to popular consultation on highly polarised topics – like the prohibition of firearms in Brazil in 2005 (Lafferriere 2009; Lissovsky and Szabó de Carvalho 2008). Moreover, the Ecuadorian referendum in 2011 indicates that institutional and policy change may be pursed at the same time by the initiating actor. In a series of referendums held on the same day, the Ecuadorian government aimed at reforming parts of the constitution (e.g. the judicial branch) and delegating several policy questions to the citizens, including a highly controversial media control law (Ramírez Gallegos 2014).

## Power struggle

The largest cell – with twenty cases – in our classification refers to referendums in contexts with multiple veto players that aim at institutional change. As mentioned earlier, although the citizens are added as a new veto player to the decision-making process, referendums may nonetheless reduce the overall number of veto players involved (see Hug and Tsebelis 2002). Since these referendums are used to change the existing institutional equilibrium to benefit one political actor, they are especially problematic from a democratic perspective (see Durán-Martínez 2012). The case of Venezuela in 1999 is a prototypical example of this. Calling for a referendum enabled Hugo Chávez – who had been recently elected president but did not control a majority in Congress – to initiate a (controversial) constitutional reform process. In the end, Chávez managed to draft a new constitution which provided him with increased powers vis-à-vis the legislature and with a comfortable majority in Congress for his political party (*see* Massüger and Welp 2013; Negretto's Chapter Three in this volume). Another example of the use of referendums as means in a power struggle happened in Bolivia in 2006. Against the background of a highly polarised political environment and the parallel process of the elaboration of a new constitution, subnational governments in opposition to President Evo Morales initiated a referendum process aiming at increasing their power vis-á-vis the national government. While the referendum was approved in opposition-controlled departments (the 'media luna') it was overall rejected in the more densely populated departments governed by Morales party, leaving the conflict between the subnational and national governments unresolved (see Mayorga 2006). This then contributed to a series of recall referendums (against the president and eight governors) in 2008 which were triggered by President Morales himself to resolve an upcoming institutional crisis between his government and the governments in the 'media luna' (Salazar Elena 2009). Hence, these instruments may also help to resolve institutional conflicts or inter-branch blockages and bring the citizens in as a moderating power instead of leading to military takeovers (see Hochstetler 2006).

## Policy struggle

This category covers seven cases in which the referendum was used to resolve policy struggles between different political actors (as opposed to policy struggles within a political actor or within the citizenry as a whole). The Bolivian referendum in 2004 may serve as a good example here. In October 2003 the country experienced high levels of popular protest against a government proposal on the new regulation of the use of revenues from natural resources, which ultimately led to the ousting of President Sánchez de Lozada (*la guerra del gas*). To avoid a similar fate, former Vice President Carlos Mesa, on assuming office, started the process of calling for a binding referendum on natural resources.[4] In doing so he responded to what was a highly salient topic for the citizenry by removing it from the electoral agenda.

Another interesting example took place in Costa Rica in 2007 where a referendum was activated just before the signature of the Central American Free Trade Agreement (CAFTA) with United States. The agreement was strongly opposed by civil society organisations who initiated a signature collection process to call for a referendum. To prevent the destabilisation of his government through a bottom-up direct democratic process, President Oscar Arias forestalled the event by calling for a referendum by presidential decree. Despite the strong opposition of most of the social movements and after an intensive campaign of the government to promote a vote in favour of the CAFTA, in the end the agreement received the support of most of the voters (Raventós 2014; Breuer 2011). Due to the parallel processes of triggering an MDD on the issue of the CAFTA agreement, the case figures in both the policy struggle category (the MDD was finally called by a president without majority support in the legislature) and the policy responsiveness category (the first attempt to activate it came from the citizens) (*see* Table 7.2).

4. The process was only made possible by amending the Constitution, which had first introduced MDDs into Bolivia (see Ley 2769, available at http://pdba.georgetown.edu/Electoral/Bolivia/Leyes/LeyReferendum.pdf, accessed 15 April 2016).

## Empowerment

With two incidences this category covers the least number of cases in our sample (Colombia May 1990 and Venezuela 2004). This speaks to the limitations that non-veto players usually face with respect to institutional reform processes. Only half of the countries in Latin America regulate MDDs that enable minority actors or civil society groups to trigger institutional change processes.[5]

In line with the empowerment logic in Venezuela (2004) the MDD was used as a weapon in the hands of an opposition actor without institutional veto power. The case refers to the recall activated against President Hugo Chávez by the Democratic Coordinator (*Coordinadora Democrática*) with the support of the business sector as well as several opposition parties. After a long and controversial process the referendum took place and Chávez was ratified with 59 per cent of the votes (see Kornblith 2005).

Like the Costa Rican referendum in 2007, the Colombian MDD in 1990 is an exceptional case given that it involved two agenda setters. In the context of the legislative elections in March 1990, an informal vote in favour of a constitutional convention was promoted by the students' movement, *la séptima papeleta*, although MDDs on constitutional reform were not included in the present Constitution. The social pressure built up through this process convinced the electoral court to validate the votes collected in this way and in the following presidential elections in May 1990 a new but this time formal referendum was called on the same topic, ratifying the previous results and opening the way to elect a constitutional convention (Tomas Acuña 2009).

## Policy responsiveness

Finally, we assigned twelve cases to this category of which ten occurred in Uruguay. Although nine countries in Latin America provide these provisions to their citizens, only three countries in the region have actually used them.[6] As mentioned above, the case of Costa Rica in 2007 involved two agenda setters and was finally called by the president. Nevertheless, the process increased the responsiveness of the government towards the preferences of the citizens, who in the end approved the ratification of the CAFTA agreement. The Peruvian case, however, is a paradigmatic example for this category. The MDD in 2010 was the final institutional attempt by the Asociación Nacional de Fonavistas de los Pueblos del Perú (ANFPP) – a civil society actor – to demand legislation on the use of funds stemming from the formerly (unlawfully) dissolved national housing fund (Fondo Nacional de Vivienda, FONAVI). The demands to hold the political elites accountable on the issue started with a legislative initiative (a petition) in

5. These countries are Bolivia, Colombia, Costa Rica, Ecuador, Mexico, Nicaragua, Peru, Uruguay and Venezuela.

6. The countries providing these provisions are Bolivia, Colombia, Costa Rica, Ecuador, Mexico, Nicaragua, Peru, Uruguay and Venezuela.

March 2001 that was ignored by Parliament and culminated in the approval of the proposal via a direct democratic vote in October 2010 (Welp 2016).

This leaves the ten cases of policy responsiveness referendums in Uruguay. All of these events took place after the countries' transition to democracy in 1985. Especially interesting from a democratic perspective was the first MDD that took place in April 1989 about the derogation of an amnesty law on human rights violations during the former military dictatorship, which was rejected, with a majority of 57.5 per cent voting against its abolition. In the following years, Uruguayans continued to demand policy responsiveness from their governments in several occasions and participated in MDDs on topics like the privatisation of public enterprises or basic human rights (see Monestier 2011).

## Conclusion

In this chapter we developed a classification of the motives that drive political actors to trigger direct democratic mechanisms. We approached this endeavour from an actor-centred perspective and derived our classification from two criteria that structure the incentives of political actors to use these instruments. First, we focused on the normative function a MDD is aimed at, i.e. whether it sets out to change (or prevent a change in) institutions or policies. Second, we investigated the position of the agenda setter (defined through the institutional design of MDDs) within the specific political context. Through the combination of these criteria we can systematise the motivations of political actors to trigger MDDs, and to merge existing classifications, which were based either on the experience of individual countries or on the analysis of specific types of MDDs, into a comprehensive scheme.

After theorising about the specific motivations for triggering MDDs we then put our classification to a first descriptive test in mapping the Latin American experience from 1900 until 2014. A first finding from our analysis is that political elites in both single and multiple veto player constellations are by far the most frequent agenda setters of MDDs in the region. Out of the fifty-six cases analysed in this chapter, fourty-four (or 79 per cent) were triggered by an agenda setter with formal veto power. The most frequent motive to use of these instruments was to struggle for power (III), followed by the motive to legitimise power (I).

In line with this pattern, we find that most of the MDDs triggered in Latin America aim at changing the institutional equilibrium (either through constitutional change or through the strengthening of one political actor within the political system). More specifically, thirty-seven cases (or 66 per cent) in our sample fall into one of the three categories of this normative function. Framed in a positive way, this indicates that the citizens were given a say in the most important changes concerning their political systems.

However, our analysis also highlights some of the consequences of MDDs for the quality of democracy already mentioned in the literature (Altman 2011; Serdült and Welp 2012; Durán-Martínez 2012). The most problematic category with respect to the consequences for democracy as a whole refers to MDDs triggered to legitimise already powerful actors within a political system (category I). This category covers sixteen of the fifty-six cases in our sample, and is the second most frequently observed motivation for triggering these events. Many cases in this category happened under non-democratic or hybrid and transitional contexts and were aimed at legitimising non-democratic political actors' hold on power, e.g. in Chile in 1978 and 1980, in Colombia in 1957 or in Venezuela in 1957. Nevertheless, the example of the MDD in Uruguay in 1980 also shows that even powerful political actors cannot completely control the uncertainty created by these processes and the outcome of these events may well play into the hands of democratising actors. Similarly problematic is the category of the power struggle motive (III). While the cases in this cell elevate citizens to a moderating power between different branches of the government in times of crisis (see Hochstetler 2006, Pérez-Liñán 2007), their outcome, at the same time often leads to the concentration of power in the hands of one governmental branch – usually the president (see Durán-Martínez 2012).

Finally, some positive accounts become more evident through our analysis as well. More specifically, if citizens directly participate in decisions on policy change, this might strengthen several aspects of democracy. For example, MDDs may give citizens a say on highly controversial or polarising topics (either through delegation or to resolve a policy struggle) or they may enable citizens to demand (and enforce) policy responsiveness from their representatives (category VI). However, these instances are, on the one hand, less frequent in the region and, on the other hand, most of them occurred in one country: Uruguay.

This chapter provides a first step towards a systematic analysis of political motivations behind the use of MDDs. Future research may use this classification to develop hypotheses about the consequences of the individual categories, for example for different aspects of democracy or the likelihood of the use of MDDs in specific contexts.

## References

Altman, D. (2010) 'Plebiscitos, referendos e iniciativas populares en América Latina: ¿mecanismos de control político o políticamente controlados?', *Perfiles Latinoamericanos*, 18(35): 9–34.

—— (2011) *Direct Democracy Worldwide*, Cambridge: Cambridge University Press.

Auer, A. (2008) 'Una mirada suiza sobre la democracia directa en América Latina', in A. Lissidini, Y. Welp and D. Zovatto (eds) *Democracia Directa en Latinoamérica*, Buenos Aires: Prometeo: 241–52.

Barczak, M. (2001) 'Representation by consultation? The rise of direct democracy in Latin America', *Latin American Politics and Society*, 43(3): 37–60.

Bjørklund, T. (1982) 'The demand for referendum: when does it arise and when does it succeed?', *Scandinavian Political Studies*, 5(3): 237–60.

Breuer, A. (2007) 'Institutions of direct democracy and accountability in Latin America's presidential democracies', *Democratization*, 14(4): 554–79.

—— (2009) 'The use of government-initiated referendums in Latin America: Towards a theory of referendum causes', *Revista de Ciencia Política,* 29(1): 23–55.

—— (2011) 'Obstacles to citizen participation by direct democracy in Latin America: a comparative regional analysis of legal frameworks and evidence from the Costa Rican case', *Democratization* 18(1): 100–34.

Dalton, R., Bürklin, W. and Drummond, A. (2001) 'Public opinion and direct democracy', *Journal of Democracy,* 12(4): 141–53.

Durán-Martínez, A. (2012) 'Presidents, parties and referenda in Latin America', *Comparative Political Studies,* 45(9): 1159–87.

Gonnet, M. (2009) 'Chile: historia, paradojas y posibilidades', in Y. Welp and U. Serdült (eds) *Armas de Doble Filo: la participación ciudadana en la encrucijada,* Buenos Aires: Prometeo: 87–107.

Hochstetler, K. (2006) 'Rethinking presidentialism: challenges and presidential falls in South America', *Comparative Politics,* 38(4): 401–18.

Hug, S. and Tsebelis, G. (2002) 'Veto players and referendums around the world', *Journal of Theoretical Politics,* 14(4): 465–516.

IDEA (2008) *Handbook of Direct Democracy,* Stockholm: International Institute for Democracy and Electoral Assistance.

Kornblith, M. (2005) 'The referendum in Venezuela: elections versus democracy', *Journal of Democracy,* 16(1): 124–37.

Lafferriere, E. (2009) 'Argentina: La participación ciudadana como desafío', in Y. Welp and U. Serdült (eds) *Armas de Doble Filo: La participación ciudadana en la encrucijada,* Buenos Aires: Prometeo: 129–52.

Lissidini, A. (1998) 'Una mirada crítica a la democracia directa: el origen y las prácticas de los plebiscitos en Uruguay', *Perfiles Latinoamericanos,* 12: 169–200.

—— (2015) *Democracia directa en América Latina: avances, contradicciones y desafíos,* Available at http://nuso.org/ (accessed 15 April 2016).

Lissovsky, M. and Szabó de Carvalho, I. (2008) *El referéndum sobre las armas en Brasil: El elector como víctima virtual,* available at http://www.pos.eco.ufrj.br/docentes/publicacoes/mlissovsky_1.pdf (accessed 15 April 2016).

Mainwaring, S. and Shugart, M. S. (1997) *Presidentialism and Democracy in Latin America,* Cambridge, Cambridge: Cambridge University Press.

Massüger, N. and Welp, Y. (2013) 'Legality and legitimacy: constituent power in Venezuela, Bolivia and Ecuador', in F. Mendez and J. Wheatley (eds) *Constitution-Making and Popular Participation,* Farnham, UK: Ashgate Publishing: 103–18.

Mayorga Ugarte, F. (2006) 'Referéndum y Asamblea Constituyente: autonomías departamentales en Bolivia', *Colombia Internacional,* 64: 50–67.

Monestier, F. (2011) *Movimientos sociales, partidos políticos y democracia directa desde abajo en Uruguay (1985–2004),* Consejo Latinoamericano de Ciencias Sociales-CLACSO.

Morel, L. (2001) 'The strategic use of government-sponsored referendums in liberal democracies', in M. Mendelsohn and A. Parkin (eds) *Referendum Democracy: Citizens, Elites, and Deliberation in Referendum Campaigns*, New York: Palgrave: 47–64.

Pérez-Liñán, A. (2007) *Presidential Impeachment and the New Political Instability in Latin America*, Cambridge: Cambridge University Press.

Qvortrup, M. (2006) 'Democracy by delegation: the decision to hold referendums in the United Kingdom', *Representation*, 42(1): 59–72.

Rahat, G. (2009) 'Elite motives for initiating referendums: avoidance, addition and contradiction', in M. Setälä and T. Schiller (eds) *Referendums and Representative Democracy: Responsiveness, Accountability and Deliberation*, London: Routledge: 98–111.

Ramírez Gallegos, F. (2014) 'El despliegue de la democracia directa en el Ecuador Postconstitucional', in A. Lissidini, Y. Welp and D. Zovatto (eds) *Democracias en movimiento: mecanismos de democracia directa y participativa en América Latina*, Mexico: UNAM: 231–74.

Raventós, C. (2014) 'Democracia directa en Costa Rica: el referendo sobre el TLC', in A. Lissidini, Y. Welp and D. Zovatto (eds) *Democracias en movimiento: mecanismos de democracia directa y participativa en América Latina*, Mexico: UNAM: 167–94.

Salazar Elena, R. (2009) 'Bolivia: El referendo', in Y. Welp and U. Serdült (eds) *Armas de Doble Filo: la participación ciudadana en la encrucijada*, Buenos Aires: Prometeo: 217–37.

Serdült, U. and Welp, Y. (2012) 'Direct democracy upside down', *Taiwan Journal of Democracy*, 8(1): 69–92.

Setälä, M. (1999) 'Referendums in Western Europe – a wave of direct democracy?', *Scandinavian Political Studies*, 22: 327–40.

Thomas Acuña, E. (2009) 'Colombia: entre la crisis de representación y la democracia directa', in Y. Welp and U. Serdült (eds) *Armas de Doble Filo: la participación ciudadana en la encrucijada*, Buenos Aires: Prometeo: 109–28.

Tsebelis, G. (2002) *Veto Players: How Political Institutions Work*, Princeton: Princeton University Press.

Uleri, P. V. (1996) 'Italy: referendum and initiatives from the origins to the crisis of a democratic regime', in M. Gallagher and P. Uleri (eds) *The Referendum Experience in Europe*, Basingstoke: Macmillan: 106–25.

—— (2002) 'On referendum voting in Italy: yes, no or non-vote? How Italian parties learned to control referenda', *European Journal of Political Research*, 41(6): 863–83.

Welp, Y. (2008) 'La participación ciudadana en la encrucijada. Los mecanismos de democracia directa en Ecuador, Perú y Argentina', *Iconos: revista de Ciencias Sociales*, 31: 117–30.

—— (2016) 'El referéndum ante la crisis de legitimidad: ¿solución o síntoma del problema? in F. Tuesta Soldevilla (ed.) *Partidos Políticos y Elecciones: Representatción Política en América Latina*, Lima: JNE: 145–159.

Wheatley, J. (2008) 'Direct democracy in the Commonwealth of Independent States: the state of the art', *C2D Working Paper Series*, 28.

Zovatto, D. (2014) 'Las instituciones de la democracia directa', in A. Lissidini, Y. Welp and D. Zovatto (eds) *Democracias en movimiento: mecanismos de democracia directa y participativa en América Latina*, Mexico: UNAM: 13–70.

# Appendix

*Table A7.3: Facultative MDDs, Latin America (1900–2014)*

| Country | Date | Content | Agenda setter | Function | Constellation | Type |
|---|---|---|---|---|---|---|
| ARG | 25 November 1984 | Treaty of the Beagle Canal | President | PC | UG | II |
| BOL | 10 August 2008 | Constitutional reform (vote of confidence) | President | IC | UG | I |
| | 2 July 2006 | Departmental autonomy | Civil society and provincial government | IC | MA | V |
| | 18 July 2004 | Policy on natural resources | President | PC | DG | IV |
| | 11 January 1931 | Constitutional reform | Military junta | IC | UG | I |
| BRA | 23 October 2005 | Policy on fire arms | Legislative majority | PC | DG | IV |
| | 6 January 1963 | Parliamentarism *v* presidentialism | Legislative majority | IC | DG | III |
| CHL | 11 September 1980 | Constitutional reform | Military junta | IC | UG | I |
| | 4 January 1978 | Presidential leadership | Military junta | IC | UG | I |
| | 30 August 1925 | Constitutional reform | President | IC | DG | III |
| COL | 25 October 2003 | Constitutional reform and social policy | President | IC & PC | DG | III & IV |
| | 9 December 1990 | Constitutional assembly | President | IC | UG | I |
| | 27 May 1990 | Constitutional assembly | Civil society/President | IC | MA/UG | V (I) |
| | 1 December 1957 | Constitutional reform | Military junta | IC | UG | I |
| CRI | 7 October 2007 | Free trade treaty | Legislative minority/President | PC | MA/DG | VI (IV) |
| ECU | 7 May 2011 | Constitutional amendment and policies | President | IC & PC | UG | I & II |
| | 15 April 2007 | Constitutional assembly | President | IC | DG | III |
| | 26 November 2006 | Education, health and welfare policies | President | PC | DG | IV |
| | 25 May 1997 | Constitutional reform (various) | President | IC | DG | III |
| | 26 November 1995 | Constitutional reform and various policies | President | IC & PC | DG | III & IV |

*(Continued)*

Table A7.3 (*Continued*)

| Country | Date | Content | Agenda setter | Function | Constellation | Type |
|---|---|---|---|---|---|---|
| | 28 August 1994 | Constitutional reform and various policies | President | IC & PC | DG | III & IV |
| | 1 June 1986 | Electoral system reform | President | IC | DG | III |
| | 15 January 1978 | Constitutional reform | Military junta | IC | UG | I |
| GTM | 10 October 1954 | Presidential succession | Military junta | IC | UG | I |
| | 24 June 1935 | Presidential term limit | President | IC | UG | I |
| PAN | 15 December 1940 | Constitutional reform | Legislative majority | IC | UG | I |
| PAR | 4 August 1940 | Constitutional reform | President | IC | UG | I |
| | 15 August 1938 | Chaco Peace Treaty with Bolivia | Military Junta | PC | UG | II |
| PER | 3 October 2010 | Housing policy (FONAVI) | Civil Society | PC | MA | VI |
| | 31 October 1993 | Constitutional reform | President | IC | UG | I |
| | 18 June 1939 | Constitutional amendment | President | IC | UG | I |
| | 18 August 1919 | Constitutional reform | President | IC | UG | I |
| URY | 25 October 2009 | Derogation of amnesty law | Civil society | PC | MA | VI |
| | 25 October 2009 | Constitutional amendment | Legislative majority | IC | UG | II |
| | 31 October 2004 | Water and health policy | Civil society | PC | MA | VI |
| | 7 December 2003 | Alimentation policy | Civil society and legislative minority | PC | MA | VI |
| | 31 October 1999 | Fiscal independence of judiciary | Civil society and legislative minority | IC | MA | VI |
| | 31 October 1999 | Electoral reform | Legislative minority | IC | MA | VI |
| | 27 November 1994 | Social policy | Civil society | PC | MA | VI |
| | 27 November 1994 | Budget law | Civil society | PC | MA | VI |
| | 13 December 1992 | Public enterprise law | Civil society | PC | MA | VI |

(*Continued*)

Table A7.3 (*Continued*)

| Country | Date | Content | Agenda setter | Function | Constellation | Type |
|---|---|---|---|---|---|---|
| | 26 November 1989 | Pension policy | Civil society | PC | MA | VI |
| | 16 April 1989 | Derogation of amnesty law | Civil society and legislative minority | PC | MA | VI |
| | 30 November 1980 | Constitutional reform | Military junta | IC | UG | I |
| | 28 November 1971 | Electoral reform | President | IC | DG | III |
| | 27 November 1966 | Constitutional reform (various options) | Various legislative coalitions | IC | DG | III |
| | 25 November 1962 | Constitutional reform | Legislative coalition | IC | DG | III |
| | 30 November 1958 | Constitutional reform (various options) | Legislative coalition | IC | DG | III |
| a | 26 November 1950 | Constitutional reform | – | IC | DG | |
| | 24 November 1946 | Constitutional reform (various options) | Legislative coalition | IC | DG | III |
| | 27 March 1938 | Constitutional reform (various options) | Legislative coalition | IC | DG | III |
| | 19 April 1934 | Constitutional reform | Colegiado and legislative coalition | IC | DG | III |
| | 25 November 1917 | Constitutional reform | Legislative coalition | IC | UG | I |
| VEN | 15 August 2004 | Presidential recall | Opposition parties | IC | MA | V |
| | 3 December 2000 | Union law | Legislative majority | PC | UG | II |
| | 25 April 1999 | Constitutional assembly | President | IC | DG | III |
| | 15 December 1957 | Presidential succession | Military junta | IC | UG | I |

*Sources:* authors' elaboration based on www.c2d.ch (accessed 15 April 2016); Altman, 2011; Lafferriere 2009; Lissidini 1998; Lissovsky and Szabo 2008; Melo 2008; Salazar Elena 2009; Thomas Acuña 2009; Welp 2008, 2014.

*Notes:* BOL=Bolivia, BRA=Brazil; CHL=Chile, COL=Colombia, CRI=Costa Rica, ECU=Ecuador, GTM=Guatemala, PAN=Panama, PAR=Paraguay, PER=Peru, URY=Uruguay, VEN=Venezuela, PC= Policy Change, IC= Institutional Change, MA= Minority Actor, DG= Divided Government, UG= Unified Government.

a Case excluded due to missing data.

*Chapter Eight*

# Recall, Political Representation and Citizen Participation: Reflections Based on the Latin American Experience

*Rocío Annunziata*
*Translated by Julieta Lenarduzzi*

## Introduction

The practice of recalling elected officials is not new, but recently the procedure has experienced a revival, especially in Latin America. This revival leads us to question the consequences and significance recall procedures have for representative democracies. More specifically, is the incorporation of recall procedures at different levels of government in tension with the parallel transformations of democracy in the region that affect both political representation and citizen participation in these countries?

In line with the definition proposed in the introduction of this book, recall is a mechanism of direct democracy (MDD) that can be triggered by citizens to oust elected officials by means of a binding vote, after complying with certain requirements such as the collection of signatures (Welp and Serdült 2014). Historically, the mechanism was introduced in Switzerland in the nineteenth century and in the United States in 1903 – at both state and local levels of government (Welp 2015a). While it has rarely been used in Switzerland (Serdült 2015), it has been and continues to be a relevant instrument in the United States – provided for in nineteen states and in 60.9 per cent of all cities and towns (Qvortrup 2014). Until the end of the 1980s it experienced only a limited diffusion around the world, but recently it has gained momentum in the Latin American region (Welp 2014). The most remarkable case in this region is Peru, where the mechanism has been triggered more than 5,300 times at the municipal level, resulting in the effective removal of 1,737 elected officials. Consequently, Peru has become the country with the greatest number of removals of elected officials in the world. Apart from the frequent use of recalls, Peru also stands out because it warns us about the potential destabilising effects of the mechanism on democratic governance (Tuesta Soldevilla 2014; Welp 2015a).

Recalls have gained importance in other Latin American countries as well. In Ecuador, for example, 21 elected officials were removed from office out of a total of seventy-eight triggered recall processes and about 800 attempts (Castellanos Santamaría 2014). In Venezuela, five elected officials out of ten that had been subject to a recall procedure were removed. Venezuela and Bolivia, moreover, distinguish themselves from the rest of the countries because they applied the recall at the national level. Both presidents – Hugo Chávez in 2004 and Evo Morales in 2008[1] – were subject to a recall. Both were reconfirmed in office and emerged strengthened from these processes (Kornblit 2014; Verdugo Silva 2014). Since 1991, Colombia provides the recall procedure only at the local level of government; however, so far no recall process has led to the removal of an elected official (Franco-Cuervo 2014). In Argentina, the mechanism is regulated at level in six provinces as well as in the City of Buenos Aires and at the municipal level in fourteen provinces. However, requirements to trigger a recall are difficult to comply with in Argentina. So, very few processes were completed (Arqués 2014).

The contemporary revival of recalls runs parallel with important democratic transformations in Latin America, both with respect to political representation and citizen participation. How do these two processes relate to each other? Do they complement or contradict each other? To unpack the relationship between the recall mechanism and democratic transformations in political representation and citizen participation I will, first, address the descent of the mandate or promissory perspective of representation in the region. Second, I will examine the increasing relevance of 'negativity' in new forms of citizen participation in Latin America. Based on these reflections, I will suggest some participatory mechanisms in the conclusion that may be more appropriate to enhance responsiveness in Latin American democracies.

## *Recall and promissory representation*

Proponents of recalling elected officials usually mention that it encourages representatives to comply with the promises they made during their electoral campaign (García Campos 2005). Consequently, the violation of campaign promises is often cited in regulations of recall procedures as one possible reason to trigger it. Although in most cases grounds for recall may also refer to misconduct or criminal behaviour in public office, the betrayal of campaign promises or the failure to comply with government platforms are at the heart of political arguments in favour of the recall mechanism. As Welp (2014) notes, countries in which the violation of campaign promises or government platforms is grounds for recall are Bolivia, Colombia and Ecuador.

The case of Colombia is perhaps the most interesting in this sense since the recall mechanism (regulated by law 131/1994) established the programmatic vote (*voto programático*) at the local level. More specifically, candidates running for office have to register a government platform on which they campaign. Later, this platform may be referenced by anyone in order to trigger a recall. However, the requirements for recalling elected officials in Colombia are particularly demanding. For example, the number of signatures required to trigger a recall

1. The recall in Bolivia was, however, activated by the government itself to pre-empt the instrumentalisation of the mechanism by the opposition. Hence, it was not a bottom-up recall (see Verdugo Silva 2014).

needs to match at least 40 per cent of the number of votes an incumbent obtained in her election, the participation quorum should not be lower than 55 per cent of the turnout when the subjected got elected, and for the successful removal of an incumbent it is necessary to obtain at least an absolute majority of the votes. Hence, it is no surprise that of 100 triggered recall procedures only about thirty met the requirement to lead to an actual recall election and none of them resulted in the removal of an elected official (Welp and Serdült 2014).

The introduction of a programmatic vote in which the violation of campaign promises is set as a reason to trigger a recall referendum seems odd in the Latin American context in which political representation seldom follows the logic of promissory or *mandate representation* (Manin et al. 1999; Kitschelt et al. 2010), but rather a *post-promissory* form of representation (Annunziata 2014).

As Dovi (2014) notes, theoretical discussions on political representation have focused mainly on the formal procedures of authorisation and accountability and have understood the representative linkage primarily as a principal–agent relationship (see also Pitkin 1967). The centrality of elections in democratic representation and the forms of accountability related to electoral timing have characterised the most abundant literature on representation theory. Within this perspective Manin et al. (1999) distinguish between two views of democratic representation. The *mandate view* supposes that candidates or parties make proposals during campaigns on which voters base their electoral decision. The winning platform that results from an election holds the mandate of the voters to govern according to their platform. In contrast, the *accountability view* supposes that voters judge governments for their past actions – regardless of the intentions expressed in electoral campaigns – hence, governments are induced to foster policies in line with citizen preferences at the time of the next election.[2] Put differently, the mandate view assumes that citizens vote in a prospective way, while the accountability view assumes retrospective voting behaviour. In both approaches there is some form of accountability in action (forward looking in one case and backward looking in the other) but both forms of accountability are conceived as sanctions (Mansbridge 2009).

According to Mansbridge (2003), the traditional model of representation, which she calls *promissory representation*, is 'focused on the idea that during campaigns representatives made promises to constituents, which they then kept or failed to keep' (Mansbridge 2003: 515). In this model representatives represent the will of the voters at the moment of the election. The relationship between the represented and their representative is linear: it is supposed that voters express their will in elections and that during the term in office they will observe and judge the behaviour of representatives regarding to their promises and hold them accountable at the next election.

Concerning the role of campaign promises or government platforms, it is worth mentioning that these promises are not perceived as compulsory for

2. In a similar way, Powell (2000) differentiates between 'mandate' and 'accountability' governments.

representative governments. In modern democracies representatives have some kind of autonomy to refrain from following campaign promises if they believe it is in the best interest of their voters. This is a fact that is backed by the absence of legal requirements that force representatives to follow their campaign promises, i.e. modern democracies do not enforce the imperative mandate (Manin 1997). Hence, even if voters take into account the campaign promises of candidates to vote, they know that the credibility of such promises remains an open question (Manin 1997). It is possible to conceive the campaign promise as a *political representative bond* between citizens and politicians, which gives legitimacy to the decisions of incumbents during their term in office.

Mandate or promissory representation supposes a significant role for political parties as suppliers of a political identity, ideology and world views. In this line, elections may well be understood as a choice between different political paths. However, the weakening of the role of political parties, the ascent of individual political leaders, and the process of personalising politics challenges the fundament of promissory representation (Mair 2005, 2008; Rosanvallon 2015).[3] While the core idea of representation as such is not in crisis and representative government remains a resilient system (Manin 2011), the type of representative link has transformed irreversibly. Manin (1997) argues, for example, that representative democracy has developed from a party democracy to an *audience democracy*, i.e. voters no longer choose among different parties or party platforms but among the vague images political leaders offer to the electorate.

Mansbridge (2003) affirms that in recent times, there are new models of representation in which campaign promises – or mandates – are no longer central; two of them concern us here. One is the model called *anticipatory representation*, which derives from the idea of retrospective voting: representatives do not represent the will of the citizens in the past election but the will they suppose citizens will have in the future election; they represent the voter at the moment of the next election, meaning that 'representatives focus on what they think their constituents will approve at the next election, not on what they promised to do at the last election' (Mansbridge 2003: 515). Hence, anticipatory representation is very similar to the accountability view of representation or the accountability government perspective mentioned above (Manin et al. 1999; Powell 2000). What is new about Mansbridge's conception of anticipatory representation is the emphasis on the Schumpeterian initiative of leaders in shaping citizen preferences (Mansbridge 2003; Schumpeter 1942).

The second model Mansbridge (2003) mentions that goes beyond promissory representation is called *gyroscopic representation*, in which voters choose not a fixed political orientation, but a person they consider will know how to behave in the increasingly uncertain, unpredictable and contingent situations that he or

3. This also relates to the decreasing utility of the left–right dimension in the region, which undermines the *responsible party government model* (see Mair 2008; Ruth 2016).

she will necessarily face during the term in office.[4] The role of representatives as political 'compasses' in this model highlights the importance of the personal characteristics of candidates. Similarly, the unpredictability of contemporary politics is one factor that makes voters favour vague images of leaders rather than the complex policy platforms of political parties in the context of the audience democracy (Manin 1997). If it is necessary to give some degree of discretion to representatives, then it is reasonable to choose them based on their apparent ability to make decisions rather than on the basis of specific policy promises.

Anticipatory and gyroscopic representation may both be considered facets of a general model of *post-promissory representation* (Annunziata 2014). As Mansbridge (2009) notes, a common feature in these two models is that accountability (in the traditional sense of sanction) is replaced by an ongoing communication process between incumbents and the public during the governmental term. If incumbents represent a future will of the people, however shaped, they need to be informed about changes in public opinion. Moreover, the post-promissory model of representation may resort to deliberative elements through shaping public opinion and educating and informing the public on pending issues. Hence, communication between incumbents and citizens becomes more imperative in more unpredictable political scenarios. Mansbridge has recently conceptualised a narrative form of accountability according to this vision and opposite to the notion of accountability based on monitoring and sanctions: 'In *narrative* and *deliberative* accountability, the representative explains the reasons for her actions and even (ideally) engages in two-way communication with constituents, particularly when deviating from the constituents' preferences' (Mansbridge 2009: 370, original emphasis).

In post-promissory representation, responsiveness plays a major role. By the same thinking, Stimson et al. (1995) proposed the notion of *dynamic representation* to conceptualise the response of incumbents to changes in public opinion. In a context of post-promissory representation, campaign promises are replaced by the constant act of listening (Annunziata 2015a). Candidates in such systems are increasingly required to convey an image of being able to listen to the concerns of ordinary citizens, to be personally present in their neighbourhoods and share their life experiences and to show empathy and compassion for their everyday suffering. In this sense, *encouraging participation* becomes a part of *representing*, and citizens are invited by their representatives to express their concerns and hopes on a permanent basis, even during campaigns, when the life stories of ordinary men and women are placed at the centre of candidates' messages (Annunziata 2012).

Rosanvallon (2008) recently hypothesised that the dissociation of electoral legitimacy from the legitimacy of political decisions lies at the core of recent changes in political representation. He observes an increasing gap between the

4. Although Mansbridge (2003) explicitly refrains from equating gyroscopic representation with the trustee model of representation – defined, for example, by Dovi (2014) as representatives who follow their own judgment to pursue the will of the people – she recognises that gyroscopic representatives are bestowed with a high level of autonomy by their voters.

legitimacy of electoral authorisation (how representatives are appointed) and the legitimacy of their actions and decisions (how they rule until the following election) – in line with what I identify as post-promissory representation. This means that, although electoral democracy is consolidated in Latin American countries, elections are merely a process of selecting rulers, and no longer imply the choice of a concrete course of action, what Ronsanvallon (2008) refers to as 'desacralized' elections. Hence, one of the founding fictions of representative democracies is that the vote of the people legitimises a government not just at the time of an election but also during their time in office, and therefore legitimacy remains fixed throughout the whole mandate. It is exactly this fiction that is losing importance due to the contemporary transformations of democracy. Campaign promises provided the glue between electoral legitimacy and the legitimacy of the behaviour of representatives throughout their term in office; without such mandates, throughput legitimacy – i.e. the legitimacy of the actions of representatives in the democratic process – is no longer guaranteed through the ballot box (see also Scharpf 1999; Zürn 2000). The lack of throughput legitimacy has been observable in several Latin American countries where political leaders won elections with strong support at the ballot box but soon after their inauguration their behaviour in office was challenged. For example, Evo Morales in Bolivia sparked strong protest when he decided to build a route across an indigenous territory (Mayorga 2014); and Cristina Fernández de Kirchner, in Argentina, was fiercely criticised by opposition forces after her decision to raise export taxes in the agricultural sector (Cheresky and Annunziata 2012).

In sum, compared to the traditional model of mandate (or promissory) representation, post-promissory representation changes the temporal dynamic of the linkage between representatives and represented. While representative linkages based on campaign promises are durable and experience ruptures only in periodic ways, post-promissory linkages are characterised by constant adjustment, i.e. they are based on immediate, direct responsiveness (Stimson et al. 1995). Representatives need to listen constantly to public changes of opinion.

But how does the recall mechanism relate to these changing contexts of representation? Are recalls capable of strengthening the traditional model of promissory representation? What is the relationship between recalls and the post-promissory type of representation? To analyse this relationship, let us return to the Colombian case. As mentioned earlier, the regulation of the recall procedure institutionalises the enforcement of a so-called programmatic vote (*voto programático*). However, the procedure has been activated in only a limited number of cases. Does this lead to the conclusion that governors and mayors in Colombia anticipate the potential threat of a recall, and hence, are more likely to fulfil their campaign promises? Evidence based on in-depth case studies indicates two things: on the one hand, since the introduction of the programmatic vote government platforms have not become clearer or more precise, and thus do not increase the capacity of citizens to judge the promissory compliance of incumbents or lack thereof. For example, a comparative study of government programmes of the 125 mayors of the Antioquia region reveals important problems with respect to the identification of concrete policy proposals (Arenas Gómez et al. 2015). Consequently, the anticipative effect of a recall procedure may incentivise candidates to run on the basis of rather vague and imprecise policy platforms.

On the other hand, a recent analysis conducted by Uribe Mendoza (2016) of the recall attempts against two mayors of Bogotá – Samuel Moreno and Gustavo Petro – highlights that the reasons to activate a recall are not necessarily based on non-compliance with campaign promises but in one of the cases it was related to extraordinary policy decisions (which had not been part of the electoral campaign). In the case of the recall of Samuel Moreno, which was driven by citizens arguing dissatisfaction with non-compliance with the programme because he decided to restrict vehicular traffic, the necessary signatures could not be collected. In the case of Gustavo Petro the recall had been triggered based on decisions rejected by citizens that had not been included in the original programme (a decree relative to a change in the garbage collection service) (Uribe Mendoza 2016). The case of mayor Petro indicates that representatives may be subjected to a recall even if they react to political challenges that have not been on the political agenda during the electoral campaign, thereby defying any manoeuvrability implied in the mandate model of representation. In short/In brief it seems doubtful that recall referendums can reverse the transformation of representative linkages; quite the contrary, they seem to be in tension with the format of representation that is consolidating nowadays.

Post-promissory representation seems to require more communication between the represented and their representatives, spaces and channels open to the acts of listening and deliberation that can contribute to legitimising decisions that were unforeseeable during the electoral campaign. Welp and Serdült (2014) argue that 'a basic issue to consider when analysing the recall referendum refers to the grounds to initiate the process, because this conveys a definition of representation. In other words, the bases of the recall define the *mandate*' (Welp and Serdült 2014: 139, original emphasis). By referring to the breach of campaign promises as possible grounds for a recall, this mechanism supposes a definition of the representative mandate that implicitly stands against the modern definition of representative government, and against the growing dissonance between electoral legitimacy and throughput legitimacy that characterises contemporary democracies in the Latin American region.[5]

## *Recall and negative citizen participation*

Beyond the campaign promises and the mandate view of representation, the recall mechanism usually serves as a tool for citizens to express objections to the course of action a government takes. Among the arguments in favour of the recall mechanism is the idea that it can work as an institutional channel to express citizens' discontent (García Campos 2005). In fact, most legal grounds for recall

5. This relationship becomes even more problematic if we take regulations about the timing of recall procedures into account (see Rosanvallon 2006; Welp 2014).

refer to either dissatisfaction or disapproval of government actions, without the need for any proof.

Furthermore the recall is usually classified as a reactive tool of direct democracy; Breuer (2007) subsumes it among the reactive initiatives, centred on controlling public officials (rather than laws or decisions). Eberhardt (2013: 15, own translation) notes that:

> [w]ithin the framework of direct or participatory democracy, their principal function is to enable a form of 'negative' citizen participation or citizen control, rather than a 'positive' expression or implementation of citizen projects and initiatives, since it repeals the representative contract before the official end of the term of office.

Hence, at first glance, the recall appears to be an adequate institutional channel for citizens to express objections to legislation and to veto it – in other words, it would follow a trend towards negative citizen participation, which lies at the heart of democratic transformations in the Latin American region. It is in this line of thought that Rosanvallon (2006) speaks about the emergence of 'people as veto players' (*see* Welp and Ruth, Chapter Seven in this volume) as one of the most significant expressions of people's sovereignty in present times. Within the framework of a 'society of distrust', Rosanvallon (2006) conceptualised various diffuse and indirect powers that give shape to the universe of 'counter-democracy', of which the veto is one. Moreover, Rosanvallon (2006) attributes the pre-eminence of negativity to a sociological factor, i.e. the fact that reactive coalitions are easier to organise, no matter their heterogeneity. Hence, to accomplish their mission, reactive coalitions do not need to be coherent. That is because refusal is the easiest thing to aggregate: all refusals are in effect identical, no matter which motives lead to their formulation. In this sense negativity has a structural advantage at the present time, since reactive political majorities have become increasingly easier to form when political arenas are no longer structured by ideological confrontations (Rosanvallon 2006). Additionally, refusal produces quick results that are immediately effective and fully accomplish their objective.

In contemporary democracies negativity is most frequently expressed through popular protest. This characterisation is shared by Urbinati and Warren (2008) when they describe self-organised citizen movements as expressions of the 'negative power of the people'. In the last few years the world experienced an expansion of forms of protest or 'non-institutionalized forms of participation' (Manin 2015), whose most salient characteristic is negativity (Rosanvallon 2006). Street protests can take place to express an opposition to a specific policy, to individual politicians or to the *political class* in general. What unites a critical mass of citizens is not a shared project but a shared refusal. This finds its representation in the frequency of the use of the words 'No!' or 'Enough!' in protest slogans. These protests can often make the incumbents back down from certain decisions, or even make them leave office. Latin America can be seen as the world's laboratory for these new forms of negative citizen participation. To give just a few examples, one can mention the popular protest called *Cacerolazo*, which played a decisive role in the presidential fall of Fernando de la Rúa in Argentina in 2001 (see Hochstetler 2008); the student movement *#Yosoy132* in Mexico in 2012, and the protests in Brazil in June 2013 initiated by the group *Passe Livre* figure among the most recent protest wave (see Welp 2015b; Bringel and Pleyers 2015). But protests are also gaining weight at regional and municipal levels. In many cities and towns in Latin American countries the frequency of relatively confined protests around specific problems of public safety or the environment have increased.

Nevertheless, it is important to keep in mind the spontaneous and ephemeral character of these forms of participation. Manin (2015), for example, describes them as episodic, and points out that citizens participate not because of their identification with an organisation but because some events offer them a possibility for political action. Contemporary protests are usually neither organised nor mediated by traditional actors such as political parties or unions, and it is the notion of self-organised citizen participation that appeals to citizens. These self-organised forms of citizen participation entail the potential of a multiplying effect: a protest that starts as an objection to a specific decision can easily turn into against the government or politicians, who are perceived as privileged, as a caste separated from ordinary citizens (Annunziata 2015b). However, the promoters of these protests cannot be considered 'organisers' in the strict sense, nor can they maintain control of their public significance.

Urbinati (2013) has recently introduced the concept of *live broadcasting representative democracy* to describe the emergence of citizen movements that lie outside the control of traditional mediating actors like political parties, and have been encouraged by new information and communication technologies. She stresses that these new forms of citizen participation are a type of revolt against intermediary bodies and all kind of mediation (Urbinati 2015). The latest report of Latinobarómetro (2015) shows that citizens are increasingly participating, but they do it outside traditional organisations:

> Protesting citizens are not affiliated to any political organization, they do not protest from inside the political or social system, but from the outside, as individuals. They do not constitute a critical mass to be incorporated into the political system, since they act alone and switch allegiances without a forming permanent attachments. Therefore, the political system loses its capacity to represent these empowered citizens, since it does not know how to mobilize them. (Latinobarómetro 2015: 16, own translation)

Hence, can we say that the introduction and frequent use of recall mechanisms in Latin American countries goes hand in hand with the transformations of citizen participation in recent years? As mentioned above, the recall is an essentially negative mechanism. In this respect it resembles recent developments towards negative forms of citizen participation. However, we should not forget that these new forms of citizen participation are also marked by a high level of spontaneity and the absence of the controlling hand of organised political actors.

Could recall, then become a mechanism to institutionalise objections or rather fluid forms of negative citizen participation?[6] On the one hand, Rosanvallon (2006) points out that it is not possible to institutionalise counter-democratic powers, let alone constitutionalise them. The huge amount of organisational resources needed to trigger a recall procedure makes the involvement of political parties in the process inevitable. Apart from the demanding requirements of triggering an event, recall mechanisms usually suppose a waiting period in order to accomplish the goal of ousting an elected official (Welp 2014). This element contradicts the spontaneity that characterises these protests or citizen movements. Hence, it seems that it is neither possible nor desirable to institutionalise this type of citizen activity through the recall mechanism.

On the other hand, research shows that, especially given the need for timing and organisation of resources the mechanism predisposes organised actors to use the recall in their own interest, thereby distorting the mechanism and institutionalising the electoral struggle between government and opposition beyond periodic elections (Tuesta Soldevilla 2014; Welp 2015a). This is what the experience in Peru reveals, where the recall has become a mechanism used by losers in elections to produce a new electoral process (Tuesta Soldevilla 2014). Welp (2015a) notes on the Peruvian case that 'recall procedures create unexpected incentives for politicians to use them as an extension to "normal" electoral competition' (Welp 2015: 11), and consequently the recall does not necessarily promote the empowerment of citizens 'despite being a bottom up procedure, it has been perverted by top down instrumentalization' (Welp 2015a: 17). But this instrumentalisation by political actors is not exclusive to countries with a high frequency of effective recalls such as Peru; take for example the Argentinean case, where we find some experiences of recall processes at the local level (Arqués 2014). On the one hand, the mayor of the City of Buenos Aires, Aníbal Ibarra, promoted a recall against himself in 2005 to successfully prevent his impeachment, since the recall process did not succeed due to high signature requirements. Another example happened in Villa Ascasubi, in the Province of Cordoba in 2011, where a recall process against two city councils was promoted by the mayor and his political party.

To sum up, the recall appears to be a mechanism of citizen control in the hands of parties: 'the main promoters are not the citizens, but political organisations, parties or political leaders' (Welp 2014: 161).

6. In this sense Lissidini (2014) recently posed the question of whether it is possible to institutionalise protest in Latin American democracies. She concludes that in contexts like Uruguay, direct democratic mechanisms have been useful to channel demands, even negative ones, blocking spending cuts and privatisation. But it is important to note that the Uruguayan party system and direct democratic practice in the country are the exception rather than the rule in the Latin American region.

## *Conclusion: recall and contemporary transformations of democracy*

The popularity of the recall mechanism in Latin American countries appears to be in tension with parallel changes in political representation and citizen participation in these democracies. This leads to the question of whether it is possible to revitalise party platforms and campaign promises by introducing the recall mechanisms, or if the recall, on the contrary, reinforces a political dynamic that no longer works.

As argued in the first part of this chapter, the discontent towards representatives does not usually derive from the breach of government platforms or campaign promises, but from unexpected events such as the decisions or actions of the incumbents. For example, in the case of Colombia the recall did not induce governments to keep their campaign promises but rather led to an increased vagueness of party platforms and campaign promises during elections. Above all, post-promissory representation calls for forms of consultation, communication and deliberation with the citizens that provide better throughput legitimacy than non-deliberative procedures. These channels for listening can play the role of expanding and going beyond traditional models of representation, instead of limiting them. Hence, post-promissory representation builds on a different temporal logic of legitimacy, while the recall mirrors a simplified legitimising logic of the mandate model of representation – based on an electoral mechanism (see Urbinati 2006; Rosanvallon 2008).

Apart from these tensions with respect to the temporality of representation as well as the establishment of throughput legitimacy, the recall mechanism also experiences a conflictive relationship with new forms of negative citizen participation. As has been argued in the second part of this chapter, in a context in which citizens express themselves mostly by means of inorganic protests of veto or rejection, the recall does not seem to be an appropriate tool: it is usually organised by actors who, as a consequence of the high demands for the implementation of the mechanism, have the capacity to promote and trigger it. Hence, the recall mechanism paradoxically requires the organisational help of political parties or powerful political actors to enable citizens to express their distrust of the *political class*. What the Latin American experience shows is that the recall is used by the political class to solve disputes among them rather than between them and their constituents. Due to its central role in the political struggle between government and opposition, the recall referendum appears to be rather an instrument of political parties and powerful political leaders than a tool of effective citizen participation.

Again, the existence of more permanent channels of listening that would allow for the communication between the represented and their representatives in the face of unexpected situations seems to be more in accordance with contemporary democratic transformations. Consequently, since the recall builds on an electoral mechanism it remains within the authorisation logic of democracy through which incumbents attain democratic legitimacy (Rosanvallon 2015). In contrast, the model of 'interactive democracy' requires representatives to become more responsive to citizens' demands and public opinion throughout their term in office (see Rosanvallon 2015; Stimson et al. 1995). Such an interactive perspective on democracy transcends the formalistic, elections-centred, and principal–agent view of traditional models of political representation (see Dovi 2014).

In conclusion I will provide some suggestions as to how it might be possible to actually enhance responsiveness and empower citizens in contemporary democracies. Considering the dissociation between electoral legitimacy and the legitimacy of decisions, one solution might be to strengthen procedures of direct citizen review of policy decisions. Several countries around the world already provide for direct democratic mechanisms that institutionalise such a popular veto on policy decisions, such as abrogative and derogative citizen initiatives (e.g. Hug and Tsebelis 2002; Breuer 2007; Serdült 2015). These initiatives are more in line with contemporary transformations of democracy since they enable citizens to voice their objections to policy decisions directly and not by denouncing the political actors who propose the policies. Additionally, these initiatives are less attractive to opposition parties or challengers who hope to be able to exploit the removal of such political actors to their own advantage.

Considering the importance of narrative and communicative accountability in contemporary democracies, it seems reasonable to also think about deliberative institutions in which citizens could contribute to the development of policies and in which representatives could explain and defend their decisions (e.g. Dryzek 2010; Goodin 2008). Altman (2014), for example, proposes randomly selected commissions or panels with the purpose of creating *citizens' counterproposals* in order to complement MDD procedures. Deliberative *mini-publics* may have an interesting incidence in improving decision-making processes (Grönlund et al. 2014). Another example is large-scale deliberative forums for discussing specific public policy issues, like the innovative procedure of National Conferences (*Conferências Nacionais de Políticas Públicas*) implemented in Brazil in recent years (Avritzer 2015).

These examples show that we do not lack ideas and creativity in institutional design and that there is much room for improving communication channels between decision makers and citizens.

## Acknowledgement

I would like to thank Saskia Ruth, Yanina Welp and Laurence Whitehead for their insightful comments on this chapter.

## References

Altman, D. (2014) 'Strengthening democracy quality: reactive deliberation in the context of direct democracy', Working Paper, No. 400 (June), Kellogg Institute, Notre Dame, available at: https://kellogg.nd.edu/publications/workingpapers/WPS/400.pdf (accessed 15 April 2016).

Annunziata, R. (2012) '¿Hacia un nuevo modelo de lazo representativo? La representación de proximidad en las campañas electorales de 2009 y 2011 en Argentina', in I. Cheresky and R. Annunziata (eds) *Sin programa, sin promesa. Liderazgos y procesos electorales en Argentina*, Buenos Aires: Prometeo: 45–87.

—— (2014) 'Más allá de la promesa electoral. Repensar la representación en Argentina', *Sudamérica: Revista de ciencias sociales*, 3: 137–53.

—— (2015a) 'Liderazgos de proximidad y procesos electorales: los casos de Sergio Massa y Martín Insaurralde en las legislativas de 2013', in R. Annunziata (ed) *Pensar las elecciones. Democracia, líderes y ciudadanos*, Buenos Aires: Clacso-IIGG: 95–128.

—— (2015b) 'Democracia participativa: ideales, experiencias y desafíos', in A. R. Lazzeretti and F. M. Suárez (eds) *Socialismo & Democracia*, Mar del Plata: EUDEM: 143–63.

Arenas Gómez, J. C., Bedoya Marulanda, J. F., Echeverry López, L. M. and Hernández Sánchez, Y. C. (2015) 'Propuestas programáticas y perfil político de los mandatarios de Antioquia (2012–2015)', University of Antioquia, Colombia, available at http://www.escuelagobierno.org/escuela/index.php?sub_cat=26138 (accessed 15 April 2016).

Arqués, F. (2014) 'Argentina: una herramienta de los gobernados en manos de los gobernantes', in Y. Welp and U. Serdült (eds) *La dosis hace el veneno. Análisis de la revocatoria del mandato en América Latina, Estados Unidos y Suiza*, Quito: Instituto de la Democracia: 159–86.

Avritzer, L. (2015) *Los desafíos de la participación en América Latina*, Buenos Aires: Prometeo.

Breuer, A. (2007) 'Institutions of Direct Democracy and Accountability in Latin America's Presidential Democracies', *Democratization*, 14(4): 554–79.

Bringel, B. and Pleyers, G. (2015) 'Les mobilisations de 2013 au Brésil: vers une reconfiguration de la contestation', *Brésil(s). Sciences humaines et socials*, 7: 7–18.

Castellanos Santamaría, A. S. (2014) 'Ecuador: la transformación de las reglas del juego y sus consecuencias (1998–2013)', in Y. Welp and U. Serdült (eds) *La dosis hace el veneno: análisis de la revocatoria del mandato en América Latina, Estados Unidos y Suiza*, Quito: Instituto de la Democracia: 83–110.

Cheresky, I. and Annunziata, R. (2012) 'Los desafíos de la democracia argentina. La primera presidencia Cristina Kirchner', in I. Cheresky and R. Annunziata (eds) *Sin programa, sin promesa: liderazgos y procesos electorales en Argentina*, Buenos Aires: Prometeo: 13–42.

Dovi, S. (2014) 'Political representation', in E. N. Zalta (ed) *The Stanford Encyclopedia of Philosophy*, Stanford: Stanford University Press, available at http://plato.stanford.edu/archives/spr2014/entries/political-representation/ (accessed 15 April 2016).

Dryzek, J. S. (2010) *Foundations and Frontiers of Deliberative Governance*, Oxford: Oxford University Press.

Eberhardt, M. L. (2013) 'Crisis de representación en las democracias presidencialistas latinoamericanas: ¿La revocatoria como opción?' *Elecciones*, 12(13):13–51.

Franco-Cuervo, A. B. (2014) 'Colombia: Instituciones, líderes políticos y abstención electoral (1991–2013)', in Y. Welp and U. Serdült (eds) *La dosis hace el veneno: análisis de la revocatoria del mandato en América Latina, Estados Unidos y Suiza*, Quito: Instituto de la Democracia: 57–81.

García Campos, A. (2005) 'La revocación del mandato. Un breve acercamiento teórico', *Quid Iuris*, 1(1): 25–40.

Goodin, R. E. (2008) *Innovating Democracy: Democratic theory and practice after the deliberative turn*, Oxford: Oxford University Press.

Grönlund, K., Bächtiger, A. and Setälä, M. (eds) (2014) *Deliberative Mini-Publics: Involving citizens in the democratic process*, Colchester: ECPR Press.

Hochstetler, K. (2008) 'Repensando el presidencialismo: desafíos y caídas presidenciales en el Cono Sur', *América Latina Hoy*, 49: 51–72.

Hug, S. and Tsebelis, G. (2002) 'Veto players and referendums around the world', *Journal of Theoretical Politics*, 14(4): 465–515.

Kitschelt, H., Hawkins, K. A., Luna, J. P., Rosas, G. and Zechmeister, E. J. (eds) (2010) *Latin American Party System*, Cambridge: Cambridge University Press.

Kornblit, M. (2014) 'La revocatoria de mandato en Venezuela: definición y puesta en práctica', in A. Lissidini, Y. Welp and D. Zovatto (eds) *Democracias en movimiento: mecanismos de democracia directa y participativa en América Latina*, Mexico DF: UNAM-Instituto de Investigaciones Jurídicas: 111–33.

Latinobarómetro (2015) 'Informe 1995–2015', Santiago de Chile, available at http://americanuestra.com/wp-content/uploads/2015/09/INFORME-LB-2015-3.pdf (accessed 15 April 2016).

Lissidini, A. (2014) 'Paradojas de la participación en América Latina. ¿Puede la democracia directa institucionalizar la protesta?' in A. Lissidini, Y. Welp and D. Zovatto (eds) *Democracias en movimiento. Mecanismos de democracia directa y participativa en América Latina*, Mexico DF: UNAM-Instituto de Investigaciones Jurídicas: 97–132.

Mair, P. (2005) 'Democracy beyond parties', Working Paper, 05-06, Center for the Study of Democracy. Irvine: University of California, available at http://escholarship.org/uc/item/3vs886v9 (accessed 15 April 2016).

—— (2008) 'The challenge to party government', *West European Politics*, 31(1–2): 211–34.

Manin, B. (1997) *The Principles of Representative Government*, Cambridge: Cambridge University Press.

—— (2011) 'La résilience de la démocratie représentative', paper presented at the Conférence du Groupe de Recherche Interuniversitaire en Philosophie Politique, University of Quebec, Montreal, 18 November.

—— (2015) 'La democracia de audiencia revisitada', in R. Annunziata (ed.) *¿Hacia una mutación de la democracia?*, Buenos Aires: Prometeo: 19–41.

Manin, B., Przeworski, A. and Stokes, S. (1999) 'Elections and representation', in A. Przeworski, S. Stokes and B. Manin (eds) *Democracy, Accountability and Representation*, Cambridge: Cambridge University Press, 29–54.

Mansbridge, J. (2003) 'Rethinking representation', *American Political Science Review*, 97(4): 515–28.
—— (2009) 'A "selection model" of political representation', *Journal of Political Philosophy*, 17(4): 369–98.
Mayorga, F. (2014) *Incertidumbres tácticas: ensayos sobre democracia, populismo y ciudadanía*, La Paz: Plural.
Pitkin, H. (1967) *The Concept of Representation*, Los Angeles: University of California Press.
Powell, G. B. (2000) *Elections as Instruments of Democracy: Majoritarian and proportional visions*, New Haven: Yale University Press.
Qvortrup, M. (2014) 'La experiencia estadounidense de 1776 a 2012', in Y. Welp and U. Serdült (eds) *La dosis hace el veneno: Análisis de la revocatoria del mandato en América Latina, Estados Unidos y Suiza*, Quito: Instituto de la Democracia: 207–24.
Rosanvallon, P. (2006) *La contre-démocratie: la politique à l'âge de la defiance*, Paris: Seuil.
—— (2008) *La légitimité démocratique Impartialité, réflexivité, proximité*, Paris, Seuil.
—— (2015) *Le bon gouvernement*, Paris: Seuil.
Ruth, S. P. (2016) 'Clientelism and the utility of the left–right dimension in Latin America', *Latin American Politics and Society*, 58(1): 72–97.
Scharpf, F. W. (1999) *Governing in Europe*, Oxford: Oxford University Press.
Schumpeter, J. (1942) *Capitalism, Socialism and Democracy*, New York: Harper & Row.
Serdült, U. (2015) 'The history of a dormant institution: legal norms and the practice of recall in Switzerland', *Representation*, 51(2): 161–72.
Stimson, J. A., Mackuen, M. B. and Erickson, R. S. (1995) 'Dynamic representation', *American Political Science Review*, 89(3): 543–65.
Tuesta Soldevilla, F. (2014) 'Perú: entre la participación y la gobernabilidad local (1997–2013)', in Y. Welp and U. Serdült (eds) *La dosis hace el veneno: análisis de la revocatoria del mandato en América Latina, Estados Unidos y Suiza*, Quito: Instituto de la Democracia: 7–30.
Urbinati, N. (2006) *Representative Democracy: Principles and genealogy*. Chicago: University of Chicago Press.
—— (2013) 'Mobilisations en réseaux, activisme numérique: les nouvelles attentes participatives', *Esprit*, 8: 87–97.
—— (2015) 'A revolt against intermediary bodies', *Constellations*, 22(4): 477–86.
Urbinati, N. and Warren, M. (2008) 'The concept of representation in contemporary democratic theory', *Annual Review of Political Science*, 11(1): 387–412.
Uribe Mendoza, C. (2016) 'La activación de la revocatoria de mandato en el ámbito municipal en Colombia. Lecciones del caso de Bogotá', *Estudios Políticos*, 48: 179–200.
Verdugo Silva, J. T. (2014) 'Bolivia: entre la expectativa de uso y los intentos fallidos de activación', in Y. Welp and U. Serdült (eds) *La dosis hace el veneno. Análisis de la revocatoria del mandato en América Latina, Estados Unidos y Suiza*, Quito: Instituto de la Democracia: 135–58.

Welp, Y. (2014) 'De venenos y fármacos. La regulación y prácticas de la revocatoria del mandato en Suiza y las Américas', in Y. Welp and U. Serdült (eds) *La dosis hace el veneno. Análisis de la revocatoria del mandato en América Latina, Estados Unidos y Suiza*, Quito: Instituto de la Democracia: 247–66.

—— (2015a) 'Recall referendums in Peruvian municipalities: a political weapon for bad losers or an instrument of accountability?', *Democratization*, 22(1): 1–21.

—— (2015b) 'Cuando todo lo sólido se desvanece en twitter: Análisis del movimiento social #Yosoy132 (México 2012)', *PostData. Revista de Reflexión y Análisis Político*, 20(2): 417–39.

Welp, Y. and Serdült, U. (2014) 'Cuando es peor el remedio que la enfermedad. Análisis de la revocatoria del mandato en los municipios de los países andinos', in A. Lissidini, Y. Welp and D. Zovatto (eds) *Democracias en movimiento. Mecanismos de democracia directa y participativa en América Latina*, Mexico DF: UNAM-Instituto de Investigaciones Jurídicas: 133–56.

Zürn, M. (2000) 'Democratic governance beyond the nation state', *European Journal of International Relations*, 6(2): 183–221.

*Chapter Nine*

# The Levelling Up of a Political Institution: Perspectives on the Recall Referendum

*Uwe Serdült and Yanina Welp*

## Introduction

The recall referendum is defined as a mechanism of direct democracy (MDD) that allows for the removal of elected officials from office before the end of their term by a popular vote. It can be direct, when the people collect signatures to activate the vote, and in this case it is known as a bottom-up MDD. Alternatively it can be indirect, when the legislature starts the process, and it is then defined as a top-down MDD. In this chapter we focus on direct recall.

In general, recall can be seen as a counter power in the configuration of checks and balances of democratic institutions. It can be used against individual office holders as well as against whole parliaments or governments. According to Lijphart (1984: 200) the rationale of the recall referendum is that it allows a number of voters who are dissatisfied with their representatives to ask for a special election in which they can eventually be removed.

Where it is regulated, recall is normatively expected to give citizens a tool to hold representatives accountable. Since the mechanism serves to remove bad representatives, it should in return incentivise responsiveness (Qvortrup 2011, Annunziata, Chapter Eight in this volume). But evidence of the extent to which the mechanism contributes to this goal is difficult to evaluate. On one hand, only a few countries have regulations that have been implemented for a sufficient period of time; examples include some Swiss cantons, where recall has been regulated since the nineteenth century (Serdült 2015), some states and municipalities in the USA, where it has been in place since the early twentieth century (Zimmerman 2013 [1928]), as well as a few Argentinian provinces, the first one starting in 1923 (Arques 2014). On the other hand, the historical path followed by these countries has been quite different. In Switzerland and Argentina the institution has been used only a few times during more than a century, whereas in the United States it has been activated relatively frequently.

What we would like to highlight in particular in this chapter, however, are more recent global developments related to the practice of the recall. We can observe that the legal provisions allowing for the recall procedure have been introduced more frequently since the 1990s. Just to give some examples, Germany introduced this procedure at the subnational level after the fall of the Berlin wall, Poland did so during the transition to democracy, and many South American countries followed (Colombia in 1991, Peru in 1993, Ecuador in 1998 and Venezuela in 1999, among others). Later examples of recall practice include California (against

Governor Gray Davies in 2004), Venezuela (against President Hugo Chávez in 2004), the city of Lima (against Mayor Susana Villarán in 2013)[1] and the city of Warsaw (against Mayor Hanna Gronkiewicz-Waltz, in 2013). These cases have attracted media attention, possibly because the recall procedure is reaching the bigger cities, and even the presidency as in the case of Venezuela, whereas it mainly seemed to be confined to smaller municipalities before. These cases seem to stress the potential of recall referendums to channel citizens' dissatisfaction with a government's performance (Bowler 2004). However, some scholars also suggest that recall referendums are mainly being activated as a strategic option in fierce struggles between elites over political power (Tuesta Soldevilla 2014, Welp 2015).

Given the growing interest in the subject and the scarcity of comparative studies, this chapter aims to identify countries where legal provisions to activate recalls by citizens exist, from the nineteenth century to 2015. Thus, our first goal is to draw a map of *direct recall referendums* around the world, identifying the levels and institutions at which they are targeted (national and/or local, the executive and/or the legislature).

Second, we want to contribute to the study of political institutions, going beyond its normative notion alone (*see* also Welp and Ruth, Chapter Seven in this volume). By looking at recall experiences in capitals and cities with more than 500,000 inhabitants, we want to test the extent to which the recall fulfils different functions depending on (1) the main agent initiating the process, for example a political party or civil society organisation, and on (2) the primary (to remove elected authority or resolve institutional deadlock) or secondary reason (resolve policy conflict or party struggle) that it was activated (Takanobu 2000).

The chapter is structured as follows: we start by summing up the theoretical debate on the functions of the recall to propose a framework for analysing our cases. We then draw a map of the spread and evolution of direct recall referendum regulations and practice, before offering an exploratory study of experiences of recall in big cities. Finally, we present some conclusions and perspectives for future research.

## State of the art

Scholarly research has associated the increasing use of MDDs activated by signature collection with a crisis of representative democracy (Dalton et al. 2001). Setälä (1999: 333) suggests that an increased number of citizens' initiatives can be expected if citizens become detached from the traditional parties. But MDDs include different types of instruments (*see* Whitehead, and Welp/Ruth, Chapters Two and Seven in this volume) oriented to different goals and with different outcomes. In this way, Miller (2005) suggests that the citizens' initiative is the purest form of direct democracy because it empowers citizens to bypass legislatures and governors and to directly propose laws. By contrast, neither referendums nor recalls circumvent the representative system as such but rather add checks to it. While referendums

1. For detailed case studies of California see Garret (2004) and Bowler (2004), for Venezuela see McCoy (2006) and for Lima see Vásquez Oruna (2014).

activated by signature collection express a check on the legislature, recall referendums allow voters to demand accountability before the representative's term of office has expired (Miller 2005: 138–9). In sum, whereas the initiative introduces unfiltered democratic rule, citizen-initiated referendums and recalls are oriented to increasing accountability and responsiveness of the representative system.

However, the view of MDDs as tools exclusively in the hands of the people as a pure form of democracy can be challenged. Research based on Switzerland and the US has demonstrated that organised interests are vital to the process of activating mechanisms of direct democracy (MDDs), particularly in terms of qualifying proposals for the ballot (Kriesi 2006; Garret 2004). Political parties seem to be better prepared and to have higher incentives for activating direct democratic procedures. The Italian and the Uruguayan examples have shown that parties can be reinforced by the activation of MDDs (Serdült and Welp 2012). Similar findings come from the Nordic and the French experience, showing that referendums can be useful to mobilise and increase the visibility of a small or a new party in the political arena but can also help to resolve power deadlocks or intra-party conflicts (Bjørklund 1982, Morel 1993).

However, the activation of recall referendums can be promoted by civil society actors as well as by political parties, while goals can be primary (the ones for which the institution is designed) or secondary (Takanobu 2000). Our previous research has shown that recalls are to be expected both in the context of scandals and political distrust and/or in the context of extreme political polarisation (Welp and Serdült 2014). The lack of political responsiveness and citizens' trust can promote citizens' activation of recall with at least two ends in mind. On the one hand, the aim can be to reject the authority's general performance (primary) or, on the other hand, it can be to reject a controversial policy (secondary). The former could be related to the lack of other mechanisms of direct intervention, such as referendums (Serdült 2015). On the side of the political elite, recall activations are related to cases of extreme polarisation and low institutionalisation of political party systems. The first, can be exemplified by the case of Venezuela, when the opposition to President Hugo Chávez organised a signature collection to activate the recall device in a context of intense conflict between government and opposition (McCoy 2006). The second is evident in cases in which neither political leaders nor their parties have any guarantee of survival beyond the next election. Recall procedures can then create rather unintended incentives for politicians to use them as an extension to 'normal' electoral competition (Welp 2015).

Most activations of the recall are multi-causal. Several actors are engaged, especially in cases when an activation eventually succeeded in removing the authority.[2] However, by analysing cases in depth we expect to identify the most relevant arguments behind the call and the main actors that initiate the process.

2. The study by Bowler (2004: 209) based on 254 recall activations in US municipalities (population over 2,500) in 1996 found that the most typical reasons to activate the device were a combination of disagreements over policy, specific charges of corruption and related to personnel changes (for example, councillors and the mayor may be subject to recall if they fire a popular police chief).

Thus, considering the main agent initiating the process (political actor or civil society), and the main function (primary or secondary) we propose the following classification:

1. *Direct accountability*: recall referendums can operate as a catharsis in the case of scandals or mismanagement by political elites. Voters are able to make judgements about representatives' performances and remove them from office if they choose to do so (Miller 2005: 138).
2. *Indirect accountability*: recall can turn into a so-called second-order recall (Serdült 2015). In that format, the recall vote is actually targeted against a specific policy and not the political authority per se (Twomey 2011: 46). This could provide an explanation for the cases of Liechtenstein and Switzerland, in which recall has tended to become rather obsolete: the more direct democracy options there are, the less politically antagonistic forces will resort to recall (Serdült 2015).
3. *Institutional struggle*: recall could be a tool used by political parties or political leaders to unblock gridlock between democratic powers (legislative versus executive, mayors versus parliaments but also judicial forces).
4. *Party competition*: recall could provide political parties with an additional option in the game of party competition. Smaller parties might use the recall in the first instance to make themselves known, bigger ones might see the recall as an opportunity to call for an early election, especially if they are almost as strong as the biggest party – particularly in contexts of weak party system institutionalisation (Welp 2015; Tuesta Soldevilla 2014).

## Mapping the evolution of recall referendums

Despite the growing introduction of legal provisions to activate recall referendums, to date a little over twenty countries in the world allow for this procedure. There are remarkable differences between countries regarding the level (national or subnational) at which the procedure can be applied or the authorities that can be removed by a direct recall referendum (*see* Table 9.1).

Recall can be activated against all the elected authorities in five countries, four of them in Latin America (Bolivia, Ecuador, Venezuela and Cuba) and in Taiwan. In Cuba it means that only delegates at the bottom level can be removed by referendum (as this is the only level that is elected), so the device has a very insignificant impact (Guzmán Hernández 2014). In Liechstenstein the whole council can be removed, as at the cantonal level in Switzerland. Then, in nine countries recall can be activated against MPs (Russia, Ethiopia, Kyrgyzstan, Kiribati, Nigeria, Liberia, Panama, Palau and Uganda). In the case of Colombia recall is regulated only to remove executive authorities at the subnational level. In the other three cases (Japan, Poland and Peru) executive and legislative authorities at the subnational level can be removed through a recall process. In addition, there

*Table 9.1: Regulation of direct recall referendums in the world*

| Level of regulation | Authorities that can be removed | Country (year of introduction) |
|---|---|---|
| National | All elected authorities | Bolivia (2009), Cuba (1976), Ecuador (1998), Venezuela (1999), Taiwan RC (2003) |
| | Parliament as a whole | Liechtenstein (1921) |
| | Members of Parliament | Russia, Ethiopia, Kiribati, Kirghistan, Nigeria, Liberia, Uganda, Panama and Palau |
| | Executive and/or legislative authorities at the subnational and local level | Colombia (1994), Japan (1947), Poland (1991), Peru (1994) |
| Subnational | All elected authorities | Switzerland: Uri (1915) |
| | Parliament and/or Government as a whole | Switzerland: Bern (1846), Solothurn (1869), Schaffhausen (1876), Thurgau (1869), Ticino (1892) |
| | Members of Parliament | Canada: British Columbia (1995) |
| | Regulated by the state, or province | Argentina[a], United States of America[b], Mexico[c] |
| | Executive authorities at the local level (mayor) | Germany: Brandenburg (1993), Sachsen (1994), Schleswig-Holstein (1996) and North-Rhine Westphalia (2011) Switzerland: Uri (1915), Ticino (2011) |

*Sources:* Based on the c2d database, IDEA Handbook of Direct Democracy (2008), Serdült and Welp (2012) (for the national level), official website of British Columbia (http://www.elections.bc.ca/index.php/referenda-recall-initiative/recall/, accessed 11 October 2013), Serdült (2015) for Switzerland, Welp and Serdült (2014) for Latin American countries; for USA see www.ncsl.org; and for Mexico from Rosa Ynés Alacio Garcia (personal communication via email).

a In Argentina recall is regulated at the provincial level in Chaco (1957), Chubut (1994), Córdoba (1923, 1987), Corrientes (1960), La Rioja (1986), Rio Negro (1988), Santiago del Estero and Tierra del Fuego (1991); other provinces include it for their municipalities, namely, Entre Ríos (1933), Neuquén (1957), Misiones (1958), San Juan (1986), San Luis (1987). It is also included in Ciudad de Buenos Aires (1996). Source: Arques (2014).

b United States: Alaska, Arizona, California, Colorado, Georgia, Idaho, Illinois, Kansas, Louisiana, Michigan, Minnesota, Montana, Nevada, New Jersey, North Dakota, Oregon, Rhode Island, Washington and Wisconsin.

c In Mexico recall is regulated in the state of Oaxaca (2013).

are another seven cases in which the regulation comes from the subnational level only. In this group, there are cases in which recall is available only against MPs (British Columbia), Switzerland (see above) and four cases (Argentina, Germany, USA and Mexico) where the legislature and executive can be removed according to the law introduced by some subnational governments.

But how can we explain the introduction of legal provisions to activate recall referendums? Explanations from case studies stress different but sometimes complementary reasons. On the one hand, it can be a request coming from the citizens; a prime example is that of Los Angeles, the first US city to introduce recall (in 1903), where its introduction was the result of the influence of the progressive movement, which associated direct democracy with the capacity of the citizenry to control corruption (Spivak 2004; Zimmerman 2013 [1928]). In Japan, the rise of direct democratic procedures, including recall, is related to an awakening of Japanese civil society in the 1990s (Igarashi 2006; Twomey 2011). On the other hand, recall referendums are sometimes associated with the introduction of direct election of mayors and more decentralisation; the introduction of recall in Germany at the municipal level is closely related to the shift from appointed mayors to directly elected mayors starting in Bavaria (1952), Baden-Württemberg (1956) and all the other Länder during the 1990s (Vetter 2006). In Peru under Alberto Fujimori the recall procedure was a way to overcome the condemnation and international blockade that occurred after the closure of the Congress in 1992 (known as *autogolpe*). In 1993 a new Constitution was approved that included many mechanisms for citizen participation, including recall.

Scholarly research mostly based on case studies relates activations of recall to three sets of quite often interrelated reasons: scandals, the impact of digital media, which add a new speed and scope for campaigning, and the leadership of political parties activating recall referendums against their opponents. In some states of the US, the increase in the number of activations has also been related to low levels of electoral participation because that reduces the number of signatures required to start a recall process (given that in most of the US cases it is a percentage of the votes cast in the election of the authority, see Zimmerman 2013 [1928]: 40–1) while digital media diffusion facilitates fast and cheap campaigning (Spivak 2004). In other cases, the current increase in the number of activations has been explained by policy differences that cannot be rejected through other mechanisms, as in the case of Japan (Twomey 2011: 54).

Other cases show the trend towards more activations combined with an attempt at changing the rules to make activation more difficult. As a reaction to the many recalls in the German Land of Brandenburg, the regional parliament increased the signature requirements to trigger the procedure. It went up from ten to twenty-five or fifteen (depending of the number of inhabitants) per cent and stayed at a relatively high level of 25 per cent in the case of Schleswig-Holstein, and one-third (or twenty per cent in bigger cities) in Saxony. However, Böhme (2008: 84) reports that during the past fifteen years in Germany only ninety of all (direct or indirect) recall procedures ended with a vote.[3] In Peru between 1997 and 2013 there were 5,303 activations of recall procedures against elected authorities in 747 out of a total of 1,645 Peruvian municipalities (45.5 per cent), most of them in units with less than 5,000 electors (Tuesta Soldevilla 2014). In Poland, after its introduction the use of recall increased, reaching a peak during the 1998–2002 legislature with a total of 195 recall votes (Piasecki 2011: 131). Since that peak, the use of the recall has tended to meander slightly below or above 100 cases per legislature with a

3. For a detailed case study of MDDs at the German subnational level *see* Geissel, Chapter Ten in this volume.

*Table 9.2: Direct recall referendums at the subnational level*

| Country | Period | Attempts[a] | Votes | Removed authorities | Attempts in big units | Votes in big units |
|---|---|---|---|---|---|---|
| Argentina | 1923–2014 | 10 | 2 | – | 3 (2002, 2005, 2014) | – |
| Bolivia | 2012–3 | 216 | – | – | – | – |
| Canada | 1995–2015 | 26 | 0 | – | – | – |
| Colombia | 1991–2013 | 169 | 54 | – | 2 (2014) | – |
| Ecuador | 1998–2013 | 786 | 78 | 21 | 1 (2001) | – |
| Germany | 1993–2008 | n/d | 17 | ~7 | 1 | 1 (2012) |
| Japan | 1947–99 | 1,250 | 397 | 262 | 1 | 1 (2010) |
| Liechtenstein[1] | 1921–2015 | 1 | – | – | – | – |
| Mexico | 2012–14 | 1 | – | – | – | – |
| Peru | 1997–2013 | 20,000 | 5,303 | 1,737 | 1 | 1 (2013) |
| Poland | 1990–2014 | n/d | 656 | 79 | 1 | 1 (2013) |
| Switzerland | 1846–2015 | 12 | 4 | 1 | – | – |
| United States | 1903–89 | ~6,000 | ~4,000 | n/d | 3 | 1 (2004) |
| Venezuela | 1999–2013 | 167 | 10 | 5 | – | – |

a In decentralised countries (Argentina, Germany, USA) data is not easily accessible so the figures have to be considered as provisional. In the case of Peru the figure is estimated based on the number of sold kits (5,800), i.e. templates to collect signatures. In the other cases attempts are coded based on the registration of a process at the corresponding electoral office which is the first legal step to initiate the process (Welp 2015).

*Sources:* Bolivia: Verdugo Silva (2014: 150); Colombia: Franco-Cuervo (2014: 62–3). MOE 2012: 13–24; Ecuador: Castellanos (2014: 93–104); Ramírez (2014: 255–66); Germany: Fuchs (2007: 65); Böhme (2008: 48); Japan: personal communication by Mitsuhiko Okamoto; Liechtenstein: Marxer (forthcoming); México: Rosa Alacio, research in progress (personal communication), Perú: Tuesta Soldevilla (2014), Welp (2015); Poland: Piasecki (2011: 131); Referenda localne (2013), http://www.prezydent.pl; Switzerland: Serdült (2015: 169); USA: Cronin (1989: 142); Venezuela: Kornblith (2014: 237, 241).

1. In Liechtenstein there was one attempt at a recall in 1928. The reason was a banking scandal. The Prince, however, stepped in and dissolved Parliament before a vote could take place (see Marxer forthcoming).

success rate of roughly 15 per cent on average. Bednarz (2013: 52) concludes that recall has made its way into the action repertoire of Polish local politics.

To summarise, Table 9.2 shows how prevalent recall experience at the subnational level can be. The data suggest a movement from small units to big cities, as can be observed in the last column: all activations of recall in big cities were registered after 2000. In the next section we will analyse these cases.[4]

4. We are not able to conduct a fully representative comparative study of the recall yet. For many countries the phenomenon is not well documented or accessible, partly due to language barriers.

## Case studies

In this section, we briefly summarise the experiences of recall in big cities (of about 500,000 inhabitants), paying attention to the main agent initiating the process (political actor or civil society) and the main goal of the activation (primary or secondary).

### *California 2003 (USA)*

As probably one of the most prominent recalls of the world the case of California in 2003, when Arnold Schwarzenegger became State Governor, has been well documented (Garret 2004; Kousser 2004; Miller 2005). In brief, the chain of events is as follows. Gray Davis (Democratic Party) came to power in 1999 with a clear victory (58 per cent of the vote). Once in office he tried to come up with an educational reform but faced resistance by his own party in the legislature. Complaining about the non-cooperative role of parliament, which did not share his visions, he seemed to have created political enemies within his own party (Kousser 2004: 307). The energy crisis in California cost the state billions of dollars and further eroded Davis' public approval rates. Furthermore, there was a scandal involving fundraising. Davis apparently accepted an important donation from Oracle after he secured a large state contract with the company (Miller 2005).

In the run-up to the 2002 state elections Davis' approval ratings dropped to 39 per cent and further down to 25 per cent in March 2003. However, he managed to get re-elected in a race marked by low turnout and much more support for minor party candidates than usual (Kousser 2004). Soon after the re-election the Republicans discussed the option of a recall. The promoters were members of the Republican Party. A group lead by Ted Costa formally initiated the process accusing Davis of 'gross mismanagement of California finances by overspending taxpayers' money, threatening public safety by cutting funds to local governments, failing to account for the exorbitant cost of the energy fiasco, and failing in general to deal with the state's major problems until they get to the crisis stage.' (Quoted in: Miller 2005: 140)

Recall proponents gathered signatures through a volunteer effort that combined the forces of conservative radio shows and the internet (25 million hits for the pro recall website 'Rescue California'). However, only when Republican Representative Darell Issa provided hundreds of thousands of dollars did the process reach the number of signatures required. More than double the necessary signatures came in. After some legal quarrels, the recall election was fixed for 7 October 2003 (Kousser 2004: 310).

The particular design of the recall election in California, where an election for Davis' successor was on the same ballot as the recall question, opened room for Arnold Schwarzenegger. The former movie-star-turned-political-activist (shortly before the election he had promoted a ballot initiative to introduce after-school activities for students) immediately become the top contender. Davis was ousted with 55.4 per cent in favour of recall. Schwarzenegger received 48.4 per cent support as a replacement among a total of seven viable candidates in a vote that split mostly along party lines (Kousser 2004). For the second time in US history and the first time in more than eighty years a governor was removed from office midterm.[5]

### *Nagoya 2010 (Japan)*

Due to the high hurdles Japanese citizens have to overcome in order to implement a local referendum ordinance (Okamoto et al. 2014), which allows them to take a – still non-binding – vote on *policy issues*, they often have no other choice than to confront parliament or the mayor with a recall (which is regulated at the national level). In his assessment of Japanese efforts to decentralise politics, and as a part of this process of increasing local direct democratic practice, Takanobu (2000: 28) observes that this shift from the primary function of the recall to a secondary one is rather directed at policies (Jain 1991: 560).

Already during the struggle and preparations for the first Japanese local policy referendum ever in 1996 in the town of Maki (Niigata Prefecture), part of the conflict was institutional in the sense that the ruling mayor at first refused to pass a local referendum law making a policy referendum possible. He then tried to delay it further when public pressure increased due to an informal referendum organised by a citizens' movement (Igarashi 2006; Okamoto et al. 2014: 14). As a reaction to the delaying tactics, the citizen groups in favour of a referendum started to collect signatures to recall the reluctant mayor. However, after more than ten thousand signatures were in, the mayor preferred to step down voluntarily. Under the new mayor the policy referendum could be held and the plan to build a nuclear power plant was voted down (Igarashi 2006: 320). The citizens thus used the recall procedure in order to achieve their initial goal, which was a policy referendum (Twomey 2011: 54–5).

As in our other case studies, the recall practice in Japan has moved a level up from smaller municipalities to bigger ones such as Nagoya, a city with 1.8 million inhabitants. The case is most peculiar because it was in fact the newly elected mayor of Nagoya, Takashi Kawamura, who initiated a recall in order to resolve a political conflict between him and the municipal parliament.[6] Trying to keep his electoral promises Kawamura (co-founder of the anti-tax party Genzei Nippon) wanted to cut taxes and reduce the size of parliament by half (Samuels 2013). After a half-hearted implementation of the tax cut by parliament the mayor threatened

5. In 1921 South Dakota removed Governor Lynn Frazier. A vote qualified in Arizona in 1988 against Governor Evan Mecham but the legislature impeached the governor before the referendum (Zimmerman 2013).

6. See http://www.japantimes.co.jp/news/2010/08/21/national/nagoya-mayor-petitions-to-recall-city-assembly/#.VuKd7FQzrlZ, accessed 11 March 2016. As a political strategy, although following different procedures, this is similar to the one activated by Bolivian President Evo Morales in 2008 (see Welp and Serdült 2014).

parliament with the recall as a last resort. In case of success he would step down as well and seek re-election in order to govern with a newly elected parliament more favourable to his reforms. In order to trigger the recall roughly 366,000 signatures had to be collected within a month – a task the supporters of the reformist mayor were not able to achieve, as they were around 12,000 signatures short. The large number of 111,000 signatures declared invalid, however, caused a further quarrel.[7] A second validation round then resulted in a reversal of the previous count.[8] The recall vote finally took place on 6 February 2011 with a positive outcome for the mayor. Parliament thus got recalled and new elections were held. This conflict between the mayor and parliament reveals a conflict between political institutions but also has to be interpreted within the larger context of administrative reforms and local government decentralisation in Japan.

### *Duisburg 2012 (Germany)*

The recall is available in most German Länder nowadays. However, the procedure can be initiated directly via signature collection only in four Länder, Brandenburg, Sachsen, Schleswig-Holstein and North Rhine-Westphalia. It can be initiated indirectly in all the other Länder except two by parliamentary majorities of varying thresholds (Böhme 2008: 33).[9] Although the institutional hurdles are relatively high, recall practice and success are not infrequent. Most recall votes, however, take place in municipalities with less than twenty thousand inhabitants (Böhme 2008: 81) and are getting initiated by parliaments in an indirect way. However, in Germany we can observe the same pattern as in our other examples, namely that also in larger cities such as Potsdam with 160,000 (1998) inhabitants, Cottbus with 100,000 (2006) and the presented case of the City of Duisburg with almost 500,000 inhabitants, recall votes are being conducted.

The case of Duisburg is connected to the Love Parade 2010 when twenty-one people died and five hundred were injured in a stampede. First held in 1989 in Berlin as a techno party in the streets of Berlin with 150 participants (Schwarz 2012: 431) the festival turned into an increasingly commercialised event attracting 1.5 million people at its peak in 1999. Due to a lack of sponsors in Berlin the Love Parade was moved to the Ruhr Valley in 2007. For the 2010 Parade in Duisburg the festival took place in an area surrounded by rail tracks that was only accessible via tunnels. Overcrowding occurred and the following panic among visitors trying to leave the area led to the deadly catastrophe. In a blame game between the organiser, the police and the authorities, the Mayor Adolf Sauerland from the Christian Democratic Union (CDU) was finally asked to take political

7. See http://www.japantimes.co.jp/news/2010/11/25/national/nagoya-recall-petition-fails/#.VuLGplQzrlY, accessed 11 March 2016.

8. See http://www.japantimes.co.jp/news/2010/12/16/news/in-reversal-nagoya-assembly-faces-recall/#.VuLJhFQzrlY, accessed 11 March 2016.

9. Not in Bavaria and Baden-Württemberg, which were actually the first to have the mayors elected directly.

responsibility for having allowed the festival to take place in an unsuitable area. However, he was unwilling to step down.

A first attempt in the form of a parliamentary motion to trigger the recall vote in 2010 did not receive the required two-thirds majority. Parliament, however, managed to change the Local Government Act on 18 May 2011 through a simple majority, explicitly in order to make this recall against Mayor Adolf Sauerland possible. North Rhine-Westphalia was thus the fourth Land in Germany to introduce the citizens' initiated recall procedure. Once the legal basis was laid down, a committee called 'New Start for Duisburg' started to collect signatures in order to demand a recall referendum. For Duisburg as a city with more than 100,000 inhabitants, signatures from 15 per cent of the electorate had to be collected. The quorum was therefore at roughly 55,000 signatures. With 67,000 valid signatures this hurdle was easily overcome. On 12 February 2012, 85.8 per cent voted in favour of recalling Mayor Sauerland. Because of the minimum turnout rule the most efficient strategy for opponents of the recall was simply not to go to the polls. However, turnout was at 41.6 per cent (the minimum turnout for the vote to be valid is 25 per cent)[10] and the mayor of Duisburg was recalled.

### *Warsaw 2013 (Poland)*

In Poland as well as in many other countries providing for the recall as a direct democratic instrument we can observe practice moving up from the local level to medium-sized and bigger cities (Piasecki 2011: 131), and in 2013 finally up to the capital. This is why we are highlighting the Warsaw recall vote of 13 October 2013 as the latest and so far most spectacular case in Poland. The recall was initiated by the mayor of one of Warsaw's boroughs and rather small local citizen groups opposing such policies as the rise of local transport ticket prices and the cost of rubbish collection as well as delays in the construction of the second metro line – all projects were the responsibility of the mayor of the political party that was in power also at the national level, the Civic Platform (PO). The opposition party, Law and Justice (PiS), later jumped on board and contributed to the collection of 134,000 signatures in favour of the recall.

Before moving to the capital, the PiS tested PO mayors with recall procedures in other towns such as Elbląg in the North of Poland in April 2013. Electoral turnout was higher than the required minimum of three-fifths of the turnout in the previous local elections. Hence the formal requirement regarding the participation quorum was fulfilled. The incumbent was eventually recalled and the PiS candidate narrowly defeated the opposing PO candidate in the subsequent local elections in Elbląg (Jasiewicz and Jasiewicz-Betkiewicz 2014: 254).

As the Freedom House country report 2014 for Poland puts it, the Warsaw 2013 recall was 'a contest between the governing Civic Platform (PO) and the opposition party PiS' (Czesnik 2015: 470). The recall attacked Warsaw mayor, Hanna

---

10. All figures from http://nrw.mehr-demokratie.de/abwahl-sauerland.html, and http://duisburg.de/news/102010100000379601.php, accessed 4 February 2016.

Gronkiewicz-Waltz, the first woman in this position (in office since 2006, re-elected in 2010) and the deputy-leader of the PO, two years before national parliamentary elections took place. The ballot stated only one question: 'Should Mrs Hanna Gronkiewicz-Waltz be recalled from the position of President of Warsaw before the end of the term of office?' However, due to the required turnout threshold the recall vote was not valid (26 per cent instead of the required 29 per cent) despite the fact that a large majority, 94 per cent of the participants, voted against her. The political elite of the ruling political party, including the prime minister and the president (who is actually meant to take on a more neutral stance on such matters), were asking people to stay at home and not to turn out (Bednarz 2013: 55–6; Jasiewicz and Jasiewicz-Betkiewicz 2014: 255). For the then opposition party PiS, the Warsaw 2013 recall thus served as a much welcomed test bed for the upcoming elections in 2015, which they won. However, at the local level, mayor Gronkiewicz-Waltz managed to stay in power for yet another term in the 2014 local elections, which she won against the candidate of PiS in the second round.

After the victory of PiS in the national parliamentary elections in 2015 it is quite likely that the party will continue to use the recall before the next regular local elections as a tactic to gain political control over cities that are still PO-ruled.

### *Lima 2013 (Peru)*

Twenty years after its introduction in Peru, the recall procedure reached the capital city Lima, where Susana Villarán from the party Fuerza Social unexpectedly became the first female mayor in 2010 (Vásquez Oruna 2014). The electoral race was particularly open this time because the incumbent, Luis Castañeda Lossio (mayor since 2003), stepped down despite very high popularity ratings in order to run for President in 2011 (for which he came fifth with 10 per cent of the vote). At the beginning of the electoral campaign Villarán did not seem to stand a chance of winning these elections. With only 6 per cent support she clearly came in last among the three top candidates in the opinion polls three months before the election. Her surge started when the National Jury of Elections (Jurado Nacional de Elecciones, JNE) prevented the up to then second most popular candidate, Alex Kouri Bumachar, from competing in the elections. He was not able to give adequate proof of having been a resident of Lima for more than two years prior to the election date (Vásquez Oruna 2014: 38). Despite a media campaign mainly against her and having been accused of being a candidate of the radical left, Susana Villarán became the main opponent of the front runner Lourdes Flores Nano from the Partido Popular Cristiano (PPC). Since the majority of the supporters of Kouri Bumachar apparently transferred their votes to Villarán, she managed to win the elections by a margin of 0.83 per cent. Her party did not win in any of the forty-two voting districts of Metropolitan Lima but thanks to the electoral law the coalition of five Fuerza Social parties (including the one called Fuerza Social) was able to win an absolute majority in the city council by one seat (Welp and Rey 2014).

After barely a hundred days in office, she presented the results of an audit denouncing the mismanagement of public funds by the previous mayor, Castañeda

Lossio. In addition, she was determined to get a firm hold on the regulation of the local public transport system, controlled by *mafias*. Later, she supported the lesbians, gays, transsexuals and bisexuals movement in a country where the conservative faction of the Catholic Church still has a strong influence. Closing the oldest and most populated market – La Parada – with the help of police in October 2012, and trying to relocate about two thousand shop owners resulted in riots with two dead and several injured. Later in the year, the urban development project Parque Rio Rimac resulted in a financial disaster for the city (Vásquez Oruna 2014: 47). Under such political circumstances and given her disputed reform projects, an attempt to activate the recall was not unexpected. Furthermore, the recall nowadays follows a well established action repertoire in Peruvian politics, facilitated by the sale of the so-called 'recall kit' (venta de kits) containing manuals and templates helping to organise the process (Tuesta Soldevilla 2014). The recall procedure was initiated by Marco Tulio Gutiérrez, a former adviser of Castañeda Lossio (Vásquez Oruna 2014: 36). From the very beginning, the recall initiative was backed by the groups most affected by Villarán's reforms and factions of the church (Vásquez Oruna 2014).

In July 2012, the promoters presented 400,396 signatures to recall the mayor and the whole council (forty members), with the intention of removing at least two-thirds of the authorities and then allow for a new election. The PPC, led by Lourdes Flores, who had lost the elections against Villarán, was against the recall, arguing that regular elections were the best mechanism to exercise accountability. Other major political players such as opposition leader Keiko Fujimori's Fuerza Popular and President Ollanta Humala did not release an official statement on the matter. After some administrative problems regarding the control of signatures, the JNE, however, set the date for the recall vote (17 March 2013). After a fierce and intense campaign the vote resulted in the recall of twenty-two council members (twenty from Fuerza Social alone) but not of the mayor. As the regulations for local elections prescribe (Tuesta Soldevilla 2014: 26) the recalled council members were first replaced with the candidates in waiting positions from the 2010 municipal elections for an interim period until new councillors were elected on 24 November 2013 (to replace the twenty-two recalled ones). By the next regular local election on 5 October 2014 the popular former mayor Castañeda Lossio had returned from national politics, ran again as a mayor and won a majority in parliament (twenty-three seats). Ex-mayor Susana Villarán's party, despite her surviving the recall vote, won only four seats.

## Conclusions

This chapter focused on the increasing spread and use of recall referendums on a global scale. A growing interest in the mechanism can be related to the relatively recent restoration of democracy in many parts of the world such as the so-called third wave of democratisation in Latin America as well as with a crisis of representative democracy. Both of these factors led to a demand for reinvigorating democracy through more direct citizen participation. While scandals place recall directly on the political agenda, the replacement of constitutions such as those that occurred in several Andean countries, and constitutional reforms in general, also create a window of opportunity to introduce the mechanism. The availability of an additional political institution increases the action repertoire of all political actors able to mobilise enough citizens for signature collection. As more options for political action become available politics is also becoming more complex.

Looking at the twelve countries in which recall is available at the local level we observe that while in some countries activations are limited (Argentina, Switzerland) in others they have been increasing over time (especially in the US, Japan, Poland and Peru). From our overview and the selected case studies we can also observe the levelling up of the recall from small municipalities to provinces or bigger cities. Among the driving forces for this development, an increasing mediatisation of politics – including social media – and the professionalisation (and hence nationalisation) of party systems can be listed as likely candidates. Bigger cities such as capitals are the bigger stage and often of national interest and therefore media are much more likely to cover them. For political parties and prominent candidates, hijacking the recall therefore pays off in several ways. They can mobilise potential voters for upcoming general elections, make themselves known and also gather information about the mobilisation and support they can find among voter segments in different constituencies. Whereas the initiators of the recall collect the benefits from such 'probing via recall' in the form of valuable information for future campaigns, the financial costs are paid by volunteers for signature collection and the state budget for the organisation of the vote.

Our study of five recall processes in cities with more than 500,000 inhabitants showed that we must often deal with a set of controversial policy decisions (California, Lima, Warsaw, and to some extent Duisburg and Nagoya as well), combined with a shaky political basis (California, Lima) as well as political forces seizing a window of opportunity. When we look at the initiation of the recall procedure we encounter cases that are quite clear cut: the procedure is used to promote a nascent political party or to compete with an almost equally strong opponent between regular electoral contests. Some cases are, however, less clear cut when political parties are not at the origin of a signature collection process but jump on the occasion to profit from it politically. In sum, when looking at the recall procedure through our case studies it becomes evident that their use is multifunctional and mainly depends on the actor constellation within a given polity at a given time.

Whereas the recall is directed at elected agents in a democracy, such as MPs, presidents, mayors or judges, the referendum is directed at democratic actions such as laws and policy measures. In an ideal world with a balanced institutional framework these two main citizen-initiated democratic counter powers would be available at equal cost and all political actors would have equal resources. Recall would thus be able to fulfil its primary function whereas the availability of referendums would prevent its use as a weapon against unpopular policy measures. However, a well documented study testing the relationship between referendums and the recall is still missing and would be desirable for further research.

From an institutional design perspective it would be preferable to limit the use of political institutions to their primary purpose within the intended boundaries. As we can see, however, these events rarely refer exclusively to the primary purpose for which they were intended. If the primary, intended or even 'good cause' for calling a recall referendum is to account for obvious cases of mismanagement or reckless behaviour by political elites and to eventually resolve institutional deadlocks, we would like to avoid – to a maximum degree – the more problematic use of secondary, unintended purposes of the recall. On one hand this concerns the instrumental use of the recall to maximise media attention or to avoid accepting political defeat in regular elections. On the other hand in the case of opposition to clearly identifiable but unwanted policy decisions it is rather the lack of appropriate institutional options – for example in the form of citizen-initiated referendums – that leads political actors to using the recall instead. In polities with a trend for the recall to level up to bigger cities or national governments, the increased use of the instrument can reach a stage of self-perpetuating path dependency, leading the authorities to think about changes in institutional design (as in Germany and Peru). Two options come to mind: on one hand the thresholds for signature collection and the validity of the recall vote can be made more difficult to achieve; on the other hand it would be possible to introduce other direct democratic mechanisms such as referendums – especially as many activations of the recall are aimed against policies rather than against democratically elected bodies.

## References

Arques, F. (2014) 'Argentina: una herramienta de los gobernados en manos de los gobernantes', in Y. Welp and U. Serdült (eds) *La dosis hace el veneno: la revocatoria del mandato en Suiza, Estados Unidos y América Latina*, Serie Ciencia y Democracia, Quito: Consejo Nacional Electoral: 159–86.

Bednarz, H. (2013) 'The development of direct democracy mechanisms in Poland', *C2D Working Paper Series*, 44, Aarau: Centre for Research on Direct Democracy.

Bjørklund, T. (1982) 'The demand for referendum: when does it arise and when does it succeed?', *Scandinavian Political Studies*, 5: 237–60.

Böhme, D. (2008) *Die Abwahl von Bürgermeistern – Institution und Praxis* [Verwaltungswissenschaftliche Beiträge 38], Bamberg: University of Bamberg, available at http://www.econbiz.de/archiv1/2010/133361_abwahl_von_buergermeistern.pdf (accessed 15 April 2016).

Bowler, S. (2004) 'Recall and representation: Arnold Schwarzenegger meets Edmund Burke', *Representation*, 40(3): 200–12.

Castellanos, A. S. (2014) 'Ecuador: la transformación de las reglas del juego y sus consecuencias (1998–2013)', in Y. Welp and U. Serdült (eds) *La dosis hace el veneno: la revocatoria del mandato en Suiza, Estados Unidos y América Latina*, Serie Ciencia y Democracia, Quito: Consejo Nacional Electoral: 83–110.

Cronin, T. E. (1989) *Direct Democracy: The Politics of Initiative, Referendum and Recall*, Cambridge and London: Harvard University Press.

Czesnik, M. (2015) 'Poland', in S. Habdank-Kołaczkowska and Z. Csaky (eds) *Nations in Transit: Democratization from Central Europe to Eurasia*, New York/Washington, DC: Freedom House: 469–88.

Dalton, R., Bürklin, W. and Drummond, A. (2001) 'Public opinion and direct democracy', *Journal of Democracy*, 12: 141–53.

Franco-Cuervo, A. B. (2014) 'Colombia: instituciones, líderes, políticos y abstención electoral (1991–2013)', in Y. Welp and U. Serdült (eds) *La dosis hace el veneno: la revocatoria del mandato en Suiza, Estados Unidos y América Latina*, Serie Ciencia y Democracia, Quito: Consejo Nacional Electoral: 57–81.

Fuchs, D. (2007) *Die Abwahl von Bürgermeistern – ein bundesweiter Vergleich.* KWI-Arbeitshefte 14. Potsdam: Kommunalwissenschaftliches Institut der Universität Potsdam.

Garret, E. (2004) 'Democracy in the wake of the California Recall', *University of Pennsylvania Law Review*, 153: 239–84.

Guzmán Hernández, T. Y. (2014) 'Cuba: deudas pasadas y retos presentes desde la norma', in Y. Welp and U. Serdült (eds) *La dosis hace el veneno: la revocatoria del mandato en Suiza, Estados Unidos y América Latina*, Serie Ciencia y Democracia, Quito: Consejo Nacional Electoral: 187–205.

Igarashi, A. (2006) 'Japan – against oppressive national policies: rebellion by the people', in J. Hwang (ed.) *Direct Democracy in Asia: A Reference Guide to the Legislations and Practices*, Taipei: Taiwan Foundation for Democracy: 311–22.

International Institute for Democracy and Electoral Assistance (2008) *Direct Democracy: The International IDEA Handbook*, Stockholm: International IDEA.

Jain, P. C. (1991) 'Green politics and citizen power in Japan: the Zushi Movement', *Asian Survey*, 31(6): 559–75.

Jasiewicz, K. and Jasiewicz-Betkiewicz, A. (2014) 'Poland', *European Journal of Political Research Political Data Yearbook*, 53: 250–6.

Kornblith, M. (2014) 'Revocatoria de mandato en Venezuela: Examen de los procesos presidencial, regional y local' in F. Tuesta Soldevilla (ed.) *Una onda expansiva*, Lima: Jurado Nacional de Elecciones: 209–55.

Kousser, T. (2004) 'The California Governor's recall', in K. Chi (ed.) *The Book of the States*, Vol. 36. Lexington, KY: Council of State Governments: 307–15.

Kriesi, H. (2006) 'Role of the political elite in Swiss direct-democratic votes', *Party Politics*, 12(5): 599–622.

Lijphart, A. (1984) *Democracies: Patterns of Majoritarian and Consensus Government in Twenty-one Countries*, New Haven: Yale University Press.

Marxer, W. (forthcoming) *Direkte Demokratie in Liechtenstein* [Liechtensteinische Politische Schriften] Schaan: Verlag der Liechtensteinischen Akademischen Gesellschaft.

McCoy, J. (2006) 'The 2004 Venezuelan Recall Referendum', *Taiwan Journal of Democracy*, 2(1): 61–80.

Miller, K. P. (2005) 'The Davis Recall and the courts', *American Politics Research*, 33(2): 135–62.

MOE (2012) *Mecanismos de Participación Ciudadana en Colombia –20 años de ilusiones*, Misión de Observación Electoral, Bogotá, September.

Morel, L. (1993) 'Party attitudes toward referendums in Western Europe', *West European Politics*, 16(3): 225–44.

Okamoto, M., Ganz, N., Serdült, U. (2014) *Direct Democracy in Japan. c2d Working Papers Series* 47, Aarau: Centre for Democracy Aarau (ZDA).

Piasecki, A. K. (2011) 'Twenty years of Polish direct democracy at the local level', in T. Schiller (ed.) *Local Direct Democracy in Europe*, Wiesbaden: VS Verlag: 126–37.

Qvortrup, M. (2011) 'Hasta la vista: a comparative institutional analysis of the recall', *Representation*, 47(2): 161–70.

Ramírez Gallegos, F. (2014) 'El despliegue de la democracia directa en el Ecuador post constitucional', in A. Lissidini, Y. Welp and D. Zovatto (eds) *Democracias en Movimiento*, Mexico DF: UNAM: 231–74.

Samuels, R. J. (2013) *3.11 – Disaster and Change in Japan*, Ithaca and London: Cornell University Press.

Schwarz, A. (2012) 'The love parade in Duisburg: lessons from a tragic blame game', in A. M. Schwarz and C. B. Pratt (eds) *Case Studies in Crisis Communication: International Perspectives on Hits and Misses*, New York/London: Routledge: 340–58.

Serdült, U. (2015) 'A dormant institution – history, legal norms and practice of the recall in Switzerland', *Representation – Journal of Representative Democracy*, 51(2): 161–72.

Serdült, U. and Welp, Y. (2012) 'Direct democracy upside down', *Taiwan Journal of Democracy*, 8(1): 69–92.

Setälä, M. (1999) 'Referendums in Western Europe: a wave of direct democracy?' *Scandinavian Political Studies*, 22: 327–40.

Spivak, J. (2004) 'California's recall: adoption of the "Grand Bounce" for elected officials', *California History*, 81 (2): 20–63.

Takanobu, T. (2000) 'Local self-governance in Japan: the realities of the direct demand system', *National Institute for Research Advancement Review*, 7(2): 26–9.

Twomey, A. (2011) 'The recall of Members of Parliament and citizens' initiated elections', *University of New South Wales Law Journal*, 34(1): 41–69.

Tuesta Soldevilla, F. (ed.) (2014) *Una onda expansiva*, Lima: Jurado Nacional de Elecciones.

Uribe Mendoza, C. (2016) 'La activación de la revocatoria de mandato en el ámbito municipal en Colombia: lecciones del caso de Bogotá', *Estudios Políticos*, 48: 179–200.

Vásquez Oruna, E. M. (2014) 'Cuando los vientos revocadores azotaron Lima', in Y. Welp and U. Serdült (eds) *La dosis hace el veneno: la revocatoria del mandato en Suiza, Estados Unidos y América Latina*, Serie Ciencia y Democracia, Quito: Consejo Nacional Electoral: 31–56.

Vetter, A. (2006) 'Modernizing German local government: bringing the people back', in V. Hoffmann-Martinot and H. Wollmann (eds) *State and Local Government Reforms in France and Germany: Divergence and Convergence*, Wiesbaden: VS Verlag: 253–68.

Welp, Y. (2015) 'Recall referendums in Peruvian municipalities: a political weapon for bad losers or an instrument of accountability?', *Democratization*, 12 August 2015, available at http://www.tandfonline.com/doi/full/10.1080/13510347.2015.1060222 (accessed 15 April 2016).

Welp, Y. and Rey, J. (2014) 'Revocatoria de mandato y democracia: análisis de las experiencias recientes en Lima y Bogotá', *Democracias*, 2: 189–208.

Welp, Y. and Serdült, U. (eds) (2014) *La dosis hace el veneno: La revocatoria del mandato en Suiza, Estados Unidos y América Latina*, Quito: Consejo Nacional Electoral.

Zimmerman, J. (2013 [1928]) *The Recall: Tribunal of the People*, New York: State University of New York Press.

*Chapter Ten*

# Direct Democracy and its (Perceived) Consequences: The German Case

*Brigitte Geissel*

## Introduction

Democracy is a resilient and adaptable system. It changes over time due to altering problems, challenges and public demands. Today, most democracies seem to be troubled by several challenges, summarised in the rhetoric of 'democratic disenchantment', unsatisfying policy outcomes and decreasing governability (e.g. Cain et al. 2003; Dalton et al. 2004). Democratic theory as well as the 'real world of politics' reacted, discussing and introducing various democratic innovations, especially direct democratic instruments, in order to cope with these challenges (e.g. Barber 1994; Bertelsmann Stiftung 2011; Denters and Klok 2010; Pateman 1970, 2012). But how successful are these instruments?

The Federal Republic of Germany is an especially interesting case for scrutinising direct democratic instruments. Since its founding in 1949, the German political system has rested firmly on the principles of representative democracy. The framers of the Basic Law, fearing anti-democratic popular tendencies, designed moderating institutions between the people and the exercise of power. Political parties became the most important of these, and Germany is even characterised as a 'party-state'. Today, however, the concepts of representative democracy and the 'party-state' are under stress and participatory concepts are gaining ground. Although there has been no direct democratic experience at the national level, the situation looks quite different at the level of states and municipalities. Since the 1990s all German federal states (*Bundesländer*) have introduced referendums at the state and local levels that can be launched by respective authorities or by citizens.

In this chapter I first inform about direct democratic instruments in Germany at the national, state, and local level, referring to their regulations as well as to their usage. Then I discuss the state of the art on their impact. Empirical data on actual effects are rare, but some information about expected and perceived effects of direct democratic instruments is available. The chapter presents the first documented evidence on the matter.

### *Direct democratic instruments in Germany – regulations and usage*

This section gives an overview of the regulations relating to direct democratic instruments at all levels of the German federal system and describes the actual usage of these regulations.

### *The national level*

The Federal Republic of Germany is one of the few countries with no direct democratic experience at the national level. The German Constitution ('Basic Law') does not require referendums on constitutional changes. Article 146 of the German Constitution states that a completely new constitution should be agreed on by 'the people'. The only issue in which a referendum is mandatory is the changing of state boundaries (polity domain). More specifically, state boundaries can only be altered if the citizens living in the respective states agree to the change (Art. 29). However, there has never been a nationwide referendum about any restructuring of state boundaries at the national level; two referendums were held at state level on the (re-)construction of the respective state boundaries of Baden-Württemberg as well as those between Berlin and Brandenburg. Bottom-up MDD are not considered in the Basic Law.

Although German citizens have no experience with referendums at the national level, there is a strong demand for direct democratic instruments. Public opinion surveys show that a majority of German citizens would prefer to have a direct say on national issues. For example, 87 per cent support referendums at the national level in 2012 (Emnid 2013).

### *The state level*

Until the beginning of the 1990s only seven states offered direct democratic instruments at the state level. Most of these states provided for obligatory referendums in case of constitutional amendments. However, during the 1990s all German states changed their state constitutions adding a variety of direct democratic instruments at state level as well as at local level (*see* Figure 9.1).

Since 1996 citizens have been allowed to trigger MDDs in all German states (Eder and Magin 2008: 266). However, if citizens want to launch a citizen initiative, they always have to go through an application process (*Antrag auf Volksbegehren, Volksinitiative*).[1] The collection of signatures for the citizen initiative (*Volksbegehren*) can only begin, if the application is accepted. After achieving the number of required signatures, the state parliament can either agree to the proposal or submit the proposal to a referendum (*Volksentscheid*). The referendum is decisive if either the majority of votes or a specific proportion of the electorate casts its vote in favour of the proposal (*see* Table 10.1). The quorum of agreement differs between votes aimed at changing normal laws and constitutional changes. The quorum of agreement to change laws ranges from the requirement of 33 per cent of the electorate in Baden-Württemberg favouring the

1. There is a difference between the *Antrag auf Volksbegehren*, which aims to trigger a direct democratic decision, and the *Volksinitiative*, through which citizens can set a topic on the legislative agenda. Most states only provide for the *Antrag auf Volksbegehren*, a few states only for the *Volksinitiative*, and some states provide for both options. The acceptance of the *Antrag* is decided by the respective state parliament, while the *Volksinitiative* is often decided by an administrative authority.

*Figure 10.1: Mechanisms for direct democracy (state and local levels)*

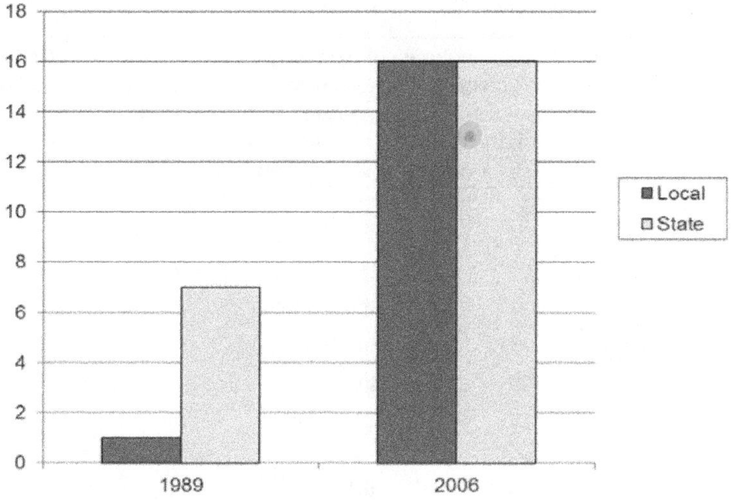


issue at stake to a simple plurality requirement in Bavaria, Hesse, and Saxony (*see* Table 10.1).

How many direct democratic procedures took place at the federal state level? The number of actual direct democratic procedures varies significantly in the literature on German direct democratic instruments. Some authors include the application for a citizen initiative (around 300), some authors take into account citizen initiatives/*Antrag auf Volksbegehren* (around 90), and other studies only include actual referendums, launched through bottom-up as well as top-down processes (around 50) or only referendums launched through bottom-up processes (around 20). The last two columns in Table 10.1 show the number of actual citizen initiatives and referendums launched by citizens or state authorities. These figures show that some states are more active than others. Bavaria is the most active user of referendums at the state level, whereas most German states use them rather sparingly.

Whether the required quorums with respect to the signature collection and the agreement in a referendum are achieved or not depends on aspects like the topic and the ability of the actors to mobilise voters.[2] For example, the quorum of agreement was reached in a referendum, in Berlin in 2014 on the use of a former airport and airfield as a park rather than as a construction site for industrial and apartment buildings. The referendum in Berlin on the renationalisation of the power supply company in 2013, however, failed to meet the threshold of agreement. With 24 per cent of the electorate favouring renationalisation, agreement was 1 per cent short

2. Voter turnout is also higher when referendums are held in conjunction with other elections (local, state, national elections or elections for the European Parliament).

*Table 10.1: Direct democratic instruments in Germany, regulation and usage at the state level (2014)*

| | Citizen initiative: signature quorum (%) | Referendum: agreement quorum (laws) (% of electorate) | Referendum: agreement quorum (constitutional) (% of electorate) | Citizen initiatives (Volks-begehren), N | Referendums (Volks-entscheide), N |
|---|---|---|---|---|---|
| Baden-Württemberg | 16.7 | 33 | 50 | 0 | 2 |
| Bavaria | 10 | P | 25 | 20 | 21 |
| Berlin | 7 | 25 | 50 + 2/3 of votes | 9 | 9 |
| Brandenburg | 4 | 25 | 50 + 2/3 of votes | 11 | 3 |
| Bremen | 5 | 20 | 40 | 4 | 3 |
| Hamburg | 5 | 20 | 2/3 of votes | 16 | 7 |
| Hesse | 20 | P | not available | 1 | 11 |
| Mecklenburg-West Pomerania | 8.5 | 33 | 50 + 2/3 of votes | 4 | 1 |
| Lower Saxony | 10 | 25 | 50 | 3 | 0 |
| North Rhine-Westphalia | 8 | 15 | 50 + 2/3 of votes | 2 | 1 |
| Rhineland-Palatinate | 10 | 25 | 50 | 1 | 2 |
| Saarland | 7 | 25 | 50 + 2/3 of votes | 1 | 0 |
| Saxony | 13 | P | 50 | 4 | 1 |
| Saxony-Anhalt | 11 | 25 | 50 + 2/3 of votes | 3 | 1 |
| Schleswig-Holstein | 5 | 25 | 50 + 2/3 of votes | 5 | 2 |
| Thuringia | 8/10 | 25 | 40 | 5 | 1 |

*Notes:* P=plurality of valid votes.

*Sources:* Schiller (2014); http://www.mehr-demokratie.de/volksentscheide_in_deutschland.html (accessed 15 April 2016); http://www.mehr-demokratie.de/volksbegehren-deutschland00.html (accessed 15 April 2016).

of the threshold of 25 per cent. The same topic attracted enough proponents in Hamburg in 2013, where the threshold was only 20 per cent.

The topics of bottom-up direct democratic referendums at the state level are manifold. Topics refer to democratic reforms, education and schooling, public infrastructure, the prevention of privatisation or demands for remunicipalisation/renationalisation and environment/health questions. More than half of the

*Volksentscheide* covered questions within these dimension of politics; other referendums refer, for example, to policies on smoking or on religious education in schools.

### *The local level*

The issue of direct democracy is in Germany especially alive at the local level. By 1990, only Baden-Württemberg had provided direct democratic procedures at the local level (since 1956). Nevertheless, after unification in 1990, all eastern German states introduced direct democratic elements in their state constitutions. This resulted mainly from the idea that citizens should get comprehensive participatory rights to impede any new kind of unwarranted state control. The western *Bundesländer* followed during the 1990s. Today, local direct democratic instruments are institutionalised in all German states (for example, see Schiller 2007).

Referendums can be launched by the local councils or by the citizens themselves. Like the procedure at the state level a citizen initiative (*Bürgerbegehren*) has to start with an application process. During this process it is checked to see whether the proposal covers an issue that is allowed to be put to a referendum. While some states allow a very limited range of issues (e.g. Rhineland Palatinate), other states are more flexible (e.g. Bavaria, Hamburg, and Berlin). Most states also require a citizen initiative to include a plan for covering the costs of the proposal (exceptions are Bavaria, Hamburg and Berlin). Usually, the local council decides if an application is accepted, but in some states local administrative authorities, e.g. district offices, make this decision. There are no studies covering the difference between local councils or authorities in the rate of acceptance. However, to the best of my knowledge, applications are generally accepted if they comply with the formal requirements. If the application is accepted, the collection of signatures for the *Bürgerbegehren* can start. Citizen initiatives (*Antrag auf Bürgerbegehren*) can aim to 'correct' a decision of a local council (*Korrekturbegehren*), put a topic on the political agenda that had been neglected by local political representatives, or suggest a new law.

In any case, a *Bürgerbegehren* requires a quorum of signatures (*Unterschriftenquorum*), i.e. a certain number of supporting signatures, to be regarded as valid. The quorum for supporting signatures – expressed as a percentage of the electorate – differs vastly between municipalities within different German states. In Berlin, for example, it is as low as 3 per cent and in Brandenburg as high as 10 per cent (*see* Table 10.2). Other regulations differ as well, for example, where signatures for a *Bürgerbegehren* can be collected (either only in the city hall or anywhere), the timeframe for collecting the signatures (the number of weeks), and the option for postal votes. If the *Bürgerbegehren* is signed by the required number of citizens, the issue must be discussed within the local council. At the next stage, the local council can either accept or refuse the proposal. If the council accepts the proposal, it issues a respective regulation; if the council refuses the proposal, the issue is put to a referendum (*Bürgerentscheid*). Hence, either a referendum takes place – or the local council decides according to the *Bürgerbegehren*. Consequently, we can say that a *Bürgerbegehren* combines the instrument of political agenda setting with the instrument of direct democratic decision-making.

A *Bürgerentscheid* is decisive if a minimum percentage of the electorate agrees with the proposal – support by a majority of votes cast is not sufficient (the exception is Hamburg, *see* Table 10.2). The required quorum of agreement depends on the state as well as on the size of the municipality, varying between 10 and 30 per cent of the electorate. In contrast to most European countries, referendums on the local level in Germany are binding if they reach the required quorum. Table 10.2 provides information about the regulations of local MDDs (by state), as well as the number of local initiatives and referendums (initiated by citizens or local authorities) until 2013.

*Table 10.2: Direct democratic instruments in Germany, regulation and usage at the local level (2013)*

| | **Citizen initiative: signature quorum (%)** | **Referendum: agreement quorum (%)** | **Citizen initiative (Bürger-begehren), N** | **Referendum (Bürger-entscheid), N** |
|---|---|---|---|---|
| Baden-Württemberg | 5–10 | 25 | 552 | 332 |
| Bavaria | 3–10 | 10–20 | 2,075 | 1,517 |
| Berlin (districts) | 3 | 10 | 36 | 13 |
| Brandenburg | 10 | 25 | 134 | 160 |
| Bremen (city) | 5 | 20 | 6 | 1 |
| Hamburg (districts) | 2–3 | None | 100 | 20 |
| Hesse | 3–10 | 25 | 388 | 137 |
| Mecklenburg-West Pomerania | 2.5–10 | 25 | 89 | 47 |
| Lower Saxony | 10 | 25 | 280 | 86 |
| North Rhine-Westphalia | 3–10 | 10–20 | 667 | 194 |
| Rhineland-Palatinate | 6–10 | 20 | 166 | 80 |
| Saarland | 5–15 | 30 | 15 | 0 |
| Saxony | 5–10 | 25 | 211 | 159 |
| Saxony-Anhalt | 4.5–10 | 25 | 92 | 190 |
| Schleswig-Holstein | 4–10 | 8–20 | 388 | 201 |
| Thuringia | 4.5–7 | 10–20 | 155 | 40 |
| Baden-Württemberg | 4.5–7 | 10–20 | 155 | 40 |

*Source:* http://www.mehr-demokratie.de/5968.html (accessed 15 April 2016); http://www.mehr-demokratie.de/bb-bericht2014.html (accessed 15 April 2016).

Comparing the number of local referendums within European countries, Germany is currently leading the list (see Walter-Rogg 2008). However, there are huge differences between the states. As at state level, Bavaria is most active at the local level as well, with about 2,000 initiatives and 1,500 referendums. This is probably also due to the rather low hurdles in Bavaria, both with respect to the signature quorum as well as the agreement quorum. In contrast, states with especially high hurdles, like Saarland or Thuringia, have experienced only few local direct democratic procedures.

What are the topics of direct democratic procedures on the local level? Since Bavaria is the most active state in Germany, most studies tend to examine procedures based on this state (e.g. Rehmet and Wenisch 2005; Schoen et al. 2011). Until 2005 two-thirds of all the processes in Bavaria concerned the 'public infrastructure and provision of basic services' (23 per cent), 'town planning' (23 per cent), and 'roads and transport planning' (20 per cent). Several initiatives also aimed at hindering the building of hypermarkets, malls and retail parks (e.g. in Bayreuth) (Rehmet and Wenisch 2005, 6).

### *The consequences of direct democratic procedures in Germany – state of the art*

Research on direct democratic instruments and procedures in Germany have proliferated for about a decade. However, most studies have analysed legal and historical aspects or they have aimed at explaining the number of procedures, voter turnout and similar basic information (e.g. Bertelsmann Stiftung 2011; Feld et al. 2010; Grotz 2009; Heußner and Jung 2009; Jung 2005; Kost 2008; Paust 1999; Scarrow 1997; Schiller and Mittendorf 2002; Schiller 2007, 2014). Research units such as the Forschungsstelle Bürgerbeteiligung (Bergische Universität Wuppertal), the Forschungsstelle Bürgerbeteiligung und direkte Demokratie (Philipps-Universität Marburg) and the non-governmental organisation Mehr Demokratie e.V. (2012), have contributed to the collection of a relatively comprehensive descriptive database on citizen initiatives and referendums at state and local levels, concerning both their regulation and usage. However, research on the effects of direct democratic instruments in Germany is still rare.

### *Findings on perceived consequences*

Recently, two public opinion surveys scrutinised the expected and perceived effects of direct democratic procedures at the local level: one of these surveys was conducted by the Bertelsmann Foundation in twenty-seven German municipalities (2,700 citizens, 2014), and the other study was conducted in the context of the Baden-Wurttemberg Democracy Monitoring (see below).

The survey of the Bertelsmann Foundation (2011) showed the clear preferences of the German citizenry. When asked 'What is crucial when making a political decision?', most citizens opted for a 'dialogue with citizens' (80 per cent) and for direct democratic decision making (69 per cent). Obviously, German citizens prefer more involvement in political will-formation and decision-making. The concept of democracy as just selecting representatives is no longer the only game in town.

Most respondents (60 per cent) expect an improvement of public decisions when they are made via referendums. In contrast, only 39 per cent are convinced that decisions are of better quality when city councils decide alone. Respondents believe that the involvement of citizens via direct democratic instruments has a positive effect on public policy outcomes, because citizens provide more and better information and ideas than (local) authorities. Moreover, they are convinced that citizen involvement in public decision-making avoids bad investment. The survey also showed that, at the same time, the institutions of representative democracy will not lose importance. The majority of respondents do not expect the importance of the institutions of representative democracy (city councils, political parties and politicians) to decrease if citizen involvement increases.

The second study on the perceived impact of direct democratic procedures is the Baden-Württemberg-Study on the 'effects of local citizen participation' ('Wirkungen lokaler Bürgerbeteiligung'), which is part of the 'Democracy Monitoring' programme of the state government (Baden-Württemberg Stiftung 2015). In this study more than a hundred interviews were conducted with different actors (politics, administration, citizens, and the media) in more than ten middle-sized municipalities of Baden - Württemberg. The interviewees were asked to retrospectively evaluate (both direct - democratic and dialogue - oriented) participation processes, which took place in their communities. The Baden-Württemberg-Study (Baden-Württemberg Stiftung 2015) differentiates between effects of these processes on 'policy-related output' (effectiveness, acceptance of decisions), 'democratic self-development' (political awareness, external efficacy, democratic values), 'politics and polity related outcomes' (responsiveness), and 'political culture and social capital' (political support, trust etc.) (Vetter and Geyer 2014).

The study revealed mainly positive perceptions of participatory instruments. Especially aspects of democratic self-development were perceived to be enhanced by participatory procedures. But the effects on policy-related output, responsiveness and political culture were also considered to be rather positive than negative. However, in the context of this chapter, the perceived effects of direct democratic instruments are especially of interest. Vetter and Geyer (2014) found that local referendums are considered to contribute to an improved acceptance of political decisions, to increase political elite's responsiveness and sensitivity for people's interests and to enhance effectiveness. Direct democracy is also perceived to have positive effects on citizens' democratic skills and attitudes (see Benz and Stutzer 2004 for Switzerland). However, potential negative effects are mentioned as well, for example, that referendums can have a tendency to polarise the community by producing clear winners and losers.

The study also showed that the perceived effects of local referendums vary vastly between municipalities and different topics and instruments. In the best case scenario, local referendums generate mainly positive effects (see also Bogumil 2002). But in the worst cases, polarisation and distrust increase, leaving a deeply divided community. Table 10.3 summarises the findings in the best as well as the worst cases.

Considering the findings on the polarisation of the community, the case of 'Stuttgart 21' shows a somewhat different picture (Brettschneider and Schuster 2013). Stuttgart 21 was a highly controversial railway project in Stuttgart that led to massive protests between 2009 and 2011. Different means were used to pacify the situation, e.g. a mediation process including all the interested stakeholders. However, the controversy continued and finally a *Bürgerentscheid* was conducted, which decided in favour of the project. Although the citizenry remains highly polarised on the topic, the direct democratic decision had a seemingly harmonising effect on the situation since the outcome of the direct democratic decision was widely accepted.[3]

### *Findings on the actual consequences*

Since data on actual effects is missing, most authors base their evaluation on impressionistic expert evaluations.[4] Schiller (2014) suspects that decisions made via referendums are highly accepted, that direct democratic instruments increase citizen as well as civil society involvement, and that the responsiveness of state and local authorities is increased. Rehmet and Wenisch (2005) conclude that in many Bavarian communities local authorities are more interested in communicating with their citizens, due to the existing direct democratic options. These local

*Table 10.3: Perceived effects of local referendums*

| | **Best case** | **Worst case** |
|---|---|---|
| Local referendums | Clear decision after referendum (effectiveness)<br>In most cases acceptance of decisions<br>Changes in the elite's behaviour, increased responsiveness<br>Self-development (improved political awareness, etc.) | Polarisation of the community (i.e. conflicts are not resolved but aggravated, which makes the process inefficient)<br>Development of distrust |

*Source:* Vetter and Geyer 2014; based on data from Baden-Württemberg study (Baden-Württemberg Stiftung 2015).

3. For the exceptional experience in 2012 of a recall referendum in the city of Duisburg *see* Serdült and Welp, Chapter Nine in this volume.

4. Data availability is much better for Switzerland and the USA, where scholars have scrutinised the effects of direct democratic instruments for many years (e.g. Benz and Stutzer 2004; Feld and Kirchgaessner 2002, 2009; Freitag and Wagschal 2007; Gebhart 2002; Grotz 2009; Kriesi 2008; Wagschal and Obinger 2000).

authorities provide comprehensive information about political issues and try to involve the public in the processes of political will-formation, thereby improving political responsiveness.

A few ‘famous’ referendums at the state level have been scrutinised more thoroughly, e.g. the referendum in Bavaria on smoking in restaurants (e.g. Schoen et al. 2011) or the referendum in Hamburg on a school reform (Toeller et al. 2011). However, these studies focused less on impacts. They scrutinised, for example, the socio-economic structure of the voters and examined the factors influencing participation (e.g. Schoen et al. 2011). Systematic studies examining the effects of direct democratic instruments on actual policies, on political institutions, or on citizens’ attitudes are still missing for Germany (Schiller 2014).

## Conclusion

This chapter discussed the regulation and usage of direct democratic instruments in Germany as well as their (perceived) effects. Impressions and findings about the effects are consistent. Most experts, as well as most citizens, regard direct democratic instruments as positive democratic innovations. For example, they perceive and expect positive effects on elite responsiveness, on policy effectiveness, on democratic self-development and on the acceptance of political decisions. Policies are expected to be more in line with citizens’ preferences and it is assumed that citizens are more often willing to accept a political decision when they were involved directly in the decision-making process.

Circling back to the questions raised in the introduction of this book, Germany presents a special case. Although German citizens are not allowed to vote on constitutional changes (polity dimension) at the national level, direct democratic mechanisms are nevertheless on the rise at the state and local levels. The consequences of direct democratic mechanisms on the subnational level are, however, manifold. On the one hand, they had the potential to resolve conflicts in situations of extreme polarisation, as the case of Stuttgart 21 showed; on the other hand, they have also been able to foster conflict, as the Baden-Württemberg-Study (Baden-Württemberg Stiftung 2015) insinuated. Considering the question of accountability, there is no sign that direct democratic mechanisms would undermine democratic accountability.

However, research on the effects of direct democratic instruments in Germany is still in its infancy. Further research on the topic needs to tackle several empirical shortcomings. First, research on Switzerland and the United States, as well as several chapters in this book, have indicated that the effects of direct democratic mechanisms differ greatly depending on the actual instrument (e.g. Freitag and Wagschal 2007; Kriesi 2008; Grotz 2009). Top-down and bottom-up procedures can have quite different effects on the polity, politics and policy domains (*see* Whitehead, Chapter Two in this volume). However, research on Germany has not yet taken into account potential variations in the effects of different direct democratic mechanisms. Second, the contexts within which direct democratic instruments are applied should be considered as well. Political cultures and institutional structures vary between German states, providing the potential for subnational comparative analyses (see similar studies on Swiss cantons in Freitag and Wagschal 2007). Especially at the local level these differences are strong, e.g. institutional structures in some municipalities are rather presidential, while others mirror the parliamentary system of government. Until now, research has not taken these differences sufficiently into account. Finally, the effects discussed in this chapter are based on subjective data, i.e. the perceptions and expectations of citizens. The collection of objective data on the political effects of direct democratic decisions is a crucial task for future evaluations. The search for a 'better democracy' is based on 'trial and error' experiences (see e.g. Bertelsmann Stiftung and Staatsministerium Baden-Württemberg 2014). Modern democracy is changing and scholars should make sure to scrutinise these experiences thoroughly with the objective of avoiding wrong directions and dead ends.

## References

Baden-Württemberg Stiftung (ed) (2015) *Demokratie-Monitoring Baden-Württemberg 2013/2014*, Wiesbaden: Springer VS.

Barber, B. R. (1994) *Starke Demokratie: Über die teilhabe am politischen*, Hamburg: Rotbuch Verlag.

Benz, M. and Stutzer, A. (2004) 'Are voters better informed when they have a larger say in politics? Evidence for the EU and Switzerland', *Public Choice*, 119(1–2): 31–59.

Bertelsmann Stiftung (2011) *Demokratie vitalisieren – politische Teilhabe stärken*, Gütersloh: Bertelsmann Stiftung.

Bertelsmann Stiftung and Staatsministerium Baden-Württemberg (2014) *Partizipation im Wandel*, Gütersloh: Bertelsmann Stiftung.

Brettschneider, F. and Schuster, W. (eds) (2013) *Stuttgart 21 – Ein Großprojekt zwischen Protest und Akzeptanz*, Wiesbaden: Springer VS.

Bogumil, J. (2002) 'Direkte Demokratie als verhandlungsdemokratischer Impuls – Wirkungen kommunaler Referenden in NRW', in T. Schiller and V. Mittendorf (eds) *Direkte Demokratie: Forschung und perspektiven*, Wiesbaden: Westdeutscher Verlag: 194–206.

Cain, B. E., Dalton, R. J. and Scarrow, S. E. (eds) (2003) *Democracy transformed? Expanding political opportunities in advanced industrial democracies*, Oxford: Oxford University Press.

Dalton, R. J., Scarrow, S. E. and Cain, B. E. (2004) 'Advanced democracies and the new politics', *Journal of Democracy*, 15(1): 124–38.

Denters, B. and Klok, P.-J. (2010) 'Rebuilding Roombeek: patterns of citizen participation in urban governance', *Urban Affairs Review*, 45: 583–607.

Eder, C. and Magin, R. (2008) 'Direkte Demokratie', in M. Freitag and A. Vatter (eds) *Die Demokratien der deutschen Bundesländer*, Opladen: Barbara Budrich Verlag: 257–308.

Emnid (2013) Umfrage des Meinungsforschungsinstitut TNS Emnid im Auftrag von FOCUS, November 2013, available at http://www.focus.de/politik/deutschland/das-volk-ruft-nach-mehr-demokratie-deutliche-mehrheit-fuer-volksentscheide-auf-bundesebene-_aid_1160857.html (accessed 15 April 2015).

Feld, L. P. and Kirchgaessner, G. (2002) 'Direkte Demokratie in der Schweiz: Ergebnisse neuerer empirischer Untersuchungen', in T. Schiller and V. Mittendorf (eds) *Direkte Demokratie: Forschung und perspektiven*, Wiesbaden: Westdeutscher Verlag: 88–101.

—— (2009) 'Wirkungen direkter Demokratie: Was sagt die moderne politische Ökonomie?' in H. K. Heußner and O. Jung (eds) *Mehr Demokratie wagen: Volksentscheid und Bürgerentscheid: Geschichte – Praxis – Vorschläge*, München: Olzog, 417–30.

Feld, L. P., Huber, P. M. and Jung, O. (eds) (2010) *Jahrbuch für direkte Demokratie*, Baden-Baden: Nomos.

Freitag, M. and Wagschal, U. (eds) (2007) *Direkte Demokratie: Bestandsaufnahmen und Wirkungen im internationalen Vergleich*, Berlin: LIT Verlag.

Gebhart, T. (2002) *Direkte Demokratie I – Die Wirkungen direktdemokratischer Verfahren: Was lehren die Erfahrungen in der Schweiz?*, Arbeitspapier Nr. 87, Konrad-Adenauer-Stiftung e.V.

Grotz, F. (2009) 'Direkte Demokratie in Europa: Erträge, Probleme und Perspektiven der vergleichenden Forschung', *Politische Vierteljahresschrift*, 50(2): 286–305.

Heußner, H. K. and Jung, O. (eds) (2009) *Mehr direkte Demokratie wagen: Volksentscheid und Bürgerentscheid: Geschichte – Praxis – Vorschläge*, München: Olzog.

Jung, O. (2005) 'Grundsatzfragen der direkten Demokratie', in Kost, A. (ed.) *Direkte Demokratie in den deutschen Ländern – Eine Einführung*, Wiesbaden: Springer VS: 312–66.

Kost, A. (2008) *Direkte Demokratie*, Wiesbaden: Springer VS.

Kriesi, H. (2008) *Direct Democratic Choice: The Swiss experience*, Lanham, MD: Lexington.

Mehr Demokratie e.V. (2012) Bürgerbegehrensbericht 2012. Mehr Demokratie e.V., Forschungsstelle Bürgerbeteiligung (Bergischen Universität Wuppertal) and Forschungsstelle Bürgerbeteiligung und direkte Demokratie (Philipps-Universität Marburg), available at https://www.mehr-demokratie.de/fileadmin/pdf/201-09-04_BB-Bericht2012.pdf (accessed 15 April 2016).

Pateman, C. (1970) *Participation and Democratic Theory*, Cambridge: Cambridge University Press.

—— (2012) 'Participatory democracy revisited', *Perspectives on Politics*, 10(1): 7–19.

Paust, A. (1999) *Direkte Demokratie in der Kommune: Zur Theorie und Empirie von Bürgerbegehren und Bürgerentscheid*, Bonn: Stiftung Mitarbeit.

Rehmet, F. and Wenisch, S. (2005) 'Report: 10 years of citizens' initiatives and referendums in Bavaria, Germany', Mehr Demokratie and Democracy International, available at https://www.mehr-demokratie.de/fileadmin/pdf/direct-democracy-bavaria.pdf (accessed 15 April, 2016).

Scarrow, S. E. (1997) 'Party competition and institutional change: the expansion of direct democracy in Germany', *Party Politics*, 3(4): 451–72.

Schiller, T. (2007) 'Direkte Demokratie auf Bundesländer- und Kommunalebene', in M. Freitag and U. Wagschal (eds) *Direkte Demokratie: Bestandsaufnahmen und Wirkungen im internationalen Vergleich*, Berlin: LIT Verlag: 115–49.

—— (2014) 'Effekte und Entwicklungen von direkter Demokratie', in Bertelsmann Stiftung and Staatsministerium Baden-Württemberg (eds) *Partizipation im Wandel*, Gütersloh: Bertelsmann Stiftung: 185–31.

Schiller, T. and Mittendorf, V. (eds) (2002) *Direkte Demokratie: Forschung und perspektiven*, Wiesbaden: Westdeutscher Verlag.

Schoen, H., Glantz, A. and Teusch, R. (2011) 'Abstimmungskampf, Informationsvermittlung und Stimmentscheidung beim Volksentscheid über den Nichtraucherschutz in Bayern', in L. P. Feld, P. M. Huber and O. Jung (eds) *Jahrbuch für direkte Demokratie*, Baden-Baden: Nomos: 295–320.

Toeller, A. E., Pannowitsch, S., Kuscheck, C. and Mennrich, C. (2011) 'Direkte Demokratie und Schulpolitik. Lehren aus einer politikfeldanalytischen Betrachtung des Scheiterns der Hamburger Schulreform', *Zeitschrift für Parlamentsfragen* 3/2011: 503–23.

Vetter, A. and Geyer, S. (2014) 'New forms of citizen participation – what for?' Paper presented at the ECPR General Conference, Glasgow, UK, 3–6 September.

Wagschal, U. and Obinger, H. (2000) 'Der Einfluss der Direktdemokratie auf die Sozialpolitik', *Politische Vierteljahresschrift*, 41(3): 466–97.

Walter-Rogg, M. (2008) 'Direkte Demokratie', in O. W. Gabriel and S. Kropp (eds) *Die EU-Staaten im Vergleich*, Wiesbaden: Springer VS: 236–67.

*Chapter Eleven*

# Direct Democracy in Switzerland: The Growing Tension Between Domestic and Foreign Politics

*Pascal Sciarini*

## Introduction

While it is often seen as a model in terms of citizens' participation in public policy making, Swiss direct democracy has been under strain over the last few years. The speeding up of the globalisation and Europeanisation processes, together with the extension of direct democracy to cover a growing set of international treaties, accounts for these strains. On the one hand, in the era of globalisation domestic and international politics are increasingly blurred. Issues that used to be domestic in nature are now strongly affected by changes in the international context – and more especially in the European context. On the other hand, the progressive enlargement of judicial domains in foreign politics where direct democracy applies has granted the Swiss people a growing influence on the country's foreign policy.

In Switzerland, internationalisation means first and foremost Europeanisation. While between the mid-1990s and the late 2000s the Swiss people have repeatedly supported the Swiss government's European policy (the so-called 'bilateral way'), the acceptance of the popular initiative 'against mass immigration', introduced by the Swiss People's Party on 9 February 2014, threatens the bilateral way. The constitutional provision introduced by the popular initiative is not compatible with the bilateral agreement on the Free Movement of Persons (FMP) and may, therefore, lead to the termination of entire first package of bilateral agreements.

Against this background, the purpose of this chapter is to shed light on the growing tensions between domestic and foreign politics in Swiss direct democracy. In the next section I elaborate further on the problems raised by internationalisation/Europeanisation in a direct democratic context in general, and with regard to Switzerland's European policy in particular. In the empirical section, I start with an overview of how the use of direct democratic institutions on internationalised issues has evolved over time (from 1961 to 2015), and how far the Swiss government has been successful in the related votes. I then briefly discuss the 'double game' played by the Swiss People's Party, which uses direct democracy in foreign and immigration policy to oppose the government to which it belongs. Finally, the last subsection takes a closer look at the direct democratic vote on the popular initiative 'against mass immigration'. Based on the post-election surveys I evaluate the tensions between a domestic goal (the desire to control immigration) and a foreign policy goal (the continuation of the strategy of bilateral agreements with the EU). The fourth section concludes.

## *Internationalisation/Europeanisation and direct democracy*

Two developments account for the growing tension between domestic and foreign politics in the Swiss direct democracy: the speeding up of the globalisation and Europeanisation processes, and the extension of direct democracy to a growing set of international treaties.

### Direct and indirect internationalisation/Europeanisation

In the era of globalisation domestic and international politics are increasingly entangled. By lowering the boundaries among nation states the process of globalisation leads to the internationalisation of domestic politics. Issues that used to be domestic in nature are now strongly influenced by economic, political or technological developments at the international level; there are hardly any policy issues that have no international component. The first and most straightforward form of influence results from international negotiations or from membership in a supranational organisations, and is usually referred to as 'direct internationalisation' (Fischer 2005, 2007; Sciarini and Nicolet 2005; Sciarini et al. 2004; Sciarini et al. 2002).

Several studies have highlighted the importance of that direct form of influence. Focusing on a comparison between the early 1980s and the early 1990s, Hirschi et al. (1999) highlight the strong increase in the number of international treaties and the growing scope covered by these treaties, both substantively and geographically: these treaties tend to cover an increasing number of domestic policy fields and an increasing number of countries. Based on a more systematic analysis of the stock of domestic and international normative acts (laws and ordinances) in force in Switzerland from 1947 to 2007, Linder et al. (2009) show that the share of international law in the total of normative acts has steadily increased over the last 60 years (also Linder, 2014). Since the mid-1990s, international treaties have started to outnumber legislative acts in domestic law. In 2006, they accounted for 60 per cent of the total of normative acts. The two sets of bilateral treaties with the EU have strongly contributed to this increase.

This last result reminds us that in the European context internationalisation means first of all Europeanisation. While Switzerland is not a member of the European Union, it is nevertheless strongly affected by European integration. After the rejection of the European Economic Area in a popular vote in 1992, Switzerland started to negotiate bilaterally with the EU. The two rounds of bilateral talks led to fifteen agreements in various fields (Afonso and Maggetti 2007; Dupont and Sciarini 2007; Schwok 2006), and enabled Switzerland to reach a 'customized quasi-membership' (Kriesi and Trechsel 2008: 189).

Second, internationalisation may arise even in the absence of formal international negotiations. This is typically the case when a state adapts unilaterally to existing international or supranational rules. This form of influence is usually referred to as 'indirect internationalisation' (Fischer 2005, 2007; Sciarini and Nicolet 2005; Sciarini et al. 2004; Sciarini et al. 2002). In several policy domains Switzerland has indeed adapted unilaterally to EU rules (Linder 2011a, 2013). According to a study on the Europeanisation of Swiss legislation a third of all legislative changes introduced from 1990 to 2010 are to some extent congruent with EU rules (Jenni 2014a, 2014b).[1] Out of the 1,124 legislative changes covered by this study 13 per cent are fully in line with EU rules, 6 per cent show a partial adaptation and 14 per cent were already EU-compatible before the policy change occurred. Indirect Europeanisation accounts for a larger share of compatibility with EU rules than direct Europeanisation (three-quarters and one-quarter, respectively).

Gava and Varone (2014) reach a similar conclusion (also Gava and Varone 2012). Looking at 'EU footprint' in primary (i.e. laws, decrees) and secondary (i.e. ordinances) legislation through a computer keyword search, they quantitatively assess the degree of Europeanisation in domestic legislative changes enacted between 1999 and 2012. Their results confirm that references to the EU are related more to indirect Europeanisation rather than to direct Europeanisation. However, this holds mainly for secondary legislation, where 13 per cent of policy changes show the EU's indirect footprint, against only 3 per cent of policy changes with a direct footprint. In primary legislation, by contrast, manifest references to the EU in policy changes are equally shared between direct and indirect Europeanisation (5 per cent each).[2]

The importance of Europeanisation also transpires from Sciarini et al.'s (2015) study of the eleven most important decisions-making processes of the 2001–6 period, which they identified based on an expert survey (also Fischer and Sciarini 2014; Sciarini 2014a). Among the eleven most important processes, three are directly Europeanised (the extension of the bilateral agreements with the EU on the FMP, the agreement regarding Switzerland's participation in the Schengen–Dublin agreements, and the bilateral agreement on the taxation of savings), and two are indirectly Europeanised (the revision of the law on foreigners and the telecommunication act).[3]

Finally, in addition to direct and indirect internationalisation, I wish to point to additional forms of influence that internationalisation may take (Sciarini et al. 2002). First, even in the absence of international or supranational rules, a state may have to react to more informal economic or political pressures. For

1. The assessment of the extent of EU-related adaptation is based on the coding of the message published by the Federal Council (or by the responsible parliamentary commissions) in support of a given legislative change (Jenni 2014a and 2014b).

2. They further find that the share of Europeanised legal reforms per year is systematically higher for secondary legislation enacted by the Executive than for primary legislation enacted by Parliament. In addition, while the extent of Europeanisation of primary legislation tends to stagnate towards the end of the period under study, the share of Europeanised ordinances is still on the rise.

3. Note, however, that with respect to Europeanisation the most important decision-making processes are not representative of the larger set of legislative acts. Among all legislative acts subject to direct democracy (popular initiatives, constitutional changes, federal laws) of the 1995–2006 period (N=583), the share of Europeanised acts is only 9 per cent: 6.5 per cent of directly, and 2.5 per cent of indirectly, Europeanised acts.

example, it may decide to modify its legislation in order to increase its locational attractiveness (e.g. Scharpf 1998): in the era of state competition, states tend to adapt their legislation to reduce undesirable outflows of internationally mobile factors, or to attract new inflows of the same kind. Second, there are policy issues that intrinsically have a strong international dimension. Immigration policy is obviously a case in hand (Linder 2011b). As a wealthy country, Switzerland has been an important target for migrant workers and asylum seekers. The sharp increase of migrant flows – another crucial aspect of globalisation (Kriesi et al. 2008) – has exerted a strong influence on public policy making in Switzerland, and it has given rise to a number of direct democratic votes (see below). In addition to immigration policy broadly defined, internationalisation may also affect other policy fields such as environmental, monetary or transportation policy.

## Foreign policy and direct democracy

Together with federalism and neutrality, direct democracy is one of the three cornerstones of the Swiss political system, and a key element of Swiss national identity (Kriesi 1999, 2005; Sciarini et al. 2001). Direct democracy influences public policy both directly, by granting the people with a veto power on political decision-making, and indirectly, through its impact on other decision-making phases and on political actors' strategies. It is widely acknowledged that direct democratic institutions, and more especially the facultative referendum, fostered the development of the pre-parliamentary phase in the first half of the twentieth century (Neidhart 1970). The risk of failure at the end of the decision-making process led to the institutionalisation of pre-parliamentary procedures such as extra-parliamentary committees and consultation procedures, which help actors to compromise at an early stage of decision-making processes. Powerful interest groups – those able to jeopardise the process with a 'referendum threat' – are granted access to these procedures and can thus increase their influence on political decision-making. As a result, the pre-parliamentary phase is deemed crucial in Swiss politics (Kriesi 1980), even if it has lost some importance during the last three decades (Sciarini 2014a, 2015).

Until the late 1980s, foreign policy was to a large extent immune from direct democracy, meaning that many international treaties were not subject to referendum. Constitutional amendments in 1977 and in 2003 have, however, extended the judicial domains in foreign politics where direct democracy applies. This extension has granted citizens with additional co-decision rights on foreign policy formulation and increased the impact of referendums on public policy (Linder 2009). As a result of the 2003 extension of the scope of international treaties subject to direct democracy, the number of international treaties that can be attacked by the optional referendum has strongly increased (Burri 2007: 321). While before the reform this number hardly exceeded ten by legislative period (of four years), it nearly reached fifty after the reform. In that sense, one may say that the internationalisation of domestic politics went hand in hand with the democratisation of foreign policy.

The democratisation of foreign policy imposes severe constraints on the Swiss government, and Swiss diplomacy has increasingly become subject to both layers of direct democracy: treaty ratification and the related incorporation in (or adaptation of) domestic legislation (Germann 1994a, 1994b, 1995; Hug and Sciarini, 1995). Furthermore, there is an important difference between domestic policy and foreign policy proposals. In domestic policy, the failure of a policy proposal in a direct democratic vote is of course painful for the Federal Council and for the Swiss Parliament. However, a correction is always possible. That is, it is always possible to start a new decision-making process and come up with a new – and hopefully more acceptable – solution. Alternatively, it is also possible to put the process on hold and wait for more favourable conditions before restarting it. In foreign policy, by contrast, a defeat in popular vote is more problematic, since it also affects the negotiation partner(s) with whom the agreement was concluded. In such a situation, restarting a new process is obviously more complicated, since it depends on the willingness of the negotiation partner; a 'wait and see' position might not be an option either. In that sense, in foreign policy a single negative vote may lead to a deadlock from which the Government may then have a hard time to escape. Similar problems arise when a direct democratic vote on a given issue contradicts previous international commitments made by Switzerland in related fields.

This does, however, not mean that citizens' direct participation in foreign policy making is inherently problematic and should therefore be banned, as some classics would let us believe (Almond 1950; Lippmann 1965 [1922]). Quite to the contrary, a range of studies on opinion formation and voting behaviour in referendums on foreign policy in Switzerland show that voters do not treat foreign policy as different from other policy areas in referendums, and do not behave differently in this field (Bützer and Marquis 2002; Marquis 2006; Marquis and Sciarini 1999; Sciarini 1996; Sciarini and Marquis 2000; Sciarini and Tresch 2009, 2011). First, the 'Swiss laboratory' contradicts the widespread view that citizens are poorly informed about and little interested in foreign affairs, or that foreign policy votes are more emotional than domestic policy votes. Second, opinion formation in foreign policy shows similar patterns as in domestic policy, that is, it consistently depends on the interactions between the elite's discourse and citizens' political predispositions and political competence, as they are conceptualised in Zaller's (1992) theory. Third, and still in line with Zaller's (1992) model, in both domestic and foreign policy we witness a 'mainstream' and 'polarisation' effects, depending on the level of conflict among the elite, and depending on the framing of referendum campaigns. Fourth, and relatedly, foreign policy votes show some distinctive characteristics mainly with respect to the conditions under which opinion formation occurs, i.e. with respect to the line-up of partisan coalitions and to the intensity and direction of political messages.

## European policy: constraining dissensus rather than permissive consensus

Increasing the influence of the people on foreign policy – be it deliberately, through the extension of citizens' direct legislation or incidentally, because of the increase of internationalised issues brought about by the globalisation and Europeanisation processes – is not necessarily a problem, as long as the elite's preferences and the public's preferences converge. However, policy proposals arising from the international environment often touch the established domestic order and are thus likely to foster conflict domestically.

In the EU, the deepening of the integration process was to some extent premised on the depoliticisation of EU-related issues. The resulting 'permissive consensus' among the public allowed elites to take important steps towards building the EU (Inglehart 1971, Lindberg and Scheingold 1970). The 'permissive consensus' reached its limits with the Maastricht treaty (Franklin et al. 1994, Gabel and Palmer 1995), and then turned into 'constraining dissensus' (Hooghe and Marks 2009).

In Switzerland, by contrast, the necessity to submit EU membership to compulsory referendum and bilateral agreements to optional referendum has prevented the emergence of a 'permissive consensus' over European integration (Afonso et al. 2014). Instead, from the outset direct democratic institutions have created a 'constraining dissensus' and contributed to the politicisation of EU matters. No wonder then that there have been more direct democratic votes on European integration in Switzerland than in any member state of the EU.

After the rejection of the European Economic Area (EEA) in 1992, the Swiss Federal Council enjoyed consistent popular support for its strategy of bilateral agreements with the EU. The list of successful direct democratic votes is indeed impressive: the rejection of a popular initiative calling for a withdrawal of the membership application in 1997 (74 per cent no); support for the first set of bilateral agreements in May 2000 (67 per cent yes); the rejection of a popular initiative asking for a reactivation of the membership application in 2001 (77 per cent no); support for the agreement on Switzerland's participation in Schengen–Dublin in 2005 (55 per cent yes); support for the extension of agreement on the FMP to the ten new EU member states in 2005 (56 per cent yes); support for the federal law on cooperation with eastern European countries (Switzerland's contribution to the EU's cohesion fund) in 2006 (53 per cent yes); renewal of the agreement on the FMP and its extension to Romania and Bulgaria in 2009 (60 per cent yes); support for the introduction of biometric passports and travel documents as part of Schengen regulations in 2009 (50.1 per cent yes).[4]

These repeated successes reinforced the credibility of the Swiss government as a negotiation partner. However, as we will see below the Swiss government has suffered from some major defeats in direct democratic votes during the last few years.

4. An in-depth study of the decision-making process regarding two of these issues (the extension of the free trade agreement with the EU and the Schengen–Dublin agreement) shows that the successful outcome was notably due to the ability of decision-makers to form an oversized coalition in support for their plans (Fischer 2012). This ability, in turn, owes much to the proactive and inclusive strategy of executive state actors (Fischer and Sciarini 2013).

## Empirics

Table 11.1 provides an overview of the evolution of direct democratic votes on internationalised issues. In line with the discussion above, the internationalisation category comprises three distinct sets of votes: *directly* internationalised issues, which to a large extent correspond to the field of *foreign/European* policy (i.e. Switzerland's membership of international organisations such as the UN or the IMF/World Bank, and bilateral agreements with the EU); *indirectly* internationalised issues, that is, domestic legislative acts relating to international or EU rules that Switzerland adapts to unilaterally, or to international organisations with which Switzerland intends to cooperate (e.g. the creation of a blue helmet corps in the field of security policy); and a residual category of domestic legislative acts that have a *strong international component*. The latter category includes mostly policy issues in immigration and asylum policy, or issues relating to the acquisition of Swiss citizenship (naturalisation) or of real estate by foreigners.

Table 11.1 (first row) shows that the number of direct democratic votes dealing with internationalised issues has substantially increased over time. While this number amounted to less than ten votes per decade during the 1960s, it has exceeded twenty since the 1990s. In each decade, the issues of immigration, asylum and foreigners provide a larger number of votes, ahead of foreign/European policy. The growth of votes on internationalised issues gets even clearer when calculated in relative terms, i.e. as a share of votes on internationalised issues considered against the total number of votes in a given decade. That share has increased from 17 per cent in the 1960s to 30 per cent in the 2000s. In other words, Table 11.1 suggests that the number of direct democratic votes on internationalised issues has increased at a faster pace than that of direct democratic votes in domestic politics.

*Table 11.1: Frequency of direct democratic votes and government success on internationalised issues (1961–2015)*

| | **1961–70** | **1971–80** | **1981–90** | **1991–2000** | **2001–10** | **2011–15** |
|---|---|---|---|---|---|---|
| Total number of direct democratic votes | 29 | 87 | 66 | 106 | 82 | 42 |
| N direct democratic votes on internationalised issues<br>(among which foreign/European policy)<br>(among which immigration/asylum policy) | 5<br>(0)<br>(1) | 16<br>(4)<br>(3) | 15<br>(1)<br>(7) | 26<br>(5)<br>(5) | 25<br>(8)<br>(10) | 13<br>(2)<br>(4) |
| Direct democratic votes on internationalised issues as a share of all direct democratic votes (%) | 17 | 18 | 23 | 25 | 30 | 31 |
| Government success on internationalised issues (%) | 100 | 81 | 60 | 80 | 64 | 69 |

*Source of data:* Swissvotes (until 2012), C2D (since 2013); author's own calculations.

As already mentioned, issues relating to the broad category of immigration, asylum, foreigners and naturalisation have strongly contributed to this trend. In fact, about a third of all votes on internationalised issues of the whole 1961 to 2015 period pertain to immigration broadly defined. Note, however, that almost all votes on immigration policy correspond to the third category of domestic issues with a strong international component, whereas European policy accounts for the bulk of popular votes on directly internationalised issues.

The last row of Table 11.1 provides information about the success rate of the Federal Council in direct democratic votes on internationalised issues. The success rate is measured as the share of direct democratic votes ending up with an outcome that was in line with the Federal Council's voting recommendation. The success rate has remained stable and high (above 60 per cent) across the decade. It has thus been as high in foreign politics as in domestic politics (Sciarini and Tresch 2014). In other words, while an increase in the frequency of direct democratic votes has offered additional opportunities to oppose policy proposals, the Federal Council has still been able to get support in most popular votes. However, as mentioned above, a failure in a direct democratic vote on foreign policy is more consequential. Unlike in domestic politics, it is not always possible to restart a decision-making process, and a 'wait and see' position may not be an option either. Switzerland had its first traumatic experience of such an outcome with the rejection of the EEA agreement in 1992, and it faced a similar deadlock with the acceptance of the popular initiative 'against mass immigration' in February 2014.

In the late 2000s, the Swiss people and the cantons provided – unexpected – support for a series of popular initiatives sponsored by the Swiss People's Party. The first vote came as a warning and caused mainly reputational damage, but did not directly affect Switzerland's foreign policy: In November 2009, a majority of the Swiss people (58 per cent) and the cantons (19.5 out of 23) said yes to a popular initiative asking for a ban on new Islamic minarets. The acceptance by a majority of voters (53 per cent) and cantons (17.5), almost exactly one year later (November 2010), of the popular initiative requesting the expulsion of criminal foreigners was more problematic, since that initiative contradicts both the European Convention on Human Rights and the bilateral agreement with the EU on the FMP. This time, the target of the Swiss People's Party's popular initiative was not a specific culture or religion, but criminal foreigners in general: the initiative called for the automatic deportation of foreigners who had committed various forms of criminal offences, from murder to breaking and entering, or welfare fraud.[5]

The most recent – and most problematic – clash took place on 9 February 2014. On that day, a very narrow majority of the Swiss people (50.3 per cent)

5. Swiss voters were faced with a choice between the hardline option of the Swiss People's Party and a compromise submitted by moderate right parties that would have allowed for a case-by-case examination of criminals' deportation. They nevertheless opted for the more extreme proposal that would lead to the automatic removal of convicted foreigners.

but a large majority of cantons (14.5) supported the popular initiative 'against mass immigration' launched by the Swiss People's Party. The initiative is in full contradiction to the bilateral agreement with the EU on the FMP, since it aims to reintroduce control over immigration through quotas on foreign workers, and preference for national workers on the job market. According to the initiative, the Swiss government must renegotiate international commitments within three years to put them in line with its requirements. At the time of writing it is not yet clear whether and how this popular initiative can be implemented without breaching the agreement on the FMP. This breach, in turn, might put the whole first set of bilateral agreements at an end.

From the outset of the first round of bilateral negotiations in 1993, the EU insisted on the 'parallelism of the talks', i.e. that any agreement (both for signature and ratification) on a given topic was dependent on the acceptance of an agreement in the other issue areas (Dupont and Sciarini 2001, 2007). Thus if one element was rejected by the Swiss, the whole package would fall. Given the EEA experience, the EU wanted to protect itself against a possible new popular rejection that would hurt the overall balance of concessions. For the same reason, the first set of bilateral agreements includes a so-called 'guillotine clause', according to which the termination of a given agreement would automatically lead to the termination of the six other agreements.

## The double game of the Swiss People's Party

The three direct democratic votes mentioned in the previous subsection exemplify the propensity of the Swiss People's Party to resort increasingly to popular initiatives as part of its 'policy-seeking' strategy (Müller and Strom 1999), i.e. in order to influence the content of public policy. It does so by bypassing 'standard' decision-making channels and by calling for a direct and binding decision by the people. The Swiss People's Party has proven extremely successful in that respect (Varone et al., 2014). While the overall success rate of popular initiatives is about 10 per cent, on average, over the last ten years the success rate of the Swiss People's Party has exceeded 30 per cent. In addition, that party uses popular initiatives not only for 'policy-seeking' purposes, but also as part of its 'vote-seeking' strategy (Müller and Strom 1999), i.e. in order to increase its electoral strength.

Thus, direct democratic institutions enable the Swiss People's Party to play the 'double game' of being in government and in opposition at the same time. In the Swiss 'assembly-independent system' (Shugart and Carey, 1992) votes of confidence and coalition agreements between governing parties do not exist. Therefore, governing parties do not need to be loyal to the Federal Council. Quite to the contrary, they may resort to popular initiatives and to referendums to bypass or oppose the government. In addition to the right-wing conservative Swiss People's Party, the other pole party of the 'governing' coalition, the leftist Social Democratic Party also extensively relies on such a 'double game' strategy. As a result, both parties frequently oppose the Swiss government in direct democratic votes (Sciarini 2014b).[6] Between 2003 and 2011, either the Swiss People's Party or the Social Democratic Party (or both!) have opposed the Federal Council in all direct democratic votes held as a result of popular initiative, in nearly all votes held as a result of optional referendum, and in three out of four votes held as a result of a compulsory referendum. In other words, in the Swiss model of 'consensus democracy' (Lijphart 2012), the Government faces the opposition of (at least) one party of the governing coalition in nearly all direct democratic votes.

## The popular vote on the initiative 'against mass immigration'

As mentioned above, tension between domestic and foreign politics has reached a peak with the acceptance of the popular initiative against mass immigration, which contradicts the agreement on the FMP with the EU. As is the case for all direct democratic votes held at the federal level since 1981, a survey poll (the so-called VOX survey) was conducted among a representative sample of 1,500 Swiss citizens in the two weeks after the vote. The VOX questionnaire comprised eight questions asking respondents to position themselves on the main arguments for and against the popular initiative put forward by the political elite during the voting campaign. Table 11.2 presents the results.

Three of the four arguments in favour of the initiative are supported by roughly two-thirds of voters. These three arguments are overwhelmingly supported not only by voters who said yes to the initiative, but also by a non-negligible share of voters who said no. Thus, while the no-voters rejected the initiative, many of them share the initiators' critical view about immigration.[7] Only the argument regarding the consequences of immigration for criminality leads to polarisation between yes-voters, who strongly support the argument, and no-voters, who strongly reject it.

Arguments raised against the initiative did not fare as good as arguments in support. Only the argument that controlling immigration with quotas will increase bureaucracy and costs receives across-the-board support: it is supported by a strong majority of no-voters, and by an important minority of yes-voters. By contrast, the three other arguments receive support only from no-voters, but did not convince yes-voters. Even the argument regarding the threat on the bilateral agreements, which was the centrepiece of the no campaign, is rejected by a strong majority of yes-voters.

---

6. While the issue profile of the Swiss Peoples Party is typical of a radical populist right party, i.e. it strongly focuses on immigration, law and order and European integration, the Social Democrats emphasise both classic economic and social issues and left-libertarian issues such as environmental and gender issues (Sciarini 2010).

7 At first glance, the sizeable support for the argument that 'If control over immigration leads to the termination of the bilateral agreement with the EU, we must run this risk' by no voters does not make much sense. On closer inspection, it is likely that no voters supported the argument not because they agreed that one should take the risk of termination, but because they agreed that a yes to the initiative would threaten the bilateral agreements.

*Table 11.2: Support for the main arguments in the popular initiative 'against mass immigration'*

| | | Agree (%) | Disagree (%) | Don't know (%) |
|---|---|---|---|---|
| *Arguments in favour of the initiative* | | | | |
| Switzerland should be able to control immigration on its own | Total | 66 | 31 | 4 |
| | Yes voters | 95 | 4 | 1 |
| | No voters | 35 | 60 | 6 |
| Uncontrolled immigration puts pressures on wages and generates problems with respect to housing and transport | Total | 66 | 31 | 4 |
| | Yes voters | 86 | 13 | 2 |
| | No voters | 45 | 50 | 6 |
| To be able to control immigration, we must run the risk of terminating the bilateral agreement with the EU | Total | 63 | 33 | 5 |
| | Yes voters | 82 | 13 | 5 |
| | No voters | 42 | 55 | 3 |
| Immigration increases criminality in Switzerland | Total | 52 | 42 | 6 |
| | Yes voters | 80 | 15 | 6 |
| | No voters | 25 | 69 | 6 |
| *Arguments against the initiative* | | | | |
| Controlling immigration with quotas comes with bureaucratic costs | Total | 63 | 30 | 7 |
| | Yes voters | 41 | 51 | 8 |
| | No voters | 87 | 8 | 5 |
| Pretending to control immigration contradicts the agreement on the free movement of persons and will lead to the termination of the bilateral agreements with the EU | Total | 55 | 36 | 10 |
| | Yes voters | 33 | 56 | 12 |
| | No voters | 79 | 15 | 6 |
| The termination of the agreement with the EU on the free movement of persons will endanger an important pillar of Switzerland's economic wealth | Total | 50 | 45 | 6 |
| | Yes voters | 17 | 76 | 7 |
| | No voters | 84 | 13 | 3 |
| Pretending to control immigration will lead to Switzerland's isolation | Total | 43 | 56 | 6 |
| | Yes voters | 13 | 82 | 5 |
| | No voters | 76 | 20 | 5 |

*Source:* Sciarini et al. (2014: 57).

Table 11.3 offers a finer-grained view of the two arguments regarding the relationships between the popular initiative and the bilateral agreements. It focuses on Yes-voters and additionally excludes 'don't know' answers on the two argument questions.

The largest group (50 per cent) comprises yes-voters who disagree with the argument that the initiative will lead to the termination of the bilateral agreements, *but* nevertheless agree that it is worth taking the risk of such a termination in order to control immigration. One-third (36 per cent) of yes-voters agree that

*Table 11.3: Crosstab between the arguments among yes-voters (per cent)*

| | The initiative endangers the bilateral way | |
|---|---|---|
| To control immigration we must run the risk of terminating the bilateral agreements | Agree | Disagree |
| Agree | 36 | 50 |
| Disagree | 2 | 12 |

*Source:* Sciarini et al. (2014: 58).

the initiative leads to the termination of bilateral agreements *and* agree that one must take this risk in order to control immigration.[8] In other words, whatever their opinion regarding the compatibility between the initiative and the bilateral agreements, more than 80 per cent of voters who said yes to the initiative are ready to live with the consequences of their choice. According to these results, supporters of the popular initiative made an informed decision, meaning that they voted in full knowledge of the likely implications of the initiative for Switzerland's bilateral integration strategy.

Figure 11.1 shows the evolution over time of Swiss citizens' attitudes towards the FMP and bilateral agreements. The data stems from the VOX-surveys carried out after the 2005 vote on the extension of FMP to the ten new EU member states (Kopp and Milic 2005), after the 2009 vote on the renewal of the agreement on the FMP and its extension to Bulgaria and Romania (Hirter and Linder 2009), and after the 2014 vote on the initiative against mass immigration (Sciarini et al. 2014).[9]

*Figure 11.1: Attitudes of the Swiss public towards the FMP*

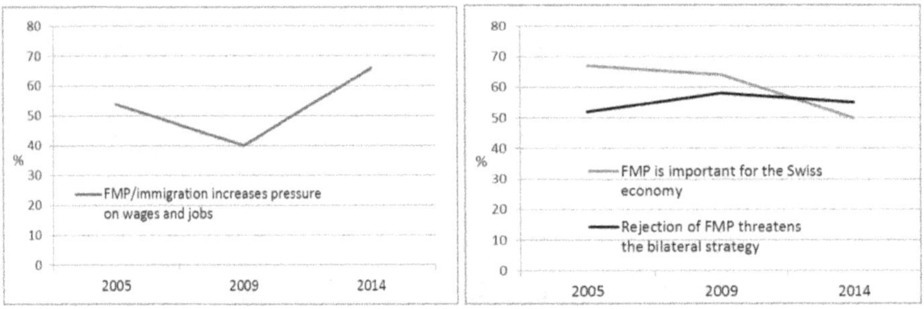


8. Only a small minority (12 per cent) disagrees with the argument that the initiative leads to the termination of bilateral agreements *and* hence also disagrees that one must take the risk of termination. Finally, a tiny share of yes voters (2 per cent) holds an inconsistent attitude, agreeing that the initiatives lead to termination but *not* agreeing to take the risk of termination.
9. The figures are not perfectly comparable, since the exact wording has slightly changed from one survey to the next.

Figure 11.1 (left hand side) shows that Swiss citizens have become highly critical towards the increase of immigration induced by the FMP. While the argument that agreeing to the FMP would increase competition on the job market and put pressure on wages was supported by a small majority of voters in 2005 and by less than 40 per cent in 2009, it was supported by two-thirds of voters in 2014. Conversely, support for the argument that the Swiss economy benefits from the FMP has strongly declined over time (Figure 11.1, right hand side), from 67 per cent in 2005 to 50 per cent in 2014. Thus, while in the 2005 and 2009 referendums the argument regarding the economic importance of the bilateral agreements strongly contributed to the acceptance of the FMP (Hirter and Linder 2009; Kopp and Milic 2005), in 2014 that argument could no longer counterbalance the negative attitudes towards growing immigration.

The argument that a rejection of the FMP would lead to the termination of the bilateral agreements displays stability over time: in 2005, 2009 and 2014, it is supported by a small majority of voters. More importantly, support for this argument is not lower in 2014 than in the two previous votes. This again suggests that the acceptance of the popular initiative 'against mass immigration' was not due to a lack of information among the public regarding its consequences for the agreement on the FMP and the bilateral way. That acceptance has more substantial grounds, namely the increase of negative attitudes about the growing inflow of migrant workers induced by the FMP.

On the political and diplomatic side, the key question has become how to get out of the deadlock caused by the acceptance of the initiative against mass immigration. Given the incompatibility between the initiative and the agreement of FMP, the Swiss government will most presumably have to call for a new decision by the people, and ask Swiss citizens to make a choice between the two goals. In a more recent VOX survey carried out in November 2014 we delved further into that crucial issue, by asking the sample two questions (Sciarini et al. 2015): a retrospective question about individuals' voting decision on 9 February 2014, and a prospective question about their likely vote in a future referendum that would ask the Swiss people to choose between the two goals.[10]

Three results are worth mentioning (Sciarini et al. 2015: 279–83). First, when faced with the dilemma between strict immigration control and a continuation of the bilateral agreements, a majority of 60 per cent of Swiss voters show support for the bilateral agreements. Second, a sizable minority (30 per cent) of voters who said yes to the initiative against mass immigration would nevertheless choose the bilateral agreements over the implementation of the initiative. This group of voters will obviously be crucial in the perspective of a new direct democratic vote. Third, our results highlight the importance of age and trust in government as determinants

10. The exact wording of the prospective question was: 'The Federal Council is attempting to respect the willingness of the Swiss people and to implement the initiative against mass immigration and, in parallel, to maintain the bilateral agreements concluded with the EU. If both goals are impossible to achieve, which one is most important for you? The implementation of the initiative against mass immigration or the continuation of the bilateral agreements?'

of attitudes towards the dilemma between immigration control and continuation of the bilateral agreements. On the one hand, among voters who said yes to the initiative against mass immigration, the likelihood of preferring a continuation of the bilateral strategy over the implementation of the initiative increases with age. In other words, young supporters of immigration control appear more intransigent in their support for implementing the initiative than older supporters, possibly because the former are less aware of the economic importance of the bilateral treaties than the latter. On the other hand, voters who supported the initiative are far more likely to favour bilateral agreements over immigration control if they trust the Federal Council. This results underlines the important role of the Federal Council, whose leadership, unity and credibility may play a central role in the future vote.

## Conclusion

As a small open economy Switzerland is heavily affected by economic globalisation, and as a country located in the middle of Europe it is critically dependent on access to the EU market. This accounts for both the strong impact that internationalisation/Europeanisation has exerted on Swiss public policies, and the close institutional ties that Switzerland has developed with the EU over recent decades. Internationalisation/Europeanisation is an ongoing process that will undoubtedly continue to influence Swiss domestic politics considerably in the years to come. The era when neutral and non-EU member Switzerland was sheltered from international politics is definitely *tempi passati*.

In Swiss direct democracy, citizens are granted an important say in public policy making. While foreign policy used to be immune from the influence of the Swiss people, both the extension of the scope of direct democracy to additional categories of international treaties and the vanishing boundaries between foreign and domestic politics have amplified the role that the Swiss public plays in the definition of foreign policy. Empirically, the number of direct democratic votes on internationalised issues has increased at a faster pace than the number of direct democratic votes in domestic politics. As a result, the Swiss government and parliament cannot count on depoliticisation and 'permissive consensus', but have been – and still are – forced to cope with politicisation and 'constraining dissensus' when designing their foreign and European policy.

This notwithstanding, the Federal Council has enjoyed a high success rate in direct democratic votes dealing with internationalised issues. Since the rejection of the EEA in 1992 the Federal Council has received support for its policy line on European matters in eight direct democratic votes in a row. Recently, however, the Federal Council has suffered from some major defeats. The acceptance of the popular initiative against mass immigration is especially problematic, since it threatens the first set of bilateral agreements with the EU. Escaping the deadlock and implementing the initiative in a way that is compatible with the requirements of FMP is a genuine challenge. In addition, if diplomats and policy makers find a way out, the Swiss people will still have to endorse the solution in a new referendum. By granting citizens so much say on the definition of foreign policy, the Swiss democracy has definitely become a specific case in comparative perspective.

**References**

Afonso, A. and Maggetti, M. (2007) 'Bilaterals II: reaching the limits of the Swiss Third Way?' in C. Church (ed.), *Switzerland and the European Union: A close, contradictory and misunderstood relationship*, London: Routledge: 215–33.

Afonso, A., Fontana, M. C. and Papadopoulos, Y. (2014) 'The Europeanisation of Swiss decision-making in comparative perspective: from outlier to normal case?', *Swiss Political Science Review*, 20(2): 246–51.

Almond, G. (1950) *The American People and Foreign Policy*, New Haven: Yale University Press.

Burri, B. (2007) 'Statistik über die Erlasse der Bundesversammlung', *Leges – Gesetzgebung & Evaluation*, 18(2): 319–26.

Bützer, M. and Marquis, L. (2002) 'Public opinion formation in Swiss federal referendums', in D. Farrell and R. Schmitt-Beck (eds) *Do Political Campaigns Matter? Campaign effects in elections and referendums*, London and New York: Routledge: 163–82.

Dupont, C. and Sciarini, P. (2001) 'Switzerland and the European integration process: engagement without marriage', *West European Politics*, 24(2): 211–32.

—— (2007) 'Back to the future: the first round of bilateral talks with the EU', in C. Church (ed.), *Switzerland and the European Union: A close, contradictory and misunderstood relationship*, London: Routledge: 202–14.

Fischer, A. (2005) *Die Auswirkungen der Internationalisierung und Europäisierung auf Schweizer Entscheidungsprozesse: Institutionen, Kräftverhältnisse und Akteursstrategien in Bewegung*, Zurich/Chür: Verlag Rügger.

—— (2007) 'Internationalization of Swiss decision-making processes', in U. Klöti, P. Knoepfel, and H. Kriesi (eds) *Handbook of Swiss Politics*, Zurich: NZZ Libro: 547–68.

—— (2012) *Entscheidungsstrukturen in der Schweizer Politik zu Beginn des 21: Jahrhunderts*, Zurich: Rügger.

Fischer, M. and Sciarini, P. (2013) 'Europeanization and the inclusive strategies of executive actors', *Journal of European Public Policy*, 20(10): 1482–98.

Fischer, M. and Sciarini, P. (2014) 'The Europeanisation of Swiss decision-making processes', *Swiss Political Science Review*, 20(2): 239–45.

Franklin, M., Marsh, M. and McLaren, L. (1994) 'Uncorking the bottle: popular opposition to European unification in the wake of Maastricht', *Journal of Common Market Studies*, 32(4): 455–72.

Gabel, M. and Palmer, H. D. (1995) 'Understanding variations in public support for European integration', *European Journal of Political Research*, 27(1): 3–19.

Gava, R. and Varone, F. (2012) 'So close, yet so far? The EU's footprint in Swiss legislative production', in S. Brouard, O. Costa and T. König (eds) *The Europeanisation of Domestic Legislatures: The empirical implications of the Delors' Myth in nine countries*, London: Springer: 197–221.

—— (2014) 'The EU's footprint in Swiss policy change: a quantitative assessment of primary and secondary legislation (1999–2012)', *Swiss Political Science Review*, 20(2): 216–22.

Germann, R. E. (1994a) 'La diplomatie référendaire de la Suisse dans l'Europe transnationale', in Y. Papadopoulos (ed.) *Présent et avenir de la démocratie directe. Actes du colloque de l'Université de Lausanne*, Geneva: Georg,: 111–19.

—— (1994b) *Staatsreform: Der Übergang zur Konkurrenzdemokratie*, Berne: Haupt.

—— (1995) 'Die bilateralen Verhandlungen mit der EU und die Steuerung der direkten Demokatie', *Schweizerische Zeitschrift für Politische Wissenschaft*, 1(2–3): 35–60.

Hirschi, C., Serdült, U. and Thomas, W. (1999) 'Schweizerische Aussenpolitik im Wandel: Internationalisierung, Globalisierung und Multilateralisierung', *Schweizerische Zeitschrift für Politikwissenschaft*, 5(1): 1–21.

Hirter, H. and Linder, W. (2009) *Analyse des votations fédérales du 8 février 2009*, Berne: Université de Berne/GfS-Berne.

Hooghe, L. and Marks, G. (2009) 'A postfunctionalist theory of European Integration: from permissive consensus to constraining dissensus', *British Journal of Political Science*, 39: 1–23.

Hug, S. and Sciarini, P. (1995) 'Switzerland – still a paradigmatic case?', in G. Schneider, P. Weitsman, and T. Bernauer (eds) *Towards a New Europe: Stops and starts in regional integration*, New York: Praeger/Greenwood: 55–74.

Inglehart, R. (1971) 'Public opinion and European integration', in L. N. Lindberg and S. A. Scheingold (eds) *European Integration*, Cambridge, MA: Harvard University Press: 160–91.

Jenni, S. (2014a) 'Europeanization of Swiss law-making: empirics and rhetoric are drifting apart', *Swiss Political Science Review*, 20(2): 208–15.

—— (2014b) 'The last Gallic village? An empirical analysis of Switzerland's differentiated European integration', Doctoral Thesis, Zurich: ETH.

Kopp, L. and Milic, T. (2005) *Analyse des votations fédérales du 25 septembre 2005*, Zurich/Berne: Universität Zurich/GfS-Berne.

Kriesi, H. H. (1980) *Entscheidungsstrukturen und Entscheidungsprozesse in der Schweizer Politik*, Frankfurt: Campus Verlag.

—— (1999) 'Introduction: state formation and nation building in the Swiss case', in H. Kriesi, K. Armingeon, H. Siegrist and A. Wimmer (eds), *Nation and National Identity: The European experience in perspective*, Chur/Zurich: Verlag Rügger: 13–28.

—— (2005) *Direct Democratic Choices: The Swiss experience*. Lanham, MD: Lexington.

Kriesi, H. and Trechsel, A. H. (2008) *The Politics of Switzerland: Continuity and change in a consensus democracy*, Cambridge: Cambridge University Press.

Kriesi, H., Grande, E., Lachat, R., Dolezal, M., Bornschier, S. and Frey, T. (2008) *West European Politics in the Age of Globalisation*, Cambridge: Cambridge University Press.

Lijphart, A. (2012) *Patterns of Democracy: Government forms and performance in thirty-six countries*, 2nd edn, New Haven: Yale University Press.

Lindberg, L. N. and Scheingold, S. A. (1970) *Europe's Would-be Polity: Patterns of change in the European Community*, Englewood Cliffs: Prentice-Hall.

Linder, W. (2009) 'The Impact of direct democracy on public policies: a historical perspective', in S. Nahrath and F. Varone (eds), *Rediscovering Public Law and Public Administration in Comparative Policy Analysis: A tribute to Peter Knoepfel*, Bern: Haupt: 63–77.

—— (2011a) 'Europe and Switzerland: Europeanization without EU membership', in A. Mach and C. Trampusch (eds), *Switzerland in Europe: Continuity and change in the swiss political economy*, London: Routledge: 43–59.

—— (2011b). 'Multicultural Switzerland and the challenge of immigration', *Journal of Minority Studies*, 5(3): 201–25.

—— (2013) 'Switzerland and the EU: the puzzling effects of Europeanisation without institutionalisation', *Contemporary Politics*, 19(2): 190–202.

—— (2014) 'Swiss legislation in the era of globalisation: a quantitative assessment of federal legislation (1983–2007)', *Swiss Political Science Review*, 20(2): 223–31.

Linder, W., Hümbelin, O. and Sutter, M. (2009) *Die Entwicklung der eidgenössischen Gestezgebungstätigkeit 1983–2007: eine quantitative analye*, Unviersität Bern: Institut für Politikwissenschaft.

Lippmann, W. (1965 [1922]) *Public Opinion*, New York: The Free Press.

Marquis, L. (2006) *La formation de l'opinion publique en démocratie directe. Les référendums sur la politique extérieure suisse 1981–95*, Zurich: Seismo Verlag.

Marquis, L. and Sciarini, P. (1999) 'Opinion formation in foreign policy: the Swiss experience', *Electoral Studies*, 18(4): 453–71.

Müller, W. C. and Strom, K. (eds) (1999) *Policy, Office or Votes? How political parties in Western Europe make hard decisions*, Cambridge: Cambridge University Press.

Neidhart, L. (1970) *Plebiszit und pluralitäre Demokratie: Eine Analyse der Funktionen des schweizerischen Gesetzesreferendum*, Bern: Francke.

Scharpf, F. W. (1998) 'Globalization: the limitations on state capacity', *Swiss Political Science Review*, 4(1): 92–8.

Schwok, R. (2006) *Suisse – Union européenne: l'adhésion impossible?*, Lausanne: Presses polytechniques et universitaires romandes – Collection le savoir suisse.

Sciarini, P. (1996) 'Opinion publique et politique extérieure', *Revue d'Allemagne*, 28(3): 337–52.

—— (2010) 'Le potentiel électoral des partis de gauche', in S. Nicolet and P. Sciarini (eds) *Le destin électoral de la gauche: le vote socialiste et vert en Suisse*, Geneva: Georg, 87–129.

—— (2014a) 'Eppure si muove: the changing nature of the Swiss consensus democracy', *Journal of European Public Policy*, 21(1): 116–32.

—— (2014b) 'Processus législatif', in P. Knoepfel, Y. Papadopoulos, P. Sciarini, A. Vatter and S. Häusermann (eds), *Handbuch der Schweizer Politik*, Zurich: NZZ Libro: 527–61.

—— (2015) 'From corporatism to bureaucratic and partisan politics: changes in decision-making processes over time', in P. Sciarini, M. Fischer and D. Traber (eds) *Political Decision-making in Switzerland: Challenges to consensus politics*, London: Palgrave/Macmillan: 24–50.

Sciarini, P. and Marquis, L. (2000) 'Opinion publique et politique extérieure: le cas de la Suisse', *International Political Science Review*, 21(2): 149–71.

Sciarini, P. and Nicolet, S. (2005) 'Internationalization and domestic politics: evidence from the Swiss case', in H. Kriesi, P. Farago, M. Kohli and M. Zarin-Nejadan (eds) *Contemporary Switzerland: Revisiting the special case*, New York: Palgrave/Macmillan: 221–38.

Sciarini, P. and Tresch, A. (2009) 'A two-level analysis of the determinants of direct democratic choices in European, immigration and foreign policy in Switzerland', *European Union Politics*, 10(4): 456–81.

—— (2011) 'Campaign effects in direct-democratic votes in Switzerland', *Journal of Elections, Public Opinion and Parties*, 21(3): 333–57.

—— (2014) 'Votations populaires', in P. Knoepfel, Y. Papadopoulos, P. Sciarini, A. Vatter and S. Häusermann (eds) *Handbuch der Schweizer Politik*, Zurich: NZZ Libro: 497–524.

Sciarini, P., Fischer, A. and Nicolet S. (2002) 'L'impact de l'internationalisation sur les processus de décision en Suisse: une analyse quantitative des actes législatifs 1995–1999', *Revue Suisse de Science Politique*, 8(3): 1–34.

—— (2004) 'How Europe hits home: evidence from the Swiss case', *Journal of European Public Policy*, 11(3): 353–78.

Sciarini, P., Hug, S. and Dupont, C. (2001) 'Example, exception or both? Swiss national identity in perspective', in L.-E. Cedermann (ed.) *Constructing Europe's Identity: The external dimension*, Boulder, CO: Lynne Rienner: 57–88.

Sciarini, P., Lanz, S. and Nai, A. (2015) 'Till immigration do us part? Public opinion and the dilemma between immigration control and bilateral agreements', *Swiss Political Science Review*, 21(2): 271–86.

Sciarini, P., Naï, A. and Tresch, A. (2014) *Analyse de la votation fédérale du 9 février 2014*, Geneva/Berne: University of Geneva/GfS.Bern.

Shugart, M. S. and Carey, J. M. (1992) *Presidents and Assemblies*, Cambridge: Cambridge University Press.

Varone, F., Engeli, I., Gava, R. and Sciarini, P. (2014) 'Agenda-setting and direct democracy: the rise of the Swiss People's Party', in C. Green-Pedersen and S. Walgrave (eds) *Agenda-setting, Policies, and Political Systems: A comparative approach*, Chicago: Chicago University Press: 105–22.

Zaller, J. (1992) *The Nature and Origins of Mass Opinion*, Cambridge: Cambridge University Press.

*Chapter Twelve*

# Direct Democracy and the European Union

*Fernando Mendez and Mario Mendez*

## Introduction

By surveying the practice of direct democracy in a supranational context, rather than a national space, this chapter would appear to take a somewhat different angle to most chapters included in this volume. Yet this would be off the mark. For a start, EU-related referendums are mostly held in a national space. Second, the challenges confronted by the EU, in terms of providing meaningful channels for citizen input, are not too dissimilar to those facing nation states in the midst of a purported crisis of representation. However, given its weakly consolidated democratic status, those challenges can take on a rather more acute form and lead to a questioning of the polity itself. Whenever such questions emerge, it seems that the tools of direct democracy are not very far away. And so it is with the EU as it confronts a series of systemic challenges, from the eurozone crisis to the refugee crisis and a more assertive Russian neighbour. Perhaps not surprisingly, as we shall see in this chapter, all three challenges, whether directly or indirectly, have led to popular votes or pledges to hold referendums.

It is because referendums have become so central to the future institutional trajectory of the EU – for instance a major referendum on whether one of the EU's most important member states will remain took place in June 2016 – that scholars have been increasingly attracted to the topic. As a result the EU's experience with direct democratic practice has become a subject of growing scholarly inquiry. In terms of direct democracy there are three broad categories of EU-related direct democratic instruments in use. The first is the referendum on EU issues. These are held either by member states, constituent parts of a member state or by non-EU states. The EU itself does not hold referendums nor does it require them, though there have been calls for it to do so (e.g. Rose 2013) and indeed there has even been debate as to its scope to proscribe certain types of referendum (see discussion in Mendez et al. 2014, Chapter 6). The second type of direct democratic instrument relating to the EU is the recent and growing phenomenon of the use of citizens' initiatives at member state level on EU issues. This second form can also be the trigger for a referendum on an EU issue, and indeed one such bottom-up EU referendum in a member state took place in April 2016 when the Dutch voted on the EU–Ukraine Association Agreement. The third type is the EU's very own fledgling instrument of transnational direct democracy, the European Citizens' Initiative (ECI), which only came into force several years ago and allows a minimum of one million citizens to request legislative action from the European Commission.

In terms of the scholarly literature, it has been the first of this category of direct democracy that has been the dominant focus. This is not without good reason, for it has the oldest pedigree, the first such referendum having been held in 1972, and has given rise to a significant body of practice with well over 50 such referendums to date. Key questions explored at length by political scientists have included why such referendums are called, the role of parties, campaigning, turnout and voting behaviour (see e.g. Hobolt 2009, and also the earlier monograph by Hug 2002). Legal scholars have also given attention to these referendums (e.g. Tierney 2013), particularly the treaty revision referendum, which in the event of a negative vote is capable of halting the integration process (de Búrca 2010). Literature on the second and third categories of EU-related direct democracy instruments is in its infancy, which is to be expected given how new these instruments are. Nonetheless the ECI was already the subject of a journal special issue shortly after it was created (*Perspectives on European Politics and Society* 2012 Issue 3) and the emerging practice is being carefully scrutinised by political scientists and legal scholars (see e.g. Bouza Garcia and Greenwood 2014; Boussaguet 2015; Organ 2014).

With a view to exploring direct democracy in the EU, this chapter is divided into four main sections. The first outlines a fourfold typology of EU referendums and provides an overview of relevant practice around this typology. The second section focuses on two key themes explored by political scientists in relation to EU referendums, why they are called and the outcomes produced. The penultimate section introduces the ECI and extant practice in relation to that instrument. The discussion in the final section brings together some of the more salient themes discussed in the preceding sections.

## Overview of the EU's referendum practice

In this section we provide an overview of the EU's referendum experience according to a fourfold typology of EU-related referendums. The typology is based on the functional properties of the particular type of referendum. The first thing to note is the relative distribution of EU-related referendums as shown in Figure 12.1, a total of fifty-seven referendum instances. We begin by offering a definition of each referendum type as well as providing illustrative examples of each type. For further details, Tables 12.3 to 12.6 contain a comprehensive list of all the referendums grouped by their category.

### *Membership referendums*

This type of referendum can take two very distinctive forms, an accession referendum and a withdrawal referendum. The former is undertaken by candidate states after a typically lengthy negotiation process. In very rare instances, a subnational entity may also undertake a separate accession referendum (as did the Finnish Åland Islands). This definition precludes the inclusion of referendums on the 'policy' of joining the EU by non-candidate states, which are thus coded

*Figure 12.1: Distribution of EU-related referendums by type*

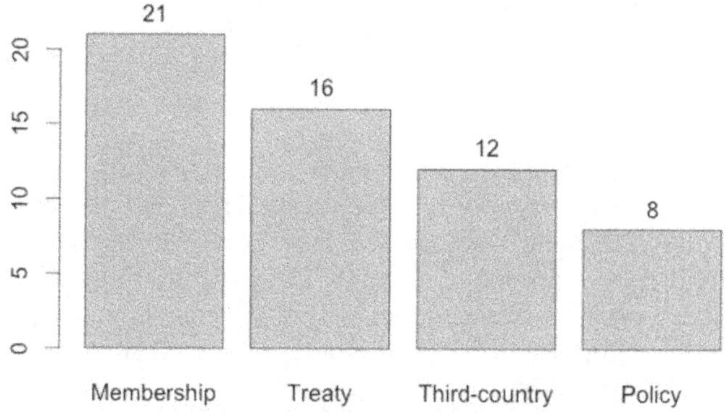


separately. The second type of referendum in this category relates to withdrawal from the EC/EU. This type of referendum can only be held by an EU member state, or a territorial entity that belongs to an EU member state.

Accession referendums account for nineteen of the twenty-one membership referendums. None of the founding member states put accession to the people. This is perhaps unsurprising given, first, that the constitutional significance of the organisation was not yet fully apparent, second, that the founding members (Belgium aside) had new clauses in their constitutions precisely for legitimising the delegating of powers to international organisations, and third, that referendum practice was then largely non-existent, indeed the German constitution would, as now, have needed an amendment to permit their use. However since the founding, sixteen of twenty-two candidate states have put accession to the people. The accession referendum emerged with the very first round of enlargement when three of the four candidate states (the UK being the exception) sought popular approval for accession. One of those four candidate states, Norway, is the only one to have ever rejected accession, which it repeated in a 1994 accession referendum. Of the five other candidate states not to have held an accession referendum, it is noteworthy that three (Greece, Spain and Portugal) joined prior to the first major change to the treaties (the Single European Act, or SEA); the other two are recent entrants (Cyprus and Bulgaria).

Withdrawal referendums account for two, soon to be three, of the membership referendums. The only withdrawal referendum held by a member state took place in 1975 when the UK, following renegotiations, held a referendum on its continued membership of the EU. Such a referendum was replicated in June 2016 as the current UK conservative government fulfilled its manifesto commitment, and legal obligation, to hold an in–out EU referendum on renegotiated terms of membership. The other express withdrawal referendum was held by a constituent part of a member state, Greenland, which in the national accession referendum in 1972 voted overwhelmingly against joining. Denmark had granted Greenland a form of home rule by the late 1970s and in 1982 Greenland held a consultative referendum in which a small majority approved of withdrawal. That decision was later approved by Greenland's parliament and led to Denmark negotiating Greenland's withdrawal, which took place in 1985.

### *EU Treaty revision referendums*

These are referendums held by member states as a precursor to ratifying a revision to the EU treaties. The existence of these referendums, and the complications to which they give rise, stems from the fact that for a treaty revision to enter into force, the EU's rules (currently Article 48 TEU) require ratification 'by all the Member States in accordance with their respective constitutional requirements'. If those domestic requirements are, or become, a referendum then this becomes a prerequisite to treaty revision taking place.

All six main rounds of treaty revision, including the attempted revision via the Constitutional Treaty, have generated such referendums. However, only six states have actually held them. Three of the states to have held them did so only once (Luxembourg, the Netherlands and Spain) precisely for the only revision, the Constitutional Treaty, to have been expressly framed in bold constitutional terms. Most EU treaty revision referendums are actually accounted for by the constitutional specificities of Denmark and Ireland. The Danish Constitution's transfer of powers clause stipulates a five-sixths parliamentary approval requirement, with popular approval required if only an ordinary parliamentary majority is obtained. The SEA did not actually fall within that clause and thus the first treaty revision referendum to have been held was Denmark's non-constitutionally required consultative referendum on the SEA. However the only other revising treaties to be subjected to popular approval in Denmark, the Treaties of Maastricht and Amsterdam, did fall within that clause and the failure to obtain the necessary five-sixths majority approval necessitated referendums. Famously the Danish no vote on Maastricht ratification in 1992 gave the EU its first experience of a negative popular vote bringing treaty revision grinding to a halt. This led to European leaders agreeing to a range of opt-outs so that Danish ratification could take place, and thus the entry into force of the Maastricht Treaty, as it did following popular approval in Denmark.

As concerns Ireland, its need for EU treaty revision referendums was unexpected and is owed to a constitutional challenge of the government's attempt to ratify the SEA using the ordinary parliamentary approval route. That challenge led to a Supreme Court ruling in 1987, which found that EU revising treaties going beyond the scope or objectives of the existing treaties, as did the SEA, would require a constitutional amendment and thus a referendum (Barrett 2009). Following this ruling, Irish governments have put all main treaty revisions to the people. This has led on two occasions (the Treaties of Nice and Lisbon) to negative votes. As with the earlier Danish example, the treaty revision process was brought to a halt and led to various assurances that allowed for a second referendum to take place in Ireland, which duly approved of the relevant treaties and thus allowed them to enter into force for all of the EU.

### *Policy referendums*

These referendums are about a specific policy field, such as monetary policy, fiscal policy or the EU's foreign policy (e.g. enlargement). Ultimately, this is somewhat of a mixed-bag category, which is most easily defined by stating what it is not: i.e. a referendum about the EU that is neither a membership referendum nor a treaty revision referendum but is nonetheless held by an EU member state. The last condition is necessary to distinguish policy referendums held by EU member states and those held by third countries on matters of EU policy, which constitute our fourth type.

From the perspective of the EU polity perhaps the most significant of the policy referendums, because of its potentially direct extraterritorial impact, was the very first EU referendum to be held: the 1972 French enlargement referendum. The EU's rules on enlargement require accession treaties to be approved by all the member states in accordance with their respective constitutional requirements. There was no such constitutional requirement for an enlargement referendum in France, but the President called this non-binding vote, and if the outcome had been a resounding no it is hard to believe that France would simply have proceeded to ratify the accession agreement nonetheless.

Two referendums have been held on adopting the Euro, but given that nineteen states have adopted the Euro one might have expected more. Part of the explanation for the paucity is that EU member states, Denmark and the UK aside, are under a legal obligation to join the Euro once they fulfil the entry conditions. This also helps explain why many states that joined the Euro relatively soon after EU accession referendums did not feel an additional Euro referendum was required (examples include Austria, Finland, Malta, Slovakia, Slovenia). It also helps to put in legal context Latvia and Lithuania's adoption of the Euro in the midst of the eurozone crisis post-2010. Yet this legal obligation, and an accession referendum less than ten years earlier, did not stop Sweden from pursuing a consultative referendum on joining the Euro in 2003. The negative outcome means that it would only be politically possible for Sweden to join following popular approval. The Swedish referendum choice was perhaps influenced by its Nordic neighbour, Denmark, which had already held the first Euro accession referendum in 2000, the people famously voting against its adoption. Denmark's referendum was however constitutionally obligatory when a five-sixths parliamentary majority was not obtained, though it was in any event politically obligatory given Danish opt-outs from the single currency following its first failed referendum on the Maastricht Treaty. Denmark's opt-outs are also responsible for another policy referendum, when in 2015 Danish voters rejected an arrangement, similar to that of the UK and Ireland, allowing them to opt-in to Justice and Home Affairs measures.

Two referendums have been held on extra-EU treaties. Extra-EU treaties are intimately connected to EU law, and indeed can make use of the EU's institutions, but are concluded between a range of EU member states. As well as being treaties born without all EU member states as parties, though all have the right to sign up later, they also do not require unanimous ratification by all contracting parties, though certain individual states can constitute veto points to entry into force. The Fiscal

Compact Treaty, which is primarily aimed at enhancing fiscal discipline by eurozone states, was the first such extra-EU treaty to be subjected to a referendum. This was successfully held in Ireland in 2012 following the government's conclusion that a popular vote was constitutionally required. The second was held in Denmark on the Unified Patent Court Agreement, which creates a court with exclusive competence over European patents. As this treaty constituted a transfer of sovereign powers, once it became clear that the Danish government could not obtain the necessary five-sixths parliamentary majority, a referendum was called for the same day as the 2014 European Parliament elections and popular approval was duly given.

This category also includes two rather idiosyncratic policy referendums: a consultative referendum held by Italy in 1989, which saw the people vote in favour of the EP being accorded a mandate to draw up a constitution for Europe; and a Greek bailout referendum in mid-2015 that followed protracted negotiations between Greece and its eurozone creditors. Its idiosyncrasy has several aspects, two of which included the shortest time between a referendum announcement and the vote (one week) and the fact that the terms of the bailout package on which the Greek people voted had already been withdrawn by the creditors.

### *Third country referendums*

Third-country referendums are referendums held on the topic of EU integration by third countries. A third country for the purposes of our referendum typology is a country that is not a EU member state nor a country that has acquired candidate status and can therefore vote on EU membership. The most recent example is San Marino's 2013 referendum on accession negotiations with the EU – which failed the quorum. As can be seen in Figure 12.1, third-country EU referendums have been even more prevalent than the policy referendum category. Most of these referendums are on treaties (or the extension thereof) signed with the EU. In practice most are accounted for by a specific country, Switzerland, with a vibrant tradition of direct democracy (Serdült 2014). It is unsurprising therefore that Switzerland has generated so many referendums related to its relationship with the EU (*see* Sciarini, Chapter Ten in this volume). More generally, thus far, third-country referendums have been only held by countries neighbouring the EU. However, this need not be the case – for instance any of the many countries in other parts of the world that are engaged in negotiating trade or association agreements with the EU could seek to have a referendum on the relevant agreement, which would be covered by the category.

### *Why EU-related referendums are held and the outcomes*

We now turn to some of the dynamics surrounding the supply of EU-related referendums and the outcomes produced. In this section we look at two aspects of this interaction that involve political elites on the one hand and citizens on the other. We shall address this in two steps: first, we consider why referendums are held and second, once called to what extent, and with what outcomes, citizens participate.

Our analysis focuses only on referendums held by EU member or candidate states. We therefore leave out the category of third-country referendums, whose inclusion would distort any of the putative associations.

We have already hinted in the previous section at the motives behind some referendums. More generally, apart from those referendums triggered by mandatory constitutional provisions, there are myriad reasons why political elites may opt for the referendum route. Indeed, there is a lively debate in the literature on the motives for holding referendums more generally (Smith 1976; Morel 2007), as well as in relation to the EU (Closa 2007; Oppermann 2013; Mendez et al. 2014). The most basic distinction is between cases where there is no political discretion, i.e. a referendum must be held because it is mandatory, on the one hand and cases where the referendum choice is at the discretion of political elites on the other. A classic example is when a referendum is not required but is held for strategic partisan motives. There is a fuzzy area between the two instances where a referendum may not be constitutionally required but it has become de facto mandatory to hold one. This gives rise to three broad categories of motives for referendums, which operate under very distinct decisional logics. We look at each logic in turn.

1. *Constitutionality*: This category is perhaps the most straightforward, though there are some nuances. In the context of EU-related referendums, the clearest example of a constitutionally mandatory referendum comes from a non-EU member state, Switzerland. Most Swiss referendums are automatically triggered by virtue of its constitutional order. In some cases they are triggered by a citizens' initiative, which if successful at the signature-gathering phase, leads to a referendum. In others, the issue at stake requires a constitutional amendment, which also triggers a mandatory referendum. In no EU member state is direct democracy so fully integrated into its constitutional order as in Switzerland. Among EU member or candidate states, constitutionally driven logic is at play in three distinct scenarios. One is where a Court decides a referendum is constitutionally required, as in the case of Ireland with the Single European Act. A second occurs, in the case of Denmark, when the legislature fails to reach the required five-sixths threshold for delivering ratification of an EU treaty, thus triggering a constitutionally mandatory referendum. Lastly, a third scenario emerges when the executive decides that a particular issue, whether membership of the EU or an EU treaty, falls within the scope of a constitutionally mandatory referendum as was the case with Austria's accession to the EU or Ireland's accession or its post-SEA EU referendums.
2. *Appropriateness*: Referendums operating under the logic of appropriateness share a trait that demarcates them from the more overtly partisan referendums described below. Broadly stated they are driven by an overriding legitimacy concern rather than overtly partisan considerations. Scholars have given different labels to these referendums, 'de facto obligatory' (Morel 2007) or to the motives for convening them, e.g. the

'rule of appropriateness' (Closa 2007). Generally, two dynamics can be at play, whereby elites are constrained either by external political factors very much outside of their control or as a result of strong internal, domestic pressure. The accession wave of referendums, when the EU expanded in 2004 to incorporate the central and eastern European countries, can be considered as an example where strong external forces were at play in the choice to convene referendums. Not only were referendums convened among candidate states because of the decisions of neighbouring countries', but they were also then programmed in chronological sequences such that countries with more favourable EU attitudes held their referendums first (Mendez et al. 2014). In contrast, with the 'de facto obligatory' referendum the propelling forces are mostly endogenously generated. Good examples include Norway's second accession referendum in 1994. Having rejected membership in 1972, it was politically inconceivable not to have consulted the people again when the question re-emerged for the 1994 enlargement wave – even though a referendum was not constitutionally required. Similarly, the Swedish referendum on joining the Euro in 2003 was not constitutionally mandatory, but politically it was obligatory despite clearly not being in the interest of the government.

3. *Partisan*: This last category includes those cases where the referendum choice was neither constitutionally required nor the result of strong internal/external pressures. Instead, these referendums are held for purely partisan motives. Two types of partisan referendums exist. The overtly 'power-reinforcing' referendum is held to boost the popularity of an incumbent leader. Classic examples of this type mentioned in the literature are the two referendums called by French Presidents in 1972 (on Enlargement) and 1991 (on the Maastricht Treaty). A second motive for convening the partisan referendum is to mediate a crisis within a party. Here the referendum operates as a crisis-resolving instrument to address conflict within a party (or coalition). The classic example is the 1975 UK continued membership referendum, which was held to resolve the internal divisions within the British Labour Party. This same referendum was repeated forty years later, but this time its manifestation was to mediate deep divisions within the Conservative Party. One of the most recent EU-related partisan referendums, the Greek 2015 referendum on a bailout package, was held because of a blend of the two motives, both to quell deep divisions within the SYRIZA party and to boost the popularity and negotiating position of the Greek leader.

Evidently, there can be a grey area when classifying referendums according to the three logics since combinations of reasons can always be given for some cases. The coding strategy has therefore focused on the overriding motive for holding a referendum when more than one motive may be at play. A consistent picture emerges when doing so. The mosaic plot in Figure 12.2 reveals the distribution of referendum type by the motive for calling a referendum. The plot takes into account the relative proportions between all the categories, so that for instance the area

*Figure 12.2: Mosaic plot of EU referendums (type of referendum by motive for calling referendum)*

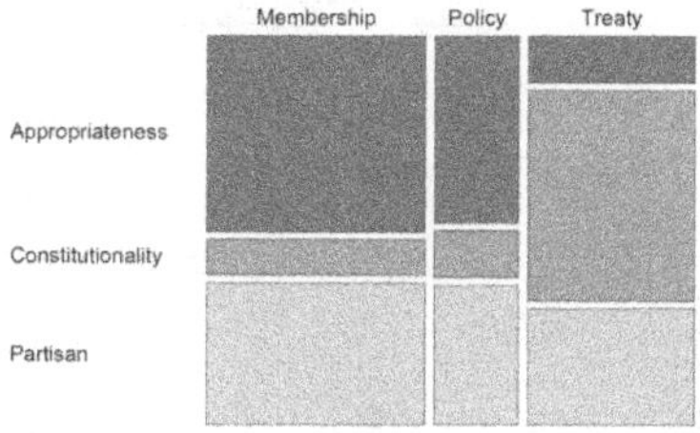


occupied by the policy referendums is smaller than the more popular membership referendums, and so on for each of the three types by three motive categories. A clear picture emerges when looking at the motives for calling the two most popular referendums, membership and treaty revision referendums. In the case of the former, most referendums have been called under the logic of appropriateness whereas with regard to treaty revision referendums most have been called because of constitutionality motives. In both cases the specific motive accounts for just over half of all referendums within the respective type of referendum. For the policy referendums a pattern can also be detected with most referendums under the logic of appropriateness. More disturbingly perhaps, what is also patently clear from Figure 12.1 is that a significant number of referendums are held for purely partisan reasons. Indeed, approximately one-third of referendums in each type are the result of partisan strategic considerations.

Some of the patterns observed are reinforced due to the fact that there are repeated instances of some types of referendum, especially treaty revision referendums, which to date have been mostly held by Ireland and Denmark. However, the units of analysis are the referendums themselves, not the member states. In terms of the patterns observed, one possible explanation for the outcomes could be that some policy referendums (e.g. joining the Euro) and membership referendums entail such consequences that the legitimating endorsement of a referendum is politically mandatory. Hence, the disproportionate number operating under the logic of appropriateness when such issues are at stake. On the other hand, the high proportion of constitutionality cases of treaty revision referendums is driven by two member states, Ireland and Denmark. Apart from these two cases, which account for more than half of all treaty revision referendums, the remainder have been mostly held for partisan motives.

Turning to our second question on the role of citizens, we now look at the outcomes across the referendum types. Table 12.1 reveals that most referendums are actually passed (see last column in Table 12.1). A number of patterns stand out, however. First, membership referendums have the highest success rate. This is perhaps not too surprising since much is at stake during a membership referendum, which has over 85 per cent success rates. On the other hand, when focusing on the failed referendums, it is noticeable that policy referendums are the most likely to fail, with a comparatively high failure rate of 50 per cent. A rejection in these

*Table 12.1: Referendum outcomes according to type and logic (per cent)*

| | Failed | Passed |
|---|---|---|
| Membership | 14 | 86 |
| Policy | 50 | 50 |
| Treaty | 31 | 69 |
| | | |
| Appropriateness | 29 | 71 |
| Constitutionality | 25 | 75 |
| Partisan | 25 | 75 |

referendums typically has the effect of preserving the status quo for the member state – certainly insofar as it remains a member state of the EU. When focusing on the motives part of Table 12.1, we see that both partisan and constitutionality based referendums are the least likely to fail. This is not surprising regarding the former, as governing elites are typically wary of calling referendums they would lose. Indeed, the failure rate of partisan referendums would be even lower if the most recent referendum in Greece had been coded differently – in that case the government specifically campaigned for a no vote, i.e. a rejection of the bailout package, and duly won its domestic vote.

The three-way interaction plots in Figure 12.3 allow us to visualise differences in average turnout rates and referendum results for the various types of referendums and their motives for being held. Looking at the first plot, it is clear that higher turnouts for both membership and policy referendums are associated with lower success rates (see also Qvortrup 2016). With regard to membership referendums, the explanation is fairly straightforward since two referendum cases – Norway in 1972 and again in 1994 – are driving the average failure rate. In both those referendums turnout rates were very high, with almost 90 per cent in the second Norwegian membership referendum. In relation to failed policy referendums, the effect is being driven again by mostly Nordic countries, where turnout is generally high, on salient referendum topics such as Euro membership. On the other hand, there is no difference in average turnout rates between failed and passed referendums on treaty revision. A similar picture emerges with regard to the motives for holding referendums in the second interaction plot in Figure 12.3. The only significant difference in referendum outcomes is with regard to the appropriateness category. The two remaining categories have very similar average turnout rates, although it also clear that partisan referendums tend to be associated with the highest turnout rates (70 per cent).

## The European Citizens' Initiative

We now take stock of some of the development in the EU's most recent democratic innovation, the ECI. Negotiated during the drafting of the Constitutional Treaty,

*Figure 12.3: Two three-way interaction plots (average turnout by referendum outcome)*

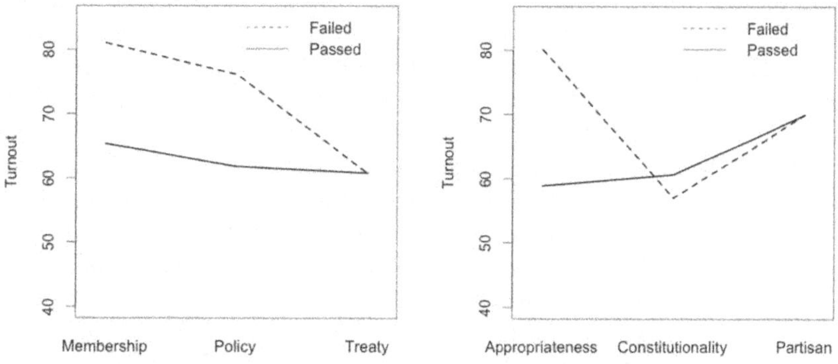


this unique instrument of transnational bottom-up direct democracy was retained in the Lisbon Treaty. Unlike the instruments of direct democracy discussed thus far, which operate at the member state or subnational level, the ECI is a truly pan-EU level institution of direct democracy. It was launched in April 2012, when the ECI Regulation entered into force, and allows one million EU citizens to invite the European Commission, within the framework of its powers, to submit a proposal for a legal act for implementing the treaties.

It is worthwhile to first situate this particular innovation in its broader EU context. Over the years, the EU has tried to experiment with various forms of democratic innovation, including experiments in participatory and deliberative democracy, which have involved citizens' conferences, deliberative polls and consultations of citizens during public policy making – to name but a few forms (see Boussaguet (2015) for a recent critical review). While such forms of democratic experimentation are mostly ad hoc and experimental in nature, the ECI is of a very different order. It represents the most significant attempt to open new institutionalised channels of citizen participation on EU affairs since direct elections were introduced for the European Parliament in 1979. Furthermore, as with the direct elections to the EP, the ECI innovation is firmly locked within the Treaty structure. Unlike many of the looser forms of EU democratic experimentation that can be abandoned at will, the ECI is here to stay. The big question in the scholarly literature is to what extent this new institution will live up to its democratic promise.

In terms of its functional properties, there is nothing especially unique about the ECI other than its supranational coverage. It has the properties of a well-understood instrument of direct democracy, the agenda-setting initiative. The latter is best understood in distinction to two other instruments, what Schiller and Setälä (2012) call a 'full-scale initiative' and a petition. All three instruments have a decidedly bottom-up dynamic in terms of putting policy issues on the political agenda while relying on an endorsement mechanism based on a signature-gathering process. What differs is the potential impact of the various instruments and the degree to which each instrument is regulated.

Briefly put, the 'full-scale initiative', as used in California or Switzerland, for example, leads to a referendum where the people directly decide on the policy proposal if it has satisfied its relevant procedural criteria. A petition on the other hand, is typically very non-committal in terms of obligations and actions placed on political elites and is also weakly regulated. Compared to a petition, an agenda initiative can be more heavily regulated, as is the case with the ECI, and while falling far short of a referendum it nonetheless typically requires a formal reaction from a political authority. Under the ECI Regulation where a registered citizens' initiative has met the one million threshold, the European Commission is legally required to (1) publish the initiative in an online register, (2) give the organisers the opportunity to explain in detail their initiative at a public hearing, and (3) set out in a public communication its legal and political conclusions on the initiative, any action it intends to take and the reasons for taking or not taking action.

In terms of the regulatory procedures the ECI is comparatively complex – though not uniquely so when compared to other agenda initiatives, such as those that exist in Austria, Argentina or Spain. In addition to the one million signature threshold, which must be obtained within one year, it includes certain regional criteria. Support must come from at least one-quarter of the EU's member states (currently seven) and for each member state a quorum (minimal number of signatures) has been defined. The process is open to all citizens allowed to vote in EP elections. Apart from Austria where the voting age is sixteen, all other member states require a minimal voting age of eighteen. Another requirement that reflects its supranational spirit is that a citizens' committee must be formed with a minimum of seven members residing in at least seven different member states. Once the citizens' committee has been formed, a request for an initiative can be registered with the European Commission. However, there is a legal admissibility test which must first be surmounted. There are several criteria involved, but all twenty of those that have been refused registration have fallen at the same hurdle: manifestly falling outside the Commission's powers to submit a proposal for a legal act for implementing the Treaties (*see* Table 12.2 for a summary of ECI outcomes). The Commission's application of the legal admissibility test has generated considerable criticism from ECI organisers, civil society, NGOs and scholars (see Anglmayer 2015). Although it was suggested that the ECI could be used for proposing treaty change (Dougan 2011), the Commission has excluded this possibility and this was a reason offered for refusing to register an initiative shortly after the system entered into force (see Organ 2014). The Commission's application of the legal admissibility test is however subject to EU level judicial oversight. Of the twenty refused registrations, six were challenged before the EU's first instance court, one of which was unsuccessful and is on appeal to the Court of Justice (case C-589/15P).

If successfully registered, the initiative enters the signature-gathering process. This is one of the most challenging stages, given the variability of rules across the member states. Particularly problematic for signature collection is the variability in rules governing personal data requirements, ranging from minimal

*Table 12.2: ECI outcomes (May 2012–January 2016)*

| Status | Frequency | Percentage |
|---|---|---|
| All proposals | | |
| Refused registration | 20 | 35.7 |
| Registered | 36 | 64.3 |
| Total | 56 | 100 |
| Registered initiatives | | |
| Completed and answered | 3 | 8.3 |
| Collection ongoing | 5 | 13.9 |
| Insufficient support | 16 | 44.4 |
| Withdrawn | 11 | 30.6 |
| Verification pending | 1 | 2.8 |
| Total | 36 | 100 |

information in Finland (name, nationality and data of birth) to countries that, in addition to the basic information, require the signatory's address, national ID card number and issuing authority. A recent EP resolution has been critical of such disproportionate requirements and the unnecessary complexity of the system (EP 2015A).

By the end of 2015, only three initiatives had met the one million signatures requirement (though five initiatives that had been registered in 2015 still had between nine and eleven months to obtain one million signatures). Those three initiatives were on respectively: legislating to implement the human right to water and sanitation and promoting their provision as essential public services ('Right2Water'); banning and ending the financing of activities destroying human embryos ('one of us'); and stopping vivisection. The Commission has since met with the organisers of these three initiatives prior to public hearings being held in the EP. However none of the Commission communications responding to the relevant initiatives have seen it willing to pursue legislative action. An EP resolution has specifically regretted 'the lack of legislative impact and the discouraging follow-up by the Commission of successful initiatives' (EP 2015A) and a separate highly critical resolution was dedicated specifically to the Commission's response to the Right2Water initiative (EP 2015B). The reasoning in the communication for the 'one of us' initiative is also being challenged by the organisers before the EU's first instance court (case T-561/14).

## Discussion

The EU's rich experience of being the object of referendum practice is destined to continue with significant implications for the EU as a polity. By way of concluding discussion, we return to three of the referendum categories central to this process

*Table 12.3: Referendums related to Membership (total 21)*

| Case | Issue |
|---|---|
| Denmark 1972 | Accession to the European Community |
| Ireland 1972 | Accession to the European Community |
| Norway 1972 | Accession to the European Community |
| UK 1975 | Remaining within the European Community |
| Greenland 1982 | Remaining within the European Community |
| Aland Islands 1994 | Accession to the EU |
| Austria 1994 | Accession to the EU |
| Finland 1994 | Accession to the EU |
| Norway 1994 | Accession to the EU |
| Sweden 1994 | Accession to the EU |
| Czech Republic 2003 | Accession to the EU |
| Estonia 2003 | Accession to the EU |
| Hungary 2003 | Accession to the EU |
| Latvia 2003 | Accession to the EU |
| Lithuania 2003 | Accession to the EU |
| Malta 2003 | Accession to the EU |
| Poland 2003 | Accession to the EU |
| Romania 2003 | Constitutional Amendment for EU Accession |
| Slovakia 2003 | Accession to the EU |
| Slovenia 2003 | Accession to the EU |
| Croatia 2012 | Accession to the EU |

with a view to highlighting some of the upcoming challenges. These referendums will shape the constitutional and political order of the EU since they define the boundaries of the polity, its constitutional evolution and how important EU policy matters may come to be decided upon. In the last section we turn to the more speculative topic of the ECI's trajectory. For the moment at least, unlike the referendum's systemic challenge, the EU's bottom-up direct democratic innovation is less likely to pose a pervasive challenge to the policy system.

Membership referendums are likely to continue to determine the future geographical contours of the EU, whether through member states joining or leaving. To that end the accession referendum has become the general norm for legitimising membership. The opposite seems to be also the case, i.e. the withdrawal of membership. Whether the EU remains as an organisation with twenty-eight member states and over 500 million citizens is shortly to be decided as its second largest member state (the UK) holds a withdrawal referendum for the second time in forty years. It seems unlikely, given the rising tide of Euroscepticism and dissatisfaction with the EU, that this will be the last of the member state withdrawal

*Table 12.4: Referendums related to Treaty ratification (total 16)*

| Case | Issue |
|---|---|
| Denmark 1986 | Single European Act |
| Ireland 1987 | Single European Act |
| Denmark 1992 | Treaty of Maastricht |
| France 1992 | Treaty of Maastricht |
| Ireland 1992 | Treaty of Maastricht |
| Denmark 1993 | Second Treaty of Maastricht vote |
| Denmark 1998 | Treaty of Amsterdam |
| Ireland 1998 | Treaty of Amsterdam |
| Ireland 2001 | Treaty of Nice |
| Ireland 2002 | Second Treaty of Nice vote |
| France 2005 | Constitutional Treaty |
| Luxembourg 2005 | Constitutional Treaty |
| The Netherlands 2005 | Constitutional Treaty |
| Spain 2005 | Constitutional Treaty |
| Ireland 2008 | Treaty of Lisbon |
| Ireland 2009 | Second Treaty of Lisbon vote |

referendums. Another important challenge to the membership dynamic – the process of acquiring or dispensing with the status of being a member state – comes from territorial restructuring within the member states themselves, specifically independence referendums, which can have significant consequences for the size of the EU. The Scottish independence referendum of 2014 is the preeminent example (*see* Tierney, Chapter Five in this volume). Such a referendum is clearly distinct from a constituent part of a member state voting exclusively and expressly on withdrawing from the EU as happened in Greenland. The challenge posed by Scottish-type independence referendums, in which the seceding entity wishes to remain within the EU, is precisely how to accommodate this. In the Scottish case there was considerable debate as to whether a seamless internal EU enlargement could take place via the treaty amendment procedure or, perhaps the more persuasive view, that a seceding entity would need to apply to join (see Armstrong 2014, contrast Douglas-Scott 2014). The no vote on Scottish independence means that this vexed issue remains unanswered yet it may soon arise again as Catalonia pursues a referendum on seceding from Spain.

Treaty revision is at the core of the EU's evolving constitutional order. Not surprisingly, therefore, the rise of the treaty revision referendum has become one of the most controversial aspects of the EU's direct democratic landscape. This is ultimately because the EU's rules of treaty change require unanimity and in the presence of a negative referendum such change cannot take place. Although few member states have held such referendums, attempts to require one through the use

*Table 12.5: Referendums related to policy (total 8)*

| Case | Issue |
|---|---|
| France 1972 | Enlargement of the European Community |
| Italy 1989 | European Parliament to elaborate a European Constitution |
| Denmark 2000 | Adopting the Euro |
| Sweden 2003 | Adopting the Euro |
| Ireland 2012 | Fiscal Compact Treaty |
| Denmark 2014 | Accession to Unified Patent Court (UPC) |
| Greece 2015 | Bailout package |
| Denmark 2015 | Opting in to Justice and Home Affairs (JHA) measures |

of constitutional challenges, the parliamentary process and bottom-up mechanisms have been a regular and growing occurrence across a wide range of member states (see Mendez et al. 2014, Chapter 2). Moreover, in 2011 the member state generally viewed as having the most Eurosceptic of populations (the UK) has legally enshrined referendum locks policed by its courts, so that further treaty revision transferring powers to the EU can only take place following popular approval (see Hodson and Maher 2014). The referendum roulette to which major treaty change in the EU has become subject has rendered this route to constitutional change increasingly unattractive. Two of the central instruments to respond to the eurozone crisis, the European Stability Mechanism Treaty and the Fiscal Compact Treaty, are not in fact EU treaties, even though they make use of the EU's institutions. Instead these are ordinary international treaties that overcome the unanimity hurdles for revising EU treaties. This may be a harbinger of future developments with the shadow of the treaty revision referendum discouraging elites from pursuing the big bang type changes that characterised European integration between the 1986 Single European Act and the 2007 Lisbon Treaty.

One area where EU referendums could be expected to proliferate is in relation to policy referendums. Although only two have been held on joining the Euro thus far, it is likely that some non-eurozone states would not countenance joining without a referendum. They need not involve issues as far-reaching as abolishing a country's currency, as Demark most recently showed with its referendum on EU Justice and Home Affairs. Other member states, such as the UK, have pre-emptively created referendum locks to cover policy issues that include transfers of power, such as signing up to a European public prosecutor (as well as joining the Euro). Ultimately, however, the consequences of the aforementioned referendums are mostly borne by the member state holding the referendum. This is not the case for policy referendums with a direct extraterritorial impact – in the sense of stopping the EU from acting. Hence the problematic nature of the French enlargement referendum in 1972 where a no vote would have jeopardised the EU's first enlargement. This may not be the last occasion on which an existing member state implements a popular veto on EU enlargement. France itself introduced its first ever constitutionally obligatory

*Table 12.6: Third-country referendums on European integration (total 12)*

| Case | Issue |
|---|---|
| Liechtenstein 1992 | Accession to EEA |
| Switzerland 1992 | Accession to EEA |
| Liechtenstein 1995 | Accession to EEA |
| Switzerland 1997 | Citizen's initiative to let people decide on joining EU |
| Switzerland 2001 | Popular initiative referendum on EU accession negotiations |
| Switzerland 2000 | Bilateral treaties with the EU |
| Switzerland 2005 (b) | Bilaterals (extension of free movement) |
| Switzerland 2005 (a) | Bilaterals (Schengen) |
| Switzerland 2006 | Bilaterals (extension to Eastern European countries) |
| Switzerland 2009 | Bilaterals (free movement to Bulgaria and Romania) |
| San Marino 2013 | Accession negotiations with the EU |
| Switzerland 2014 | Migration quotas (affects bilateral treaties) |

referendum in 2005 when the constitution was amended to require enlargement referendums following any accessions after Romania, Bulgaria and Croatia. The French Constitution was however amended in 2008 so that an enlargement referendum could be avoided via joint parliamentary supermajority approval. How this French enlargement referendum lock plays out will be of great consequence, not least if other member states follow suit. Bulgaria, for instance, witnessed a bottom-up attempt to generate a Turkish enlargement referendum using a new law on direct citizen participation (see Mendez et al. 2014).

A related intriguing development flowing from the introduction of direct democratic instruments into a member state that may be illustrative of new bottom-up dynamics is the consultative Dutch referendum due in April 2016 on the EU–Ukraine Association Agreement. If the Dutch reject the agreement, which the Netherlands has not yet ratified, and the government respects the outcome this would affect that EU Agreement's capacity to enter fully into force.

Bottom-up policy referendums have thus now also become a feature of the EU's direct democratic landscape and potentially with extraterritorial impact. Scope for an arguably more controversial type of policy referendum has emerged in the wake of the EU's response to the refugee crisis. In 2015 Hungary was one of several member states outvoted on a mandatory refugee redistribution quota leading its populist prime minister in February 2016 to propose a referendum on the measure. If a popular vote in Hungary against this EU measure does take place, it would have no legal impact on the EU measure but its political implications are another matter.

Finally turning to the EU's novel experiment with direct democracy, the ECI, it certainly does in theory have the capacity to bring Europe much closer to its citizens. And it has generated considerable activity which might, given its embryonic nature, be thought rather remarkable at least from a comparative perspective.

However the way the Commission has performed its gatekeeper role of registering proposals has meant that a significant percentage have failed this initial legal test. Interestingly, two of those that fell at this hurdle were actually about establishing EU level referendums, something for which there is no legal competence in the treaties. The fact that the Commission has ruled out the possibility of an ECI being used to pursue treaty change is one of the most significant things we have learned about the remit of this new instrument. However, there remains scope for EU courts to expand access to the ECI and cases are pending in which disgruntled citizens' groups have challenged how the registration hurdle has been applied. Legitimate cause for concern has arisen in relation both to the Commission's application of the registration hurdle and its limited follow-up to the three registered initiatives that met the one million signature threshold. It is however ultimately rather early to speculate as to the significance of this instrument, not least as reforms of the ECI Regulation to expand access to it may be on the agenda. But one very interesting spillover effect should not be lost sight of. The existence of the ECI has contributed to EU member states adopting their own domestic instruments of direct democracy, which can in turn be used in relation to EU issues. Thus Finland introduced its own citizens' initiative law, of the agenda-setting variety, at around the same time as the ECI came into effect. And it is no accident that the Netherlands has only very recently formally introduced direct democracy into its constitutional system. The very first use to which this new full-scale citizens' initiative has been put is precisely an EU issue, the EU–Ukraine Association Agreement mentioned above on which the Dutch voted in 2016. In short, the ECI's impact also has a spillover dimension with ramifications for deploying national direct democratic instruments on EU matters.

## Parliamentary resolutions

EP (2015A), Resolution of 28 October 2015 (A8-0284/2015).
EP (2015B), Resolution of 8 September 2015 (A8-0228/2015).

## References

Anglmayer, I. (2015) Implementation of the European Citizens' Initiative, European Parliamentary Research Services, available at http://www.europarl.europa.eu/thinktank/en/document.html?reference=EPRS_IDA%282015%29536343 (accessed 15 April 2016).

Armstrong, K. (2014) 'An Independent Scotland in the European Union: pathways, pitfalls and legal perspectives', *Cambridge Journal of International and Comparative Law*, 3(1): 181–95.

Barrett, G. (2009) 'Building a Swiss chalet in an Irish legal landscape? Referendums on European Union treaties in Ireland and the impact of Supreme Court jurisprudence', *European Constitutional Law Review*, 5: 32–70.

Boussaguet, L. (2015) 'Participatory mechanisms as symbolic policy instruments?' *Comparative European Politics*, 14: 107–24.

Bouza García, L. and Greenwood, J. (2014) 'The European Citizens' Initiative: a new sphere of EU politics?', *Interest Groups & Advocacy*, 3(3): 246–67.

Closa, C. (2007) 'Why convene referendums? Explaining choices in EU constitutional politics', *Journal of European Public Policy*, 14(8): 1311–32.

De Búrca, G. (2010) 'If at first you don't succeed: vote, vote again: analyzing the "second referendum" phenomenon in EU treaty change', *Fordham International Law Journal*, 33: 1472–89.

Dougan, M. (2011) 'What are we to make of the citizens' initiative?', *Common Market Law Review*, 48(6): 1807–48.

Douglas-Scott, S. (2014) 'How easily could an independent Scotland join the EU?', Oxford Legal Studies Research Paper, No 46/2014.

Hobolt, S. B. (2009) *Europe in Question: Referendums on European integration*, Oxford: Oxford University Press.

Hodson, D. and Maher, I. (2014) 'British brinkmanship and Gaelic games: EU treaty ratification in the UK and Ireland from a two level game perspective', *British Journal of Politics and International Relations*, 16(4): 645–61.

Hug, S. (2002) *Voices of Europe: Citizens, referendums, and European integration*, Lanham, MD: Rowman & Littlefield.

Mendez, F., Mendez, M. and Triga, V. (2014) *Referendums and the European Union: A comparative inquiry*, Cambridge: Cambridge University Press.

Morel, L. (2007) 'The Rise of "politically obligatory" referendums: the 2005 French referendum in comparative perspective', *West European Politics*, 30(5): 1041–67.

Oppermann, K. (2013) 'The politics of discretionary government commitments to European integration referendums', *Journal of European Public Policy*, 20(5): 684–701.

Organ, J. (2014) 'Decommissioning direct democracy? A critical analysis of Commission decision-making on the legal admissibility of European Citizens Initiative proposals', *European Constitutional Law Review*, 10: 422–42.

Qvortrup, M. (2016) 'Referendums on membership and European integration 1972–2015', *Political Quarterly*, 87: 61–8.

Rose, R. (2013) *Representing Europeans: A pragmatic approach*, Oxford: Oxford University Press.

Schiller, T and Setälä, M. (2012) 'Introduction', in M. Setälä and T. Schiller (eds) *Citizens' Initiatives in Europe: Procedures and consequences of agenda-setting by citizens*, Basingstoke: Palgrave Macmillan: 1–14.

Serdült, U. (2014) 'Referendums in Switzerland', in M. Qvortrup (ed.) *Referendums around the World: The continued growth of direct democracy*, Basingstoke: Palgrave Macmillan: 65–121.

Smith, G. (1976) 'The functional properties of the referendum', *European Journal of Political Research*, 4: 31–45.

Tierney, S. (2013) 'The people's last sigh? European referendums and the end of the state', *European Public Law*, 18 (4): 683–700.

# *Chapter Thirteen*

# Let the People Rule?

*Laurence Whitehead, Yanina Welp and Saskia P. Ruth*

'Let the people rule' is a fine democratic principle, and likely to be much more acceptable to public opinion than the alternative of others deciding for them. But, as democratic theory has long recognised, and as our case studies concerning recent experiments with direct democracy reaffirm, this principle is too broad to provide the precise guidance needed for specific decision-making procedures. The fundamental issues have been debated for centuries: Who are 'the people' in question on any given political choice? What is to count as the 'decision' that they have taken? What kinds of evidence or argumentation are required in order for the people to take a decision they have understood? Who is to be held responsible for both setting the agenda and implementing the follow-through? How is any such popularly authorised decision to be reconciled with other political developments that are not subject to direct democratic control in the same way?

In the mid-nineteenth century, John Stuart Mill propounded a canonical formula intended to satisfy the broad principle, while in practice endorsing many of the main features of the then prevailing 'Westminster System' of representative government as a workable solution:

> There is no difficulty in showing that the ideally best form of government is that in which the sovereignty, or supreme controlling power in the last resort, is vested in the entire aggregate of the community; every citizen not only having a voice in the exercise of that ultimate sovereignty, but being, at least occasionally, called on to take an actual part in the government, by the personal discharge of some public function, local or general. ... [I]t is evident that the only government which can fully satisfy all the exigencies of the social state is one in which the whole people participate; that any participation, even in the smallest public function, is useful; that the participation should everywhere be as great as the general degree of improvement will allow; and that nothing less can be ultimately desirable than the admission of all to a share in the sovereign power of the state. But since all cannot, in a community exceeding a single small town, participate personally in any but some very minor portions of the public business, it follows that the ideal type of a perfect government must be representative. (Mill 1861: Chapter 3)

Despite the great appeal of this long-run ideal, Mill was far from arguing that universal political participation was the practical solution for all times and contexts. Quite the contrary, in fact:

> Of what avail is the most broadly popular representative system if the electors do not care to choose the best member of parliament, but choose him who will spend most money to be elected? How can a representative assembly work for good if its members can be bought, or if their excitability of temperament, uncorrected by public discipline or private self-control, makes them incapable of calm deliberation, and they resort to manual violence on the floor of the House or shoot one another with rifles? … Whenever the general disposition of the people is such that each individual regards those only of his interests which are selfish, and does not dwell on, or concern himself for, his share of the general interest, in such a state of things good government is impossible. (Mill 1861: Chapter 2)

Not surprisingly, therefore, in subsequent chapters, Mill moved on from his heavily qualified ideal type to a succession of practical limitations and qualifications that served to bring these bold principles into rough concordance with Victorian political practices. His main focus was on 'good government' (recruiting the best representatives, and enlisting the skills of suitable experts) rather than on broad deliberation, active consent, or popular 'legitimacy'; and his reference point was overwhelmingly British. Following Bentham, he resisted the idea that systems of government could be chosen, so the idea that the people might rule through ratifying a written constitution was not on his agenda, and contemporary experiences such as Swiss democracy were absent from his analysis. The representatives he envisaged were individual politicians, not party-disciplined professionals.

By contrast, Maurice Duverger took a rather different view of the realities of representative democracy in the mid-twentieth century:

> In practice elections, like the doctrine of representation, have been greatly changed by the development of parties. There is no longer a dialogue between the elector and the representative, the nation and parliament: a third party has come between them, radically modifying the nature of their relations. Before being chosen by his electors the deputy is chosen by his party: the electors only ratify this choice. … In regimes which desire to remain very close to classic democracy the real ballot is preceded by a pre-ballot, through which the party chooses the candidate who will later face the electors: the American technique of the primaries is the most successful example of this tendency. But the pre-ballot is never pure and the influence of party leaders is quite clearly shown in it. (Duverger 1959: 353–4)

In fact, a large part of Duverger's classic text is devoted to tracing the diverse ways in which party elites distort or even capture the processes of popular representation, and thereby capitalise on the appearances of democratic choice while curbing its substance. If anything, the subsequent rise of a more 'presidential' style of party leadership (as signified, for example, in televised electoral debates) has reinforced this critique. By the early twenty-first century Peter Mair (2013) took this line of analysis to the next level by documenting the 'hollowing out' of these parties, thus leaving the foundational rationale of democratic representation more ungrounded than ever. The financial crisis of 2008 sharpened all such concerns, and redoubled popular distrust in ruling politicians of all parties, thereby fuelling the outbreaks of 'populist' disaffection so evident in many of the leading Western democracies in the following decade.

Here, for example, is how the Cambridge theorist John Dunn has responded to such developments:

> The key issue for this modern variant of democracy is how far it necessitates a level of alienation of will, judgement and choice which any ancient partisan of democracy could only see as its complete negation: at most a partially elective aristocracy, and at worst a corrupt and heavily mystified oligarchy. If ancient democracy was the citizens choosing freely and immediately for themselves, modern democracy, it seems, is principally the citizens very intermittently, choosing under highly constrained circumstances, the relatively small number of their fellows who will from then on choose for them. There are many obvious ways in which modern citizens have no need whatever to accept this bargain. They could insist on taking particular state decisions personally: putting them out to referenda ... A more substantial democratic opportunity would go beyond the right to vote on issues which it suits the incumbent government to put to a referendum (on terms they can largely control for themselves). It would demand as well the opportunity to put to a referendum whatever issues the citizens themselves happen to wish ... Deliberative democracy, democracy which embodies and realizes democracy at its best, attempts to prescribe how a community of human beings should wish for its public decisions to be taken ... reflectively, attentively, and in good faith. ... More exactingly still, it should take them in a way in which all can enter, and all who wish to do in fact enter, the deliberation as equal, and hold equal weight within it. ... [so there is a case that] representative democracy as it is now cannot be all for which we can reasonably hope. (Dunn 2005: 176, 177, 178, 185).

In a similar vein John Keane has recently argued not only that more should be hoped for from modern democracy, but that more is, in fact, rapidly emerging. He has coined the term 'monitory' democracy for this new historical form,

> a variety of 'post-parliamentary' politics defined by the rapid growth of many kinds of extra-parliamentary, power-scrutinizing mechanisms. These monitory bodies take root within the 'domestic' fields of government and civil society, as well as in 'cross-border' settings once controlled by empires, states and business organizations. In consequence ... the whole architecture of self-government is changing. The central grip of elections, political parties and parliaments on citizens' lives is weakening. ... In the age of monitory democracy, the rules of representation, democratic accountability and public participation are applied to a much wider range of settings than ever before. ...

> Monitory democracy is the age of surveys, focus groups, deliberative polling, online petitions and audience and customer voting … (which) … has the effect of interrupting and often silencing the soliloquies of parties, politicians and parliaments. … The number and range of monitory institutions so greatly increase that they point to a world where the old rule of 'one person, one vote, one representative' … is replaced with the new principle of monitory democracy: 'one person, many interests, many voices, multiple votes, multiple representatives'. (Keane 2010: 689–91)

So, although successive theorists of democracy have made highly persuasive arguments for 'letting the people decide' and 'setting the people free', the practical realities continue to fall far short of those alluring ideals (*see* Whitehead, Chapter Two in this volume). Nevertheless, hope springs eternal, and even unattainable political aspirations matter in practice, to the extent that they rationalise dissatisfactions and motivate new experiments. Democratic idealism is unquestionably one of the drivers of political innovation, but it is the confluence with other forces that gives it momentum, and shapes its contemporary content. In the early twenty-first century accelerated technical change is disrupting long-established givens of political organisation, and making possible hitherto unimagined means for direct democratic participation without regard for the age-old barriers of time and space. This can dethrone press barons, up-end established political parties, erode national sovereignties, and distribute access to political information (and misinformation) on an unprecedented scale. It is the combination of unresolved theoretical debates with urgent new citizenship potentialities that has placed mechanisms of direct democracy (MDDs) back at the centre of public attention. In this volume we have assembled a significant cross section of contemporary experiences, with the aim of understanding them empirically and comparatively. They also need to be studied in the light of the broader theoretical issues outlined above, since it is only in this context that their full significance – and their future prospects – can be properly evaluated.

## Creating (or reshaping) a demos – who are 'the people'?

One of the major problems that arises with MDDs is clearly defining 'the people', i.e. those who are allowed to participate in direct decision making. This question becomes even more pressing and controversial if MDDs touch upon the very core of public authority, or if the consequences of such direct decision making transcend the borders of the unit taking the decision. We have seen that secessionist referendums have the potential to redefine the scope and boundaries of a political community, and thereby to alter collective perceptions about the distribution of public authority and the identity of a 'democratic' sovereign people. Accordingly, in self-determination referendums the definition of the demos is quite often controversial. For example, the current Spanish government argues that, as a part of the larger polity Spain, the Catalans cannot decide about the independence of Catalonia on their own since this would affect the whole country. However, in other cases, such as Scotland and Quebec the question of the demos was an uncontested issue. As Tierney shows in Chapter Six in this volume, the body of voters in the Scottish referendum was largely uncontroversial. The franchise for the referendum was the same as for Scottish parliamentary and local government elections, mirroring the franchise used in the Scottish devolution referendum in 1997. Most importantly, even EU citizens residing in Scotland were allowed to vote in the independence referendum. Of course most MDDs do not directly contest the established state system in this way, but other constitutional choices (e.g. concerning international migration, or minarets) may also indirectly reconfigure collective identities. In the cases covered in this volume, the European Union seems to be the case that most strongly challenges the notion of the demos when activating direct democracy in a single country to decide on issues related to the whole EU. Mendez and Mendez highlight this problem in their analysis of EU referendums in Chapter Twelve. They discuss the controversial nature of these referendums, in which a part of the EU demos (i.e. a single country) may take decisions that influence the whole community.

## Demarcating the 'decisions' subject to direct popular adjudication

This brings us to our next point, the demarcation of the subject of MDDs. It is no easy matter to determine the timing, wording and terms of any such debate, and all too easily this kind of procedure can be misused, or rendered dysfunctional. Only a very limited subset of precisely demarcated choices can be put to the people as a whole. That is not to belittle the importance or merit of such a procedure. MDDs that allow citizens to decide between peace and war, old constitutions and new ones, the revocation of mandates and the continuation of current officeholders in power, can be profoundly consequential, and perhaps only the populace as a whole should resolve them. But such issues need to be presented in a clear-cut (usually binary) form; otherwise the outcome will invite division and delegitimation.

Although it is difficult to find conclusive results, the studies presented in the volume tend to show that in highly divisive issues the wording does not affect the results. Qvortrup, Chapter Five in this volume, compares examples of the wording of independence referendums held in peacetime over the past twenty years, and concludes that the tone of MDD questions has no effect on the outcome. But, he adds:

> it is noteworthy that the attempts to use positive language in both Quebec and East Timor – and to a lesser degree in South Sudan – failed to sway voters in massive numbers. Needless to say, the results do not tell us anything about the motives of individual voters. But we have no evidence from qualitative or quantitative research suggesting that the question mattered; if anything, the results in East Timor and South Sudan show that those who attempted to use value-laden words went down to conclusive defeats were roundly defeated. (see p.75)

Moreover, as can be seen from our studies on referendums in long-established democracies, the necessary binary decision making in MDDs is only one aspect in a much more complex process. What the chapters presented in this volume show is that while referendums ultimately produce clear-cut binary outcomes, quite often they open up new channels of communication and pose new avenues of negotiation between citizens and politicians during the process. The Scottish independence referendum serves as a good example, given that it established a new form of intergovernmental communication between the Scottish and the UK governments, beyond the yes or no vote (*see* Chapter Six in this volume). Moreover, as research on Switzerland and Uruguay indicates, MDDs have the potential to change the way indirect decision making works through a process of political learning and anticipated coordination. Hence, in political contexts that give citizens the power to influence political decision making directly, politicians may try to anticipate the positions of the people beforehand and take them into account within the process of representative decision making (*see* Chapter Eleven in this volume).

## Ensuring collective understanding of the issue at stake

It is essential to enable those who participate in collective decision making to understand the issues at stake, if the result of a referendum is to secure subsequent compliance and consent. In a modern well-educated mass society, in which information and opinion can be disseminated at a low cost, it may well be far easier and safer than before to entrust such deliberative procedures to the collective wisdom of the entire demos. In long-established democratic settings, the idea of activating a referendum quite often increases democratic legitimacy. In her study of MDDs at the subnational level in Germany, Geissel (Chapter Ten in this volume) describes perceptions of participatory instruments. The citizens consulted were particularly positive about aspects of democratic self-development, effects on policy-related output, responsiveness and political culture. However, Dunn's ideal criteria for democratic deliberation indicate that even in the most favourable of settings there is still a major disconnect between well-informed and mature collective judgements and the standard operating procedures governing all 'really existing' direct deliberations (Dunn 2005). Several chapters in this volume contradict this idea. In his study of recent experiences with direct democracy addressing EU issues, Sciarini (Chapter Eleven in this volume) finds that the 'Swiss laboratory' contradicts the widespread view that citizens are poorly informed about and little interested in foreign affairs, or that foreign policy votes are more emotional than ones on domestic policy; the author also shows that 'mainstream' and 'polarisation' effects depend on the level of conflict among the elite, as well as on the framing of referendum campaigns. Finally and more interesting in this context, Sciarini finds that votes show some distinctive characteristics mainly with respect to the conditions under which opinion formation occurs, i.e. the line-up of partisan coalitions and the intensity and direction of political messages. In the Swiss case, then, far from excluding political parties direct democracy depends on them and at the same time increases opportunities for the people to be included in the decision-making process. Relatedly, but with far different outcomes, in their study of recall referendums in big cities, Serdült and Welp (Chapter Nine in this volume) find that such referendums are often activated due to the absence of mechanisms to influence a given policy directly; this suggests that we need to deepen our understanding of recall referendums and their relationship with other mechanism of accountability.

## Who is to decide when and how the people are to be consulted?

Apart from the questions of who 'the people' are, who poses the question, and how informed citizens are about the issue at stake, it is crucial to know who has the power to call for an MDD in order to evaluate its consequences. If the rationale for direct democracy is that elected representatives cannot be fully trusted to govern for the collective good, then it would be self-defeating to give them unfettered discretion over when to make use of MMDs. A trusted authority is required to present the people with a choice and to ensure that they make one under fair conditions. Barring extreme conditions, public officeholders must be allowed qualified participation or input. But this need not be an insoluble issue; it requires due diligence.

Welp and Ruth (Chapter Seven in this volume) show that many different political actors can trigger MDDs, and that in order to understand their motivations for using MDDs it is necessary to take into account their position in the broader political context. Relatedly, Wheatley (Chapter Four) explores the manipulative potential of elite-initiated, top-down referendums in authoritarian and semi-authoritarian settings oriented towards the concentration and legitimation of power in one branch of government (identified as 'power consolidation referendums'). Moreover, Negretto's chapter on constitution making in democratic constitutional orders (Chapter Three in this volume) highlights the precarious equilibrium between new political forces and old-established elites. He shows that the asymmetry in power between these elite factions increases polarisation and conflict over new constitutions, as well as the likelihood of citizen participation in these processes. In the absence of a procedural agreement about constitutional replacements, Negretto shows that the most radical breaks with the pre-existing legal order coincide with higher degrees of citizen participation.

To prevent the manipulative use of MDDs many modern democracies have charged trusted autonomous institutions like supreme courts, electoral commissions, and other monitoring agencies with supervising some of the more contentious aspects of these procedures. But these institutions need clear mandates, defined responsibility, suitable oversight and mechanisms of accountability, and an appropriate role for political officeholders needs to be agreed in advance. The latter appears to be crucial, particularly in referendums on self-determination and constitutional replacement.

## How is an MDD to be reconciled with other political developments that are not similarly subject to direct democratic control?

Were the previous four points resolved to perfection, there would remain the major challenge of integrating the people's decisions resulting from MDDs with other government output and political contingencies. The issue of outputs can be illustrated by reference to the referendums on independence for Scotland and the UK's continued membership of the European Union. While these two crucial plebiscitary choices are made other regular government tasks cannot be suspended. Budgets must be authorised, laws enacted, and regulations enforced. Irrespective of the final outcome, the same routines must continue during and after the referendums. This does not happen automatically: it requires a major additional level of political management, without which an exercise in popular consultation could unintentionally trigger a political disaster. Similar considerations apply to the management of unplanned contingencies. For example, while the people may be called to decide on war and peace, military developments may overtake the decision-making process and create 'facts on the ground'.

We have already mentioned the legitimacy and institutional challenges faced by the European Union when countries activate MDDs on issues affecting the whole EU. One example is the bottom-up consultative referendum in the Netherlands in April 2016 on the EU–Ukraine Association Agreement. If the government respects the outcome it must reject the agreement, which would then mean that the EU–Ukraine Agreement cannot fully enter into force.

In contrast, in separation of power systems, like the presidential system in Latin America, MDDs may actually contribute to resolving political deadlock. As Welp and Ruth show in their chapter, in several cases citizen consultations have served to overcome a deadlock between the executive and the legislature, so the people have acted as a moderator to resolve institutional and policy struggles between opposing political forces. Similarly, as Negretto suggests in his chapter, in highly polarised constitutional reform processes citizens are called upon to authorise and/or ratify changes. However, as Negretto also mentions, these processes may be highly exclusionary of opposing elites and potentially contribute to the erosion of representative democracy.

In summary, MDDs can be usefully compared, evaluated and classified under these five headings, which are also relevant to the wider range of democratic innovations currently under development as remedies for the perceived crisis in standard twentieth-century methods of representation (e.g. Welp and Whitehead 2011). But more is at stake here than the mere construction of another typology of democratic experiments. The fundamental question at issue is which, if any, of these practices is likely to succeed in strengthening the legitimacy of popular rule, in what contexts, and how. 'Legitimacy' is, of course, a complex and elusive desideratum, which is multi-dimensional and difficult to measure. For us, the main tests of greatest practical relevance relate to two questions: Which innovations and design forms are most likely to improve the quality of governance outputs, rather than to generate further turmoil? And what reasons do we have to expect MDDs to improve popular support for democratic procedures, specifically, and democratic regimes in general?

These two tests of a successful democratic innovation are clearly interconnected. A substantial amount of time is required before a fair verdict can be reached, and there will always be some disagreement about the relevant counterfactuals. However, both comparative reflection and the available evidence seem to support the following provisional conclusions.

Let us turn first to the question of which innovations and design forms are most likely to improve the quality of governance outputs rather than to generate further turmoil. As several chapters in this volume highlight, the revocation of mandates provides one way of linking direct and representative democracy, but it displays a strong vulnerability to manipulation, not least because it alters the incentive structure for those holding elective office. As both Annunziata's and Serdült and Welp's chapters show, while the idea of recall referendums is to sanction representatives who stray from their promises or their duty to serve their constituents, in reality most representatives will not find themselves at risk, even though they may be failing in some of their duties. And some of those who do get sanctioned in this way will not receive a fair hearing or adequate recognition for meritorious service. In principle, the rules of the procedure regulating recall referendums may be drafted to minimise such injustices, but even in the best circumstances there are likely to be as many aggrieved victims as individuals deserving defenestration. Moreover, the media or political technicians, among others, can abuse the public theatre that a recall procedure offers, to reward and reinforce demagogic and undeserving appointments. The normal flow of the business of representative government may well be disrupted.

As mentioned above, the chances of a constructive outcome of any MDD can be increased if appropriate rules are suitably designed. The precise rules of any referendum can be hugely consequential. So design matters. The chapters in this volume highlight this, as well as the importance of democratic behaviour. The example of Bolivia in February 2016 is illustrative here: Evo Morales faced the rules enshrined in the existing constitution and was therefore unable to pass a bill to amend the Constitution and extend his term in office without calling a referendum which in the end resulted in a narrow defeat.

Turning now to the question of whether we can expect MDDs to improve popular support for democratic procedures specifically, and democratic regimes in general: MDDs have been used across very different regime types. Both democratising and already democratised systems have quite often submitted new (or 'refounded') constitutional documents for popular yes–no ratification. In all cases, provided a minimum level of uncertainty, the salutary effect is to remind political elites that the demos is the ultimate source of authority, and to limit the scope for the substitution of the popular will. However, the electorate does not always have the freedom to express its opinion. In his study of the processes of constitution making, Wheatley explores the manipulative potential of 'power consolidation referendums', showing that these are closely associated with political crises – including civil wars or revolutions – and serve to consolidate the power of new leaders, and to prevent the institutionalisation of power-sharing mechanisms or to delay the transition to democracy.

The scenario for referendums under autocratic regimes is not bright, but there is scope for some optimism. The referendum in Uruguay in 1980 and Chile in 1988 show that even dictators can be defeated. Welp and Ruth (Chapter Seven in this volume) show that 'power legitimation referendums' (for constitutional change in settings with a single veto player) do not just happen in non-democratic contexts. In Latin America, power legitimation referendums have also been held in transitional contexts, like the above-cited vote in Uruguay in 1980. In this case, Uruguayans rejected the proposal made by the autocratic regime, and thereby, opened the way for a swift and far-reaching democratic transition. Similarly, the 1999 referendum on independence for East Timor seems to have legitimated a new democracy despite the difficulties and limitations. Parallel exercises in Kosovo and South Sudan have proved more problematic.

In his comparative historical study of self-determination and secession referendums, Matt Qvortrup finds that most such pre-World War referendums were organised in an ad hoc and opportunistic manner. From the 1990s onwards, however, the number of legally regulated referendums increased considerably, after the fall of Communism in 1989 and the collapse of the Soviet Union in 1991. In many cases these referendums were held because the international community identified them as a sine qua non condition for the recognition of new states. As this range of examples suggests, although MDDs may encourage a degree of cooperation between otherwise antagonistic forces (e.g. South Africa's 1992 vote on ending apartheid) and perhaps even a degree of power sharing (as in Colombia's Frente Nacional referendum of December 1957), there is no guarantee that the outcome will always be so constructive. The 1950 and 2004 referendums in Cyprus entrenched divisions on the island, and it remains to be seen whether the next one will work differently.

Our cases also confirm that, beyond the more technical aspects of institutional design, careful attention must also be given to already existing structures of (democratic) governance. Incumbent officeholders, their parties and the insiders who support them all have strong incentives to intervene, to ensure that MDDs produce outcomes that are not too uncongenial, and they usually have the means to exert a distorting influence. Thus 'capture' or at least 'manipulation' of promising innovations is very possible, and can discredit otherwise salutary new instruments of popular rule. Transparency and citizen engagement can offer partial defences against such deviations, but there can be no permanent guarantees, even though a robust judiciary and a vigilant press can help.

Thus far we have sought the determinants of success or failure internal to each experiment or innovation. But the larger external and international context could prove equally, or perhaps even more, critical. In globally interdependent markets the success of an MDD in one country can attract a cascade of imitators (our case studies indicate widespread incidence of institutional diffusion); or competition for markets and investment capital may penalise the jurisdictions that go furthest in 'letting the people rule' (in a populist register) at the expense of those that are less democratically experimental (more reliably 'market driven' or even 'neo-liberal'). At the time of writing, this disjuncture seems sharper and more divisive than ever, with the political backlash against 'globalisation' gathering momentum. It is certainly too soon to judge whether the MDDs studied here will prove capable of extending policy time horizons and stabilising expectations in a manner that can calm speculative surges, or whether they will worsen policy dysfunctions. What can be expected is that in certain contexts some innovations will prove riskier, and potentially more counterproductive, than others.

## Concluding remarks

In conclusion, there are three basic points to keep in mind when surveying and comparing MDDs. First, however beneficial direct democracy 'add-on' provisions may be, they will prove less than democratic if they become substitutes for established processes of democratic representation. The specialised nature of most tasks of modern government in complex mass societies requires direction from a full-time stratum of professional decision makers. This will remain true no matter how much progress there may be in establishing 'monitory' supervision of the permanent political class, or how closely a more participatory and vigilant electorate holds elected officials accountable. MMDs can correct abuses by elected politicians, but twenty-first century democracies will still require the holding of periodic competitive elections for public office, with open contestation on a level playing field, and with genuine scope for alternation. This remains an integral part of a democratic regime that cannot be fully displaced by innovations in direct rule, no matter how imaginative or creative.

Second, various direct democratic innovations reviewed in this volume are very proximate to more classical processes of electoral representation. For example, a properly regulated 'recall' procedure can best be regarded as a perhaps useful modification of well established rules concerning standard calendars for election to public offices. The same might be said of party primaries. At the same time, the full toolbox of direct democratic innovations also contains other more unorthodox and experimental options, such as participatory budgeting, direct legislative initiatives, and so forth. Such measures take decision-making powers away from elected politicians and transfer them to activist groups of one sort or another. Even further towards the outer limits of what might be considered the universe of direct democratic innovations, individual 'whistle blowers' have recently shown how they can transform major areas of policy debate by revealing previously hidden information about tax practices, covert surveillance and the like. Here the boundary separating MDDs from the looser category of 'monitory' innovations becomes cloudy. Indeed, some crucial examples of recent whistle blowing arguably stray into illegality.

Third, the limits of legality merit special attention here. In a classical representative system parliament alone defines the law. As our democracies have delegated more powers to non-legislative bodies the simplicities of the 'principal–agent' relationship so beloved of our rational choice colleagues have been diluted, if not overwhelmed. With various direct democratic 'add-on' experiments stirred into the mix many key decision-making procedures risk becoming even more multi-form and opaque. If confusion, dysfunction and disorder are to be avoided it becomes essential to define which rules are applicable to which choices or arenas of decision making. Democracies need clear and neutral 'rules of the game', and modern democracies have often become increasingly 'judicialised' as the courts are called on to adjudicate between competing interpretations of such rules. Increased reliance on direct democracy supplements to classical parliamentary law making complicates the rules of the game and makes further arbitration necessary. While national courts and international arbitration may sometimes help to solve conflicts, they are not an automatic panacea. In some cases conflicting interpretations have produced deadlocks and supposedly neutral arbiters may even make the confusion worse.

Looking at MDDs in a broader context, they should be understood largely as a response to growing dissatisfaction with 'real world' representative institutions. The professionalised political classes that have crystallised around these arrangements are widely perceived as manipulative, perhaps dishonest, and out of touch with those they claim to represent. Taking the longer view, it would be a mistake to overstate the dichotomy that existed between direct and representative democratic forms even during the twentieth-century heyday of disciplined party parliamentarism. After all, as early as 1912 the state of California introduced provisions for direct voter initiatives, petition referendums and recall votes, and across the ensuing century, whatever their failings, these have proved both durable and compatible with spectacular economic expansion and societal progress. Switzerland, Uruguay and other jurisdictions all display some very longstanding and creditable records of direct democracy success. These were all settings that are much more populated and modern than had been specified as the limits by early theorists of direct democracy. In twenty-first century conditions these precedents have been taken up far more widely – and with far more uncertain results. As for the future, current and prospective developments in information technology and instantaneous global digital communications are eradicating age-old barriers to collective deliberation and participatory decision making, with consequences that are difficult to predict but likely to prove far-reaching.

So far, the fit between twentieth-century political norms and practices and the new possibilities arising in today's very different 'brave new world' is proving far from clear or stable. This is hardly surprising, and although it should be a source of concern there is also much positive potential. There are evident new risks to 'good government' – particularly in terms of policy coherence and the predictability of public decisions. In some cases, instead of shoring up the legitimacy of a democratic system, poorly chosen or badly implemented reforms may further alienate a restless citizenry. But with careful observations and well-designed comparative work it should be possible to learn lessons from mistakes and to promote 'best practice' variants of MDDs. The transformative and relegitimising potential of such experiments is clearest when they enable citizens to take fuller 'ownership' of the public choices that most concern them.

Some highly demanding conditions must be met if this new dispensation is to render durably positive results. Some of the pitfalls are already evident; others will take longer to surface. But cumulative experience indicates that successes are possible, and that MMDs can enrich and reinvigorate projects of inclusive democratic politics. Highlighting the more constructive options and guarding against the foreseeable failures is a major task for future comparative work on MDDs. This exploratory volume has aimed to set out a suitable agenda for that purpose.

## References

Dunn, J. (2005) *Setting the People Free: The Story of Democracy*, London: Atlantic Books.

Duverger, M. (1959) *Political Parties: Their Organization and Activity in the Modern State*, second English edition, London: Methuen.

Keane, J. (2010) *The Life and Death of Democracy*, London: Pocket Books.

Mair, P. (2013) *Ruling the Void: The Hollowing of Western Democracy*, London and New York: Verso.

Mill, J. S. (1861) *Considerations on Representative Government*, 2nd edn, London: Parker, Son and Bourn.

Welp, Y. and Whitehead, L. (eds) (2011) 'Caleidoscopio de la innovación democrática en América Latina', Mexico City: FLACSO.

*Afterword on Brexit Referendum, 23 June 2016*

# The 'People Ruled' that the UK Should Quit the European Union

*Laurence Whitehead*

On a turnout of 72 per cent the British electorate voted by 51.9 per cent to leave the European Union after almost 44 years of membership. The majority of over one and a quarter million votes was sufficiently large to eliminate any doubt or ambiguity, and the turnout was the highest in a British election for over two decades, reconfirming the legitimacy of the decision. The vote set in motion UK disengagement from the EU, precipitated the premature resignation of a prime minister who had won a single-party five-year term only thirteen months earlier, unleashed unprecedented turmoil at the apex of the British party system, and brought to the surface deep social cleavages between regions, classes, generations and ethnicities within the national polity. In strictly constitutional terms only 'the Queen in parliament' is sovereign, and so the referendum was not legally binding. But although it was only advisory, and a clear majority of MPs in Westminster would not in other circumstances have chosen to leave, this mandate of the people carries such moral force that it is said to be virtually unthinkable for the major parties and their leaders to defy the express will of the electorate.

However, the meaning of the decision 'to leave' is open to many diverse interpretations, both concerning the process and timetable, and the alternative arrangements. In legal terms, is Parliament required to repeal the European Communities Act of 1972? Will the government that emerges from the immediate turmoil (the immediate resignation of the pro-remain prime minister, David Cameron) be obliged to trigger the exit process specified in Article 50 of the Lisbon Treaty? Will it be the parliament elected in 2015 that takes these decisions, or might they be preceded by a new parliamentary election, possibly generating a different mandate? In the UK system not only is parliament theoretically sovereign, it is also not able to bind its successor. Therefore in legal terms a further election could produce a new parliament that is not obliged to uphold the referendum commitment. These are the immediate post-referendum constitutional imponderables. There is even the theoretical possibility that the Article 50 notification might be so delayed that parliament could invoke 'unforeseen developments' to justify a second referendum (despite the chorus of leadership voices denying any such possibility and the obvious insult to the electorate involved in such a tortuous manoeuvre). Two weeks after the Brexit vote the government rejected a petition signed by four million citizens calling for a second referendum (although not ruling out a parliamentary debate on the issue).

Those who promoted the 'leave' campaign were clear about what they were against, but divided, opaque and inconsistent about what would take its place, let alone the critical questions of sequencing and compensatory measures. But it is in the nature of a plebiscitary process to pose a stark binary choice at a single predetermined date, so that (depending upon how the campaign is conducted) the people can indeed decide to say no without necessarily agreeing in advance about the nature of the alternative. In the case of the June 2016 vote, the established status quo with Europe was destroyed, but everything about its replacement remains to be decided through non-plebiscitary political negotiations that have yet to be defined.

In due course this might even lead to a further referendum on the independence of Scotland (which voted uniformly and strongly to 'remain' in Europe), or on the eventual terms of a renegotiated deal with Brussels. But if so that would be a new political decision, not a legally required consequence of the June 2016 referendum.

Assuming that Article 50 of the Lisbon Treaty is eventually triggered, the resulting manifold repercussions and further political choices will branch out in all directions and could generate a great array of consequences, many (but not all) harmful, with some unmistakably attributable to the referendum vote, but many more that are at present highly under-determined, so that intermediating factors could have more causal weight. Such indirect 'knock-on' effects could include a second independence referendum in Scotland, destabilisation of the EU-backed peace settlement in Northern Ireland, and centrifugal consequences including demands for secessionist referendums in other European states. The EU's capacity to buffer historically entrenched nationalist rivalries, both within the British Isles, and in Europe more widely, has been significantly impaired.

Opinions about whether, on balance, the outcome brought benefits or did harm will therefore be contested and subject to interpretation. In fact, some parties in the referendum debate are already positioning themselves to deflect criticism by arguing that underlying long-term trends merely crystallised on 23 June, which should not be seen in isolation (and still less as an unintended accident, or self-inflicted wound).

In reality, there was a major fork in the road, and the close-fought vote set the country on a very different path from that in prospect had just 2 per cent of the voters decided otherwise. It seems probable that many of those campaigning for 'leave' did not really expect to succeed, and at least some of those who followed their lead may have believed that they were only registering a protest vote, rather than redirecting the entire course of national history (UKIP described 23 June as 'independence day', but did all 17.4 million voters view it that way?). On the other side, the 'remain' camp had lukewarm leadership (almost no one on either side had much positive to say about the EU, barring John Major and Sadiq Khan). A positive message about the merits of the Union – e.g. playing up its achievements in peaceful dispute resolution and co-operative institution building – was ruled out for fear of reigniting internal battles within the Conservative Party as much as because of its disappointing performance over Greece, refugees, etc. 'Remain' might have mobilised more supporters if the young, and the beneficiaries of EU largesse, had been better instructed on what was really at stake, and how close they were to defeat. Complacency was probably reinforced by Prime Minister Cameron's 'lucky escape' in the Scottish referendum of 2014, and by his general aura of overconfidence.

From a comparative perspective, this cautions against a casual approach to the convening of referendums on momentous issues of meta-political (constitutional) importance. Before the event it was common to assert that the Conservative government only authorised the referendum as a device to manage inner party tensions. But even if one accepts Cameron's claim that the referendum was held for strong and necessary reasons of profound public interest (and not as just a slick device to circumvent purely contingent divisions within a single political party), comparative evidence shows that on such a consequential matter more care could have been taken to protect against accidents and unintended consequences. As indicated in this volume, much forethought is essential concerning the precise scope of the *demos*; the wording, timing, legal force and other procedural aspects of the consultation; the quality of the ensuing debate; the political fall-out from both possible outcomes; and the task of harmonising the referendum decision with the normal flow of representative politics. Arguably Westminster paid due attention to the first two of these requirements, but fell short on the last three.

But there were lacunae also with regard to the *demos*. For example, in Australia when constitutional matters of fundamental importance to the Federation (such as monarchy or republic) are up for a vote, the status quo is preserved unless there is a majority in all six of the federated states. Likewise, in Swiss national referendums not only a popular majority, but also a qualified majority of cantons is required to approve a constitutional change. By contrast, the United Kingdom of Great Britain and Northern Ireland has four component units – each with their own democratic legislative assemblies and first ministers – two of which (Northern Ireland and Scotland) voted clearly in favour of the status quo. But they are to be dragged out of the EU against their will because a small balance of opinion in the majority unit (England) swamped their clear preferences. This feature of the referendum was questioned in advance (notably by the Scottish National Party), but no federal-style precautions were enacted. Other precautionary principles might equally well have been considered. After the event millions rallied to the view that such a major decision might have required a supermajority – say 60 per cent rather than just 50 per cent plus one; and/or that the turnout could have been set at an exacting threshold – say 75 per cent.[1] If such conditions were not met the decision would be regarded as provisional until reconfirmed with a simple majority in a second round. But although with hindsight such protective and legitimising rules might seem justified no consideration was given to them in advance.

1. A handful of voters signed such a petition to parliament before 23 June. Two weeks after the vote it had attracted 4.1 million signatures and became the most well supported petition ever. That triggers a debate, but cannot overturn a law.

How might this oversight be explained? Immediate post-referendum commentary has tended to highlight official carelessness, overconfidence and lack of interest in experiences from elsewhere. Such factors may indeed have played their part. But it should also be recalled that the main objective of the Cameron administration was to use the threat of a potential defeat in the referendum as a lever to extract concessions from the EU over issues such as immigration. Within that framework it made sense to avoid giving signs of hesitation or reluctance to leave when designing the referendum procedure. Of course this was predicated on the belief that once some renegotiation benefits had been delivered the London government could then repay those concessions with a successful 'remain' campaign. So, on this analysis, the 'no escape clause' format of the referendum would represent what game theorists classify as a 'game of chicken'. In the event Brussels did make some concessions to the Prime Minister, he therefore campaigned to remain. However – and somewhat contrary to the rationalist tenets of standard game theory – at the last moment the driver lost control over his wheel. So even within this framework the miscalculation verdict still stands.

What was the miscalculation? The 'remain' campaign seems to have assumed that once virtually the entire British establishment alerted the electorate to the irreversible economic damage that they believed would flow from leaving a majority would draw back from such a drastic break with the status quo (as Tierney's account in Chapter Six in this volume on the Scottish precedent indicates, this was thought to have tilted the 2014 referendum Cameron's way in the final days). Also, the opposition Labour Party would once again find itself corralled into delivering its support for a project basically owned by its Conservative opponents. But these were untested gambles, not safe predictions. In particular, warnings of economic damage were overused, and lost traction as the campaign proceeded. There was no last-minute counterpart in May 2016 to the reassuring 'vow' that dominated the final days of the Scottish referendum. In any yes/no divide the timing of closing messages can be critical, and the losing side can be expected to resort to increasingly desperate expedients to restore the balance. As the June 2016 campaign unfolded (and encouraged by Britain's mainly anti-EU press barons) the debate shifted from prudence and short-term economic self-interest towards wilder assertions and appeals to identity politics. Even so, it appears that the *leavers* were almost as unprepared as the *remainers* for the eventual outcome.

Although the Cameron government was the main author of the referendum rules, there was a series of debates in Westminster in the second half of 2015, when other parties also had the chance to display independence and forethought. But these parliamentary debates concentrated on less than transcendental issues, notably the precise wording of the question ('remain' or 'stay' for example); the date (would the Prime Minister be free to choose one of his own preference); and whether – as in Scotland – the franchise should be extended to sixteen- and seventeen-year-olds, given that their entire futures were at issue (no such extension was permitted in this case). If there was overconfidence and miscalculation it seems that not only the government but also the mainstream opposition parties (indeed almost the UK's entire professional political class) must share the responsibility between them. As I noted in Chapter Two in this volume, it would be a mistake to heap all criticism onto the direct democracy side of the ledger. The traditional parties and their flawed practices of representation must not be exempted from any critical assessment of this experience, which cannot simply be attributed to the vagaries of direct democracy. It also reflected the disorders of Britain's current parliamentary democracy, notably its inability to prevent intra-party conflicts from spilling over into a system-wide political upheaval.

In the aftermath of the vote to leave a variety of expedients have been aired as ways to negate the shock result: Parliament might refuse to repeal the 1972 European Communities Act; the next prime minister's personal authority to notify the EU of withdrawal under Article 50 of the Lisbon Treaty might be contested in the courts on the grounds that such an act involved the nullification of existing laws, and so could only be undertaken after full debate and approval by parliament; or even that instead of fulfilling the popular mandate of the referendum there might be a dissolution of parliament and the election of a new legislature, perhaps one pledged to overturn the directly expressed will of the people. Since the UK has an unwritten constitution, and in the opinion of some leading experts the Westminster System was already a 'mess' (see King 2007)[2] (or in my parlance a 'muddle' rather than a 'model', see Whitehead 2013) there can be no guarantee against such anti-referendum strategies, but it must be evident that any such course would bring British democracy into severe disrepute, and would risk provoking perilous anti-parliamentary responses.

This still unsettled episode provides a remarkable coda to the broader issues covered in this volume. Standing back from the drama (and farce) of this particular episode some more general conclusions are already visible. As noted throughout our studies, traditional models of representative democracy are under strain all around the world. Various forms of direct democracy have been 'grafted on' to buttress a faltering legitimacy, and to reconnect citizens who no longer feel adequately represented by their elected officeholders, and by inherited party machines. But, as stressed by our various authors, the melding of direct and representative forms of democracy is a problematic project. For example, Mendez and Mendez highlight in Chapter Thirteen in this volume (written before the Brexit vote) the challenge of integrating MDD outcomes within the EU and with the inevitable accompanying flux of outputs generated by conventional representative politics. Relatedly,

2. King states that his use of this term is purely, descriptive, and not pejorative. He also reconstructs the 1990s process whereby first John Major, and then in reaction Tony Blair responded to the challenge of potential membership of the Euro by pledging a referendum vote. 'Power, at least on this issue, had definitively spiralled downwards from the cabinet and parliament to the mass of the people. In 1997, for the first time in British history, both major parties were simultaneously pledged to hold a popular referendum on the same issue' (King 2007: 345). He points out that this was only the sovereign power to veto any parliamentary decision to take Britain into the single currency – not the option to force government ministers to join the single currency against their will. So, 'even after 1997 the people continued to lack the power of initiative. But they certainly now possessed the power of veto' (King 2007: 292–3) – and on a matter that was hugely important, and in no way trivial.

Sciarini in Chapter Twelve warns that, absent an additional level of political management, such exercises in popular consultation might unintentionally trigger a political disaster. Thoughtless admixture of direct and representative decision-making procedures has the potential to create worse dysfunctions than those it is intended to remedy.

The latest UK experience provides spectacular confirmation of the risks involved if MDDs are badly designed or carelessly deployed. But the underlying reasons why they may be needed should not be forgotten either. Whatever miscalculations may have led up to the 23 June decision, and regardless of possible unintended 'knock-on' effects thereafter, the referendum itself was a tremendously powerful source of legitimation and reorientation. It authorised a watershed decision that was contrary to the prior will and intentions of the Westminster parliamentary majority. This underscores the incompleteness of accounts of democracy that restrict their scope purely to the representational format.

One longstanding defender of the utility of referendums (when appropriately applied) provides a suitable concluding angle of vision. On the basis of his comparative study of over 600 referendums (notably including the Swiss experience) Bruno Frey (1992) has made the case for direct democracy on two main grounds. Working within the 'economics of happiness' paradigm he claims that they may mostly increase collective happiness. It remains to be seen whether the UK case will fit within that framework – initial signs of discontent and disarray suggest otherwise. Our approach expressed more concern over the potential polarising effects of MDDs, in particular those deployed as a substitute for tackling unresolved elite-level conflicts (*see* Sciarini on Switzerland, Chapter Eleven in this volume). Frey's second claim, while ambitious, is perhaps also more pertinent – referendums 'may actually improve the efficiency of government by giving the mass of the citizens the information and opportunity to frustrate efforts of the *classe politique* to form a coalition against the voters' (Frey 1992: 209). The UK electorate certainly seized that opportunity, and disrupted governing elite cohesion, in June 2016. They may not be the last to do so.

## References

Frey, B. (1992) 'Efficiency and democratic political organization: the case for the referendum', *Journal of Public Policy*, 12(3): 209–22.

King, A. (2007) *The British Constitution*, Oxford: Oxford University Press.

Whitehead, L. (2013) 'The Westminster system: "model" or "muddle"?', *Taiwan Journal of Democracy*, special issue, May: 9–38.

# Index

www.ingramcontent.com/pod-product-compliance
Lightning Source LLC
Chambersburg PA
CBHW021859020426
42334CB00013B/397
* 9 7 8 1 7 8 5 5 2 2 6 6 6 *